Selecting
Instructional Media

Selecting Instructional Media

A Guide to Audiovisual and Other Instructional Media Lists

Mary Robinson Sive

1978

Libraries Unlimited, Inc.
Littleton, Colorado

LIBRARIES UNLIMITED, INC.
P.O. Box 263
Littleton, Colorado 80160

Library of Congress Cataloging in Publication Data

Sive, Mary Robinson, 1928–
    Selecting instructional media.

    Previous ed. published in 1975 has title: Educators'
guide to media lists.
    Includes indexes.
    1. Audio-visual materials--Catalogs--Bibliography.
2. Catalogs, Subject--Bibliography.   3. Media
programs (Education)--Bibliography.   I. Title.
Z5817.2.S58   1978   [LB1043.Z9]   016.37133   77-27278
ISBN 0-87287-181-9   '

Foreword

When I reviewed the first edition of this book for *School Library Journal* in 1976, I hoped that an updated edition would appear sometime before 1980.

Now, lo and behold, a new and welcome edition has appeared early in 1978. My previous comments that it is well thought out and valuable are still relevant, but in this edition there is more of everything and it will be of value to even more people.

This is a reference book for educators. We usually think of them as teachers, but today "educators" refers to almost everyone who disseminates information— librarians, teachers, museum people, television writers, film programmers, advertising personnel, or whomever. All of them can use this book.

A great many media lists have been put together on a dare, much as many of this writer's early media lists were. When a list is needed on a certain subject, everyone in the field sits around staring at one another until someone cracks and volunteers to prepare that needed list. Now we have so many lists that they must be collated to form a "book of lists"; we have all apparently out-stared Mary Robinson Sive since she has volunteered to do the job not once, but twice so far. And a good job it is, too.

There are several things noticeable at first glance in this new edition. The addition of an "Introduction to Media Selection" is not only important but very helpful. Two new topics have been added—Values Education (a new and exciting subject for teaching in these days of decaying morality and dog-eat-dog, everybody-else-is-doing-it attitudes among the young) and Women's Studies (which is just as important and long overdue). I am certain that both these topics will grow in stature in coming editions of this guide.

Since Ms. Sive is two years younger than I (and has not yet reached "grand old man/lady of the media field" status), she can afford to be rash and opinionated. She has analyzed these hundreds of items for us with great honesty, and there is nothing in her work that is not intelligent and constructive.

Perhaps no amount of dazzling writing can put this guide in the category of something you would want to curl up with in bed at night, but it *is* very difficult to put down because each entry becomes either a confirmation or a revelation, depending upon whether or not one has encountered the item before in his or her work.

I have found many new riches in this guide and I am certain that most of you will too.

James L. Limbacher
Dearborn, Michigan

January 1978

Preface

The critical reception accorded the first edition of this work was proof that a need existed for a thorough and well-organized guide to the profusion of instructional media offered the educational market. To continue to meet that need, frequent revision is a necessity. This edition, published two-and-a-half years after the first, is planned for increased usefulness to the educational community. It differs from the first in four ways:

1.   The title has been changed from *Educators' Guide to Media Lists* to *Selecting Instructional Media* to avoid confusion with similar-sounding titles and to clarify the work's function.

2.   An essay entitled "An Introduction to Media Selection" has been added. Media selection has been termed one of the most talked about but least developed aspects in instructional media texts.

3.   Responsive to changing curricular emphases, a chapter on Women's Studies has been added, and the chapter on Environmental Education has been renamed Energy and Environment Education.

4.   Provision has been made for the expansion of Section II, Lists by Subjects, by reserving chapter numbers 23 to 29 for future additions.

5.   The Title Index is expanded to encompass titles mentioned in the text as well as those fully annotated and a new Name Index added.

Selecting Instructional Media is designed to aid teachers, media specialists, principals, film librarians, curriculum supervisors, and other educators at several tasks:

1.   **Selection and purchase of instructional media.** To achieve optimum media support for adopted curricula, educators may select from the wide range made accessible here materials to be requested for preview, evaluation, possible adoption, purchase, or rental. The important critical reviewing tools in various fields are also listed here.

2.   **Curriculum development.** The guide can be of similar help to those preparing curricula for school districts, education departments, and academic or other institutions. It will enable them to use more efficiently the library facilities available to them and to assemble tailor-made personal collections.

3.   **Classroom instruction.** Teachers may use this bibliographic guide to locate selection tools that will help implement specific teaching strategies, whether they are planning a year's course of instruction or a unit, constructing a learning activity package or prescribing individual assignments. The lists referenced here serve to expand and update mediagraphies included in curriculum guides or resource units. They can also be used to update and supplement media supplied as part of pre-packaged programs.

The aim is to provide one-stop access to instructional media, whether they may be obtained within a school system or outside it.

4.   **School media center operation.** The media specialist, who must be particularly concerned with anticipating future demands, can build a collection using the tools listed here.

While *Selecting Instructional Media* should not be considered a buying list for media centers, a section of a professional library devoted to media selection can be assembled from the publications presented here. Choices will be made on the basis of local needs, moneys available, the utility of each list, and ready availability of the more expensive ones at nearby college or public libraries. Individual teachers will want their own desk copies of the less expensive ones. While several of the film lists are appropriate acquisition tools only for regional film libraries, others make handy desk references to supplement the services of such libraries. The media specialist will wish to bring the entire range to the attention of other instructional personnel to implement paragraphs 1, 2, and 3 above.

The guide can, moreover, serve double duty as an organizing tool. Publications may simply be coded with the identification numbers used here, which would then serve to locate them in the professional library. Others may be coded as to their location in departmental libraries or elsewhere. Copies of this guide kept in each department, school, etc., thus become instant library catalogs and save extensive cataloging costs.

Among the lists included here are many that are well known to teachers and curriculum personnel but not to librarians, and others that are well known to librarians but not to other educators. Operation of successful media centers depends on the cooperation of these two groups, and it is hoped that this feature of the guide will increase such cooperation, if only in a small way.

The attentive user of this guide will identify instructional needs for which we offer little help. Where this is due to omission on our part, we hope such omission will be brought to our attention. Where it is due to a gap in the literature, an enterprising reader may be inspired to close that gap.

It is a pleasure once again to record my thanks to those who supplied encouragement and help with both this volume and its predecessor: Mary Virginia Gaver, inspiring teacher, honored me by a critical reading of the first edition and of the chapter on media selection in the present one. I continue to benefit from her discerning comments and wise counsel. John Bergeson, Director, Instructional Materials Center, Central Michigan University, Mount Pleasant, Michigan, offered valuable comments on the essay on media selection. James L. Limbacher, Audio-Visual Librarian, Henry Ford Centennial Library, Dearborn, Michigan, a careful critic turned friendly advocate, gave good advice. Dr. Peter Relic, now Deputy Assistant Secretary for Education, Department of Health, Education and Welfare, and Dr. Leo Poulos, Superintendent of Schools, Mendham, NJ made thoughtful suggestions for the first edition. My association with them taught me what education can be.

Maryann Chach and Brian Camp operate a superb reference library at the Educational Film Library Association and responded to all requests with unfailing courtesy and competence.

The Association of Media Producers, Hope Reports, Inc., ERIC Clearinghouse on Information Resources and National Information Center for Educational Media supplied various data and other assistance.

The author, of course, is solely responsible for any errors, omissions, or other shortcomings.

M.R.S.
January 1978

Table of Contents

Introduction

Selecting Instructional Media is an awareness tool that fully annotates 428 selected published lists of audiovisual and other instructional media; 132 others are mentioned in the text. Use of this edition can easily be restricted to updated or revised entries and to entries new to this edition, which are marked with an asterisk (*). These include more recent updates, new editions, or replacements for some of the entries in the first edition. The remainder of the 270 lists annotated in that edition are either reprinted here if still available, and useful, or deleted if they are known to be out of print, were periodicals that have since ceased publication, or are otherwise inapplicable.

Descriptions are sufficiently detailed so that readers can make informed decisions to use specific lists for specific needs. "Media" include audio and video recordings, sound and silent filmstrips, films, filmloops, slides, transparencies, simulation games, study prints, and multi-media kits. Beyond these, we lead the user to others important in instruction but often even more difficult to locate: art reproductions, documentaries, maps, microforms, photographs, television (both real-time and on tape or film), and recorded radio programs. As primary sources become objects of study at lower grade levels, source materials in these formats become increasingly relevant.

Only audiovisual software, exclusive of equipment, is within the work's purview.

Print materials are excluded except for government and free and inexpensive publications. The printed word has had a long history as an information medium. Bibliographic access to it is thus better developed, more refined, and more familiar than that to the world of audiovisual information.

The first edition of the present volume (entitled *Educators' Guide to Media Lists*) was the first work specifically geared to media appropriate for instructional programs K–12 and to actual purchasing practices in schools.

Similar works published since then (*Multi-Media Indexes, Lists, and Review Sources* [Dekker, 1975]; *Guides to Educational Media*, 4th ed. [ALA, 1977]) differ from this work and its predecessor in several important ways: they include some lists rejected here as too brief, too dated, or of too limited availability or use; they neglect those appearing in professional journals or as parts of books. They do not encompass government publications, other free and inexpensive publications, or simulation games. None supplies the amount and detail of information about each list that is provided here—most notably the number of entries in a list and the period covered by it.

"Media list" denotes a published list of materials marketed separately, not as components of total learning packages.

In order to stay within a predetermined maximum number and to maintain a reasonable balance, choices had to be made from among the many hundreds of publications that would fit such a definition. Inclusion of a list here is not to be deemed an endorsement or recommendation for purchase.

We have included some publications simply because they are almost universally known and it seemed important to point out clearly what well-known (and, in some cases, quite expensive) tools could and could not do. NICEM (National Information Center for Educational Media) Indexes and "Educators Guides" of the Educators Progress Service are in that category.

We have almost always included tools that are free or inexpensive (and the number of these may surprise some readers). In choosing among articles, we have picked those that appear in journals with wide distribution in schools.

Any selection process is bound to be somewhat subjective. Some subject areas had many lists to choose from, so we could afford to be quite selective. In each case we tried to identify the more recent, the less expensive, the more carefully selective. We tried to tell the reader only of publications that can be readily obtained. All groupings attempt to include critical and descriptive, retrospective and current lists, but they must reflect what is available, not some ideal distribution.

We have excluded obviously unreliable lists and, generally, any published prior to 1973. Those new to this edition, with few exceptions, were published between 1975 and June 30, 1977, and are marked with an asterisk (*), as are entries that were expanded or revised for this edition.

Also excluded are works published outside the United States and items that are excessively expensive, that have fewer than 20 entries, and that are out of print or of limited availability. (But see item 6 below.) The definition of "media list" excludes curriculum guides, resource units, teachers' editions of texts, and similar items. With one or two exceptions it excludes directories of sources and catalogs of commercial suppliers. Book wholesalers were prominent in the audiovisual business for a while, and the first edition annotated some of their catalogs published during those years. Few such catalogs are any longer available.

Distribution of entries among different subject areas reflects not the compiler's judgment but the state of the art. In the social sciences a large number of subject-oriented media lists exists. The same is true of areas of current concern, such as career education. Science and foreign languages are less well served. The instructional and conceptual requirements of each subject are, of course, among the determining factors.

MEDIA LISTS INCLUDED

The majority of the publications outlined here are published for the educational market. But where it seemed necessary we did not hesitate to add others often known only to specialized researchers. They cover the subject areas commonly taught K–12, exclusive of special education.

The media lists fall into several categories:

1.   **Separate publications (monographs).** Books, booklets, leaflets, catalogs of film libraries, producers, and publishers. Some fugitive material is included, but only if there has been assurance that a similar item will be available if the specific one listed no longer is. ED numbers are supplied for publications that may also be purchased as ERIC documents (see item 6 below).

2.   **Periodicals.** Those carrying announcements or reviews of instructional media of some scope and generally subscribed to by schools for library or individual use; also those devoted entirely or in large part to reviewing media.

3.   **Articles in professional journals.** Mediagraphies on special topics that appear in periodicals described in item 2 above and in other periodicals.

4.   **Portions of books.** Mediagraphies on special topics that appear in trade or reference books.

5.   **Periodical indexes.** Indexes to periodicals and to media reviews in periodicals.

6.   **ERIC documents.** Publications abstracted in *Resources in Education*, including output of state and local educational bodies, otherwise not readily available, and publications that are out of print in hardcopy.

All lists entered under separate identifying numbers were examined by the compiler. A few titles that were unavailable for examination but did seem to deserve mention are referred to in chapter introductions or under "Features." So are titles fitting one or several of the excluded categories.

ORGANIZATION OF MEDIA LISTS

A classification system specifically devised for this guide assigns each fully annotated media list a distinctive identifying number. The first two digits identify the chapter where the list may be found, the subsequent two reflect its place within the chapter. In Section II, 02 to 22 annotate lists dealing with specific subjects; in Section III, 30 to 45 annotate those dealing with specific media; Section I (01) is comprised of those dealing with several subjects and several media.

Each list is entered only once, according to its chief emphasis. Here, subject has been considered more significant than medium. Thus, *Films for Communication and Language Arts* is entered under Language Arts rather than Films. Subject and media indexes provide necessary interface.

Arrangement within each chapter is arbitrary; no preference should be implied from the order.

Arrangement of Entries

The entry for each media list attempts to give the reader the most detailed outline possible on how much and what kind of information can be obtained from it—grade levels covered, media covered, arrangement and indexing, and how critical or extensive the list is. The entries are constructed so that the reader can see each list's virtues and limitations at a glance. One can quickly tell if it is too short to be useful, or too long, whether it covers sufficiently recent material, etc. It should also be easy to determine whether a list can be used by itself or needs to be supplemented for certain information (such as availability, pricing, etc.).

The information for each referenced list is structured on the following pattern:

Classification and identifying number. References in the indexes are to this number. Entries repeated or updated from the first edition may be assigned a different number in the current one.

Main entry. Title of the publication, followed by author or issuing agency; name and address of the publisher (except in the case of well-known publishing houses, in which case address is omitted). The edition identified is the one actually examined, generally the latest. If a more recent edition has been published but was unavailable for examination, this is noted under "Revision and updating." Also noted: number of pages, publication date, price shown in the publication or in *Books in Print 1977/78*, S/N (ordering number for government publications), ED number (ordering number for ERIC documents), LC number (ordering number for Library of Congress catalog cards). The abbreviation "o.p." means out-of-print; "n.d." means no date shown or implied in the publication.

Purpose. Lists are defined as comprehensive or descriptive (listing without evaluation), as evaluative (listing both "good" and "bad"), or as making recommendations (listing "good" titles only). Where known, the basis of selection or standards for review are stated or quoted. The intended audience may be identified.

Grade level. Either as stated in the reference or as judged by the compiler. "All" indicates that the list is suitable for K–12, with strengths or limitations, if any, indicated under "Features." Suitability for ages below or above that range is disregarded.

Arrangement. Identifies whether media are listed by subject, title, type of medium, or some variation or combination of these. The number of groupings may be stated.

Subjects. Indicates subject designations used by the list itself.

Entries. Total number of media listed, with the information supplied about each. It is assumed that lists will state whether films and filmstrips are sound or silent, color or black-and-white. Only deviations from such expected practice are noted, as are omissions of information deemed relevant: grade level, price, release date. (Even in an inflationary period price information gives at least a clue as to relative or approximate costs.) Contents may be simply noted or more fully summarized. There may be full synopses, critical reviews, ratings, or other selection aids.

Indexes. Notes type of index(es) provided, if any, or their absence. Indexing of journals in *Media Review Digest* (01-03) is noted.

Period covered. Period during which media listed in the referenced title were published. When this could not be ascertained, descriptions such as "available at time of publication" or "current releases" (meaning the period from up to a year prior to the media list's publication to several months following it) are used. When the period is unknown this is stated.

Revision and updating. Indicates frequency of revision and new editions as well as extent of revision, if known. Also indicates other tools that may be used to update the information in the list.

Media represented. In keeping with the work's content-centered approach, media are identified in broad categories only, without specifying exact sizes of film, tape or filmloops, sound or silent films and filmstrips. "Films" includes both shorts and feature-length films and entertainment as well as instructional films and documentaries. "Subjects" and "Features" headings provide more detail or point out what media may be predominant. When books are included along with non-print media, they are disregarded in this rubric because use of this guide as a book selection tool would be entirely misleading.

Producers represented. The number and type (academic, commercial, government, etc.) are stated when they could be determined.

Features. Points out subject strengths of lists in Section III and others covering "all" or many subjects, particular applicability to certain grade levels, predominance of certain media, comparison with other lists, overall strengths or limitations, and clarifications of other word or phrase descriptions. Notes similar lists including some not chosen for separate entry. In the case of entries reprinted from the first edition, additions and revisions have occasionally been made here.

Subject terms. As many subject terms as seemed necessary are assigned, rather than an arbitrary number. A fuller explanation of how subject terms were chosen is given below ("Subject analysis"). In the case of lists in Sections I and III labeled "all subjects," reference should be made to "Subjects" or "Features" headings to determine specific strengths.

SUBJECT ANALYSIS

In constructing subject approaches, this guide attempts to follow common terminology used in schools and to highlight currently relevant topics such as values education, aging and death, futures education. Subject terms are not uniformly broad or narrow but are dictated to a certain extent by the state of the art. Thus, the science area is not well served by subject-oriented media lists and four subdivisions appeared sufficient. The social sciences, however, present an opposite situation, and 21 narrower terms are used to delineate that field. Those terms for which a reasonable number of specific media lists could be identified serve as chapter headings 02 to 22.

We have tried to emphasize interdisciplinary aspects, but the exact terms chosen reflect what is actually published. Educators may be looking for media lists to develop

> affective education
> community awareness
> concepts
> conflict resolution
> creativity
> discovery
> identity
> inquiry
> interdependence
> problem solving

Not many lists have been compiled, however, that could be entered under thematic terms such as the above. Nevertheless, perusal of information given under "Subjects" and "Features" headings will yield some.

Subject terms new to this edition are noted in the Subject Index with an asterisk (*).

INDEXES

The indexes are designed for simultaneous use.

The Media Index identifies all entries by types of media. Index terms in the Media Index are those used as chapter headings for Section III (e.g., audio recordings, filmloops, etc.).

The Instructional Level Index picks up the suitability of a given media list for primary, intermediate, or secondary education.

Besides indexing Sections I and III, the Subject Index also gives more detailed access to the groupings in Section II and to textual mention.

The Title Index identifies both media lists separately entered in Sections I through III (printed in UPPER CASE), and those mentioned in the text except journal articles (printed in lower case). Asterisks identify titles new to or revised for this edition.

The Name Index identifies compilers and authors.

HOW TO ORDER MEDIA LISTS

Please do not attempt to order lists from Libraries Unlimited, Inc., or from the author. Each entry in this guide contains sufficient information to enable readers to purchase desired lists or to find them in libraries. Complete addresses are supplied for all entries except for a few trade and reference books. Government documents should be ordered from the Superintendent of Documents, Washington, DC 20402, using S/N numbers and enclosing payment. ERIC documents may be ordered on microfiche from ERIC Document Reproduction Service, Box 190, Arlington, VA 22210, at $0.83 for up to five fiche of 98 pages each. The number of fiche may be estimated from the number of pages contained in the document. ED number and payment, including postage, must be enclosed. Hard copies may be ordered from the address shown in the entry if a price or the notation "free" is indicated.

An Introduction
to Media Selection

Each practicing media specialist and other education professional has a well-established method of selecting instructional materials. Those who were trained in a library school will generally prefer to purchase titles that have been favorably reviewed, if possible in several different sources. Whether this has been the training or not, the media specialist may simply make choices from the many catalogs and other announcements coming across the desk and, if possible, preview these before placing a purchase order.

Neither approach exposes students to the full potential that media can have in instruction. With their great variety they enable teachers to serve the needs of each student, something the slavish following of a textbook by an entire class cannot accomplish. The visually oriented can be served as can the child needing physical involvement. The non-verbal student can find expression in a congenial medium. Sound and motion convey levels of understanding that the printed word cannot.

If media are to *be* instruction, rather than supplemental aids to instruction, more sophisticated procedures are indicated. A systems approach permits media to be used in ways and in formats uniquely fitted to specific circumstances and objectives.

Teachers are told that "a medium of instruction must be selected on the basis of its potential for implementing a stated objective" (Gerlach and Ely, 1971) and that they "should base their selection of media on valid learning objectives and the unique characteristics of learners" (Erickson, 1972). This is easier said than done.

The number of non-print titles from which to choose has grown enormously to the point where there are, in 1977, some 350,000 titles of educational films, cartridged films, filmstrips, slides, transparencies, audio and video recordings on the market. To that number may be added other formats (simulation games, study prints, pictures, maps, pamphlets, etc.) and other titles not produced specifically for the educational market but of potential use. Some of that large number are dated, to be sure, although still offered for sale; that only makes the selector's task more complex. At the same time there is less money for purchases, while prices are rising.

Under these circumstances it may seem simplest to decide to produce one's own tapes or visuals in the media center or the classroom. That may indeed be a wise decision, *if* 1) it results in a product of professional quality but lower cost than the commercial equivalent, or 2) nothing on the market effectively presents the concept to be taught. Learner involvement is at its maximum when students themselves produce materials. Commercial producers, however, have access to both subject and technical expertise that few school districts can match. This does not necessarily ensure a quality product. But when it does, the added instructional value may be worth the price. Incidentally, it may be easier to achieve fine technical quality in a locally made product than to ascertain adequate subject coverage. This is particularly so in the case of a developing or relatively new topic—and those are frequently the ones for which audiovisual presentation is desired.

The remainder of this essay will summarize research reported in the literature on media selection, based on stated criteria and instructional needs, and will give some commonsense directions for educators to follow. These take into consideration budgetary and other restraints within which school people must operate.

MEDIA SELECTION IS DIFFERENT
FROM BOOK SELECTION

The differences in the critical reviewing and bibliographic coverage of print and non-print communications media are as basic as are those in their marketing. Schools and libraries buy most of their books through wholesale houses. Their audiovisual materials must generally be purchased from each individual producer or distributor. Bookbuying generally does not require consulting each publisher's catalog for prices; audiovisual buying does.

To choose books, we depend on reviews in journals, notes or bibliographies in other books, library catalogs, word-of-mouth recommendations, and major bibliographic tools. *Books in Print* is found in many libraries and bookstores.

Most of these ways of finding out are absent or difficult to come by in the case of audiovisual media.

REVIEWS

The National Information Center for Educational Media adds an average of over 20,000 new titles a year to its data base. The 150 journals that review instructional media cover some 3,000 titles. *Previews* (01-11), the only journal entirely devoted to reviewing software, considers 1500 titles a year. It is clear that only a fraction of instructional media production receives the attention of reviewers. By contrast, three book review journals (*Choice, Library Journal, Publishers Weekly*) each review 4,000 or more titles per year. *Book Review Index* in 1976 noted 38,200 reviews in 270 journals, out of a total book production of approximately the same magnitude.

In addition, the reviews for media are different from book reviews. Except for musical recordings, there is little or no comparison of new products with those already on the market, as is common in book reviewing. Librarians expect book reviews to tell them whether a title already on the shelves does the same job as a newly published one. In media reviewing, however, each new release is dealt with as a separate universe.

Cross-media approaches are unknown. Such an approach would compare filmstrip X on a given topic with multi-media kit Y on the same topic, a set of charts or study prints with an illustrated book or booklet.

All but a few of the 150 journals review only titles they recommend. But these may be so few that the reader cannot necessarily assume that a title not reviewed has been considered and turned down. Positive and negative reviews would be more helpful, but only *Previews* and a few other journals provide that service. (This aspect is not that different from major book review journals, since only a few professional journals are known for their publication of unfavorable assessments.) Reviewers' points of view need to be known.

Media Review Digest indexes almost all media reviews as *Book Review Digest* and *Book Review Index* do for book reviews. It appears less frequently, however than the review indexes for books. In any case, the lag time between publication or release date and the time review indexes appear is quite considerable, making them more useful for retrospective examination than for keeping up with current output.

Purchasing from favorable reviews alone cannot always be done even in the case of books: public libraries must stock best sellers no matter what the critics say; academic libraries must follow instructors' requests. In the audiovisual field—with the possible exception of film and musical recordings—it is almost impossible to achieve. (There are more entries for film lists throughout this work simply because there is both more reviewing of films and more selective listing of films on a variety of subjects.)

BIBLIOGRAPHIC TOOLS

There is no real equivalent to *Books in Print* (BIP) in the nonbook field. The NICEM indexes come closest. There are a total of 15 volumes to be examined, and they are considerably more expensive than BIP. In addition, three steps are required: checking the subject index, then a large number of entries in the alphabetical listing, and finally producers' catalogs to determine prices. *Subject Guide to Books in Print* gives needed bibliographic information and price with every entry. Computer searches of the NICEM data base are beginning to be available, however.

An effort at developing a nationwide data base for non-print materials is under way under the auspices of the National Commission on Libraries and Information Sciences and the Association for Educational Communications and Technology (AECT). When implemented, such a data base would enable a user to identify and track down a needed item not held in the local media collection.

Until data bases such as these are perfected and computer search facilities are more widely dispersed, the practicing media professional and other educators must depend on other means.

MEDIA SELECTION AIDS

Writers of texts on school media centers and on audiovisual instruction suggest to their readers what tools to use for selecting materials. As the following examples from such texts (published 1975-1977) show, their suggestions are not always practical.

Hicks and Tillin (1977) state that materials listed in *Resources for Learning* and *New Educational Materials*, among others, may be purchased without further evaluation. These guides were published in 1971 and 1970, respectively, are out of print, and list materials now ten or more years old!

Prostano (1977) makes no reference to any selection tools.

Delaney (1976) also tells media specialists to use *Resources for Learning* (1971, o.p.) and *Educational Screen and AV Guide,* which ceased reviewing some years ago.

The U.S. Office of Education (Moses, 1976) recommends selection aids published as far back as 1965 and several ceased serials such as *K-Eight, Media Review,* and *Blue Book of Audiovisual Materials.*

Marshall (1976) mentions no selection tools at all.

Berry (1975) lists selection aids for audiovisual materials published between 1963 and 1973.

Freeman (1975) recommends only four selection aids in addition to reviewing journals; all are aimed at elementary schools and all but one were published in 1972 or earlier.

Saunders (1975) is a concise, well-organized handbook, but when it comes to advice on selection tools, only one of those mentioned was published later than 1973 and they include, again, the defunct *Educational Screen and AV Guide* and *Media Review.*

Nickel (1975) recommends guides to free and inexpensive materials published in 1969!

Taggart (1975) resurrects the 1961 *Educational Media Index,* the very first effort at comprehensive bibliographic media coverage, and mentions other guides published 1965 to 1972.

Carter (1974) goes back to 1956 for a title to help with selecting recordings!

Guides designed for more limited circulation (Bergeson, 1976; Buckingham, 1976) do better than this.

When this is the advice media specialists and teachers receive, it's no wonder that somewhat casual procedures are the rule in media selection: examining producers' catalogs, visiting exhibits, consulting salesmen.

CHARACTERISTICS OF SERVICEABLE
SELECTION AIDS

Few writers have addressed themselves to an analysis of what makes a workable selection tool. Among those who have, Gillespie (1973) cites the authority of reviewers and editors and urges selectors to be aware of the selectivity and scope of the tools they use: know its limitations as to format, subject, time period, age group, its frequency of appearance or revision, and know also its features such as arrangement and indexing, what information reviews or annotations provide, whether there are comparisons or ratings.

DeLuca (1975) specifies that selection tools should cover all media and as many subject areas as possible, be organized by subject (subdivided by media and grade level), be consistent in their descriptions, provide both negative and positive signed free reviews, and state criteria followed by reviewers. Indexes, currency, and readability are musts.

The late Betty Fast (October 1976), recognizing the importance of vendor catalogs in media selection, asked that they be well indexed by subject, series, and individual titles, that they state whether parts of sets may be purchased separately, and that they indicate publication or release dates, applicable grade levels, full format details and contents. Citations of reviews and awards, cataloging information, specific teaching objectives and examples of art work are also helpful. Jobbers' catalogs should state the original producer.

SELECTION CRITERIA AND POLICIES

To be worthy of purchase, media should meet certain minimum standards. What these standards are is defined in statements by various organizations and individuals.

The American Association of School Librarians (1976) asks that materials "be relevant to today's world, represent artistic, historic, and literary qualities; reflect problems, aspirations, attitudes and ideals of a society; contribute to the objectives of the instructional program; be appropriate to the level of the user; represent differing viewpoints on controversial subjects; provide a stimulus to creativity" and "be of acceptable technical quality. . . ." Among objectives of selection are "to provide materials on opposing sides of controversial issues [and] . . . to provide materials which realistically represent our pluralistic society. . . ."

The National Education Association (1976) recommends that teachers have the major role in selecting instructional materials for classrooms and deplores adoption and other practices that hamper freedom of selection by local committees of professionals. Criteria encompass content, accuracy, presentation, relevance, philosophy, authorship, recency, cost, utility, physical characteristics, ease of use, and others. Media that fit the criteria are to be selected in the light of curricular objectives, their contribution to promoting sequential progress, to providing for student differentials in ability, interests, achievement and background. They should reflect our society of multiple ethnic, racial, religious, social and sexual characteristics, encourage self-instruction, and involve all senses.

Media Programs: District and School (1975) outlines procedures for media center collection building primarily in quantitative terms (so many titles and so many pieces of equipment for so many students). Obviously, a larger collection has a better chance of successfully furnishing learning materials. Purchases should be governed by an adopted selection policy so that selections will reflect curriculum, innovations in instruction, research in learning, availability of materials and equipment, and other factors. Such a policy is to reflect the principles of the Bill of Rights of the American Library Association, the School Library Bill of Rights of the American Association of School Librarians, the Students' Right to Read statement of the National Council of Teachers of English and similar professional statements on intellectual freedom, which outline procedures covering controversial materials. Titles are to be selected for purchase from published evaluations, reviews, lists of recommended titles and standard bibliographic tools.

Association of Media Producers criteria (see 01-17) ask evaluators to examine each title's content, motivation, grade level, the extent to which it achieves its stated purpose, and the nature of complementary materials provided with it.

The Educational Products Information Exchange, established to provide information to educators that would help them in their instructional materials selection urges (1973) that selection committees be composed of teachers, administrators, parents, students and other members of the school community. Its

Criterion Check List addresses authoritativeness of materials, budgeting, personnel and space requirements, age, grade and ability level, subject matter content, point of view and sequence or presentation, socioeconomic, geographic and ethnic orientation, students' learning and teachers' pedagogical styles, methodology and methods for evaluation and assessment, among other factors.

Fits and Misfits (National Committee for Citizens in Education, 1974) restates the same matter for parents and other non-professionals. But evaluation forms for various media presented by EPIE's Executive Secreatry (Komoski, 1975) essentially ask teachers to vote on whether they would use a given title again, not to evaluate them analytically.

The Educational Film Library Association asks judges at its American Film Festival to rate films on, among other factors, structure, cinematography, sound, originality, clarity of presentation, accuracy, appropriateness for intended audience.

Brown (1977) states content, purposes, appropriateness, cost, technical quality, circumstances of use, learner verification and validation as media selection criteria.

Brown, Norberg, and Srygley (1972) ask that media contribute to achieving specific instructional goals, be appropriate, authentic, organized, balanced, of satisfying technical quality, and cost-effective as compared to possible substitute titles.

Erickson's (1972) selection criteria demand that materials be useful and important to learners, interesting, sequential, authentic, typical and up-to-date, of good technical quality, carefully planned and validated, accurate, and in good taste. Prospective purchasers should examine how they deal with controversial issues and whether there is evidence of bias.

Erickson (1968) pioneered the distinction between selection at the classroom level and that at the system-wide level:

> Two levels of selection should be identified. The first is at the classroom teaching level. At this level the teacher selects from local or remote sources for a forthcoming unit and carries out an appropriate pre-use examination. The second level of selection is the system-wide, central distribution level. At this level the director of instructional media services must assume responsibility for selection of the best materials that teachers need to carry on their work effectively. The best basis for selection of materials at both levels is their probable contribution to valid teaching purposes (these of course being the best possible estimates of pupil needs), their excellence in technical quality, and their suitability for known groups of learners. The only valid reason for selection at the second level is to facilitate selection at the first.

Different criteria receive emphasis at each level. The classroom teacher may have to make do with an item not of the desired technical quality if it is the only one available to serve a particular instructional purpose. The system-wide or building-level selector, on the other hand, must anticipate all possible needs. Students' interests do not necessarily stay within the adopted curriculum and may lead them in an unanticipated direction at any time. The school library/media center exists to serve and nurture the individual interests of young people in schools as well as to support the curriculum. In addition, such interests or an event outside of school may touch off new directions for an entire classroom. Whenever this happens, the media center is expected to be ready with materials to outfit such unforeseen excursions.

How should media center collections be balanced among various subject areas, age and instructional levels, and formats?

Prostano (1977) urges that collections have "equilibrium" and be "sufficiently broad to meet the basic informational and recreational needs of students and teachers with any medium required" and "sufficiently specific in content and media to meet the direct instructional needs of the school with due regard for the age-grade-ability levels of students." But in a real world it may not be possible to provide information on each subject in each format, print and non-print. Fast (January 1976) questioned whether it may not be wiser to aim for "media saturation" for selected subjects than to try to cover all subjects with a limited number of formats.

WHO SHALL SELECT MEDIA?

The selection of instructional materials for purchase is a process that may involve persons both inside and outside the school. Committing large sums to the purchase of major learning systems or the adoption of textbooks obviously cannot be undertaken casually—but then, neither should the purchase of a set of filmstrips.

That agencies outside the school community have impact on instructional materials choices is a fact of life. Parents have a legitimate interest in what their children are taught. Community influence at its worst may take the form of censorship or attempted censorship. Professional organizations such as the American Library Association have guidelines for the proper handling of pressure groups so that legitimate concerns of both majority and minority interest groups can be reflected, and students exposed to a broad range of views.

Students are gaining impact on instructional decisions. EPIE guidelines (see p. xxi above) recommend that students be included on selection committees. That material is best which is most effective, and what is most effective may be what students best relate to.

How selection for purchase is to be divided among teachers, administrators, and media specialists is a matter of continuing debate. Teachers are anxious to reserve the right to choose classroom materials, and many teacher contracts so provide. Administrative personnel are more knowledgeable about district-wide objectives and developments in the subject field and in educational practice, but perhaps less so about levels of difficulty and manner of presentation appropriate to given situations. Librarians/media specialists know the market and bibliographic and reviewing tools, and they may have greater specific knowledge of media suitability for given purposes. Selection committees are frequently recommended, a suggestion probably valid chiefly for major expenses. Obviously, one cannot have a selection committee for the purchase of every two-dollar pamphlet. A 1970 NEA study found over half of teachers on both elementary and secondary levels participating in media selection, but the actual time given over to it was not reported (cited in Conover, 1974). Percentages were greater at the secondary than the elementary level, and in school systems with fewer than 25,000 students than in larger ones.

Data on media center expenditures and total audiovisual sales give some indication of what proportion of such purchases are made by media specialists. In 1973/74 (the latest data available from the Office of Education), library/media centers in U.S. schools spent $71,380,000 on audiovisual materials. Industry sources reported "el-hi" materials sales of $257,000,000 in 1973, $304,000,000 in 1974 (Hope Reports, Inc.). The proportions may be different four years later, but these figures do seem to bear out the observation that "the notion of the librarian or media director as responsible for nonprint media selection in the schools was found on the whole to be unfounded" (Conover, p. 52). That is the ideal advocated by the American Association of School Librarians and others who speak for the profession.

The bulk of audiovisual purchases would seem to be made by persons who do not have librarians' training in consulting reviews and recommendations before purchase. As we have noted, only a fraction of nonbook media output receives the attention of reviewers in any case.

What a reviewer says about a title is not as important as what a teacher does with it in the classroom. And the teacher is the ultimate selector when it comes to classroom use. As Erickson pointed out, district-wide selection exists only to facilitate that job for the teacher.

MEDIA SELECTION FOR
SPECIFIC LEARNING SITUATIONS

General selection criteria help to identify media worthy of purchase. But teachers need not only to identify media that are "good" but to ask "good for what or for whom?" From the many titles with accurate content, proper sequencing and vocabulary, and of fine technical quality, the teacher must select the format appropriate to the instructional objective.

Though few decisions in school can any longer be made entirely without regard to cost, cost alone should not be the determining factor in instructional media decisions. In actuality, however, a less expensive format may frequently do the job as well as a high-priced one. If color is not essential to the presentation, why use expensive color film? If motion is not essential, why use expensive moving picture film?

When questions such as these are raised, the relative popularity of films becomes puzzling. The market share of 16mm films has been decreasing, but, according to the Association of Media Producers, such sales still account for about one out of every four audiovisual software dollars.

Many films, in fact, are largely still pictures strung together with a sound track. A slide or filmstrip format with accompanying recording may actually be more effective, since it can more easily be stopped at or returned to a given frame for extended examination. These formats can be produced at a fraction of the cost of the equivalent film. Froehlich (1974) employs strong words about the misuse of the film medium, scorning "visually illiterate" films, whose entire message is conveyed by the sound track.

If the target audience is a small group or an individual, there may be no need for projection at all and a set of prints may suffice.

And we should also not forget that a book may be the most suitable medium. In Isaac Asimov's words, in a 1972 talk, the book is the "ultimately refined cassette

... self-contained, mobile, non-energy consuming, perfectly private, and largely under the control of the will."

There is no need to use electronic technology just "because it's there."

While many authors have outlined ways of integrating media selection into the instructional design process, teachers are human and "many of us select media for use on the basis of what we are most comfortable with or what is conveniently available. The choice is a subjective one, often with little consideration to objective criteria for selection" (Kemp, p. 47). Though geared to production, Kemp's text (1975) is pertinent to selection for purchase or rental as well. To provide "some basis for making logical, educated guesses," he succinctly tabulates the advantages, limitations, and local production costs of eight types of audiovisual materials (photographic prints, slides, filmstrips, recordings, overhead transparencies, motion pictures, television and display materials, and multi-image/multimedia). Kemp's Media Selection Diagrams for individual study, small group interaction, and large group presentation guide the user to examine instructional needs for visual, audio, audiovisual and multi-image, or simulation techniques, for stills, motion, or still-motion combinations.

Whether instructional objectives are in the cognitive, affective, or psycho-motor domains and whether media are to be used for learner feedback or evaluation will also determine the choice of medium or media.

Bergeson (1976) postulates seven levels of abstraction in the cognitive domain, ranging in increasing order from direct purposeful experience, to simulation, exhibits, motion pictures, still pictures, and visual-word symbols, to the spoken word. The level of abstraction and the necessity of visual, audio, and tactile components, of motion and color should determine the format chosen. The determination is further narrowed by learner characteristics and learning styles, physical and logistical considerations, and cost.

Anderson (1976), although aimed at instructors in industry training pro-grams, offers analyses equally relevant to school situations. Media selection for purposes of instruction (resulting in changed behavior) and information (no behavior change required) are distinguished, and detailed flow charts are presented for each. Variables in the choice of format are: size of group, pacing of lesson, necessity for motion, sound, and color, nature of instructional objective (cognitive, affective or psychomotor). Media are divided into audio, printed, audio-print, projected still-visual, audio projected still-visual, motion-visual, audio-motion-visual, in addition to objects themselves (realia), human and institutional resources, and computers. Bretz (1971) employs similar divisions.

Haney (1975) cautions the instructor to be sure that "a medium's capability for stimulus presentation match the requirements of the lesson objectives." Size of target group determines the form of projection and the need for short- or long-term access to visual display determines the choice of still or motion projection. In the cognitive domain, still projection and print are said to be suitable for many tasks, but dramatizations, motion pictures, and role playing are the formats of choice for learning attitudes and values (affective domain). Loop films are valuable for teaching motor skills, while multi-media presentations belong in the large-group instruction more commonly found in higher education. "When two or more media are appropriate for an instructional task, then the decision can be made on the basis of cost and availability " (p. 34).

xxvi / An Introduction to Media Selection

Armstrong (1973) is primarily addressed to special education media, but the chapter on selection outlines models for systematic selection on a construct involving internal and external dimensions of the material. The former subsume factors such as the material's target population, scope and content, sequential progression, instructional objectives, the number of lessons for which it is designed, and time required. Physical properties, packaging, availability, and transportability are among external factors.

Merrill and Goodman (1972) divide instructional media into five categories: objects, still pictures, motion pictures, audio, and written words and symbols. They single out motion pictures' ability to demonstrate human interactions and time-space relationships and their value in introducing or summarizing a unit of study. Recorded words, dramatizations, and music and written words can all be highly effective in generating attitudes and interest. With numerous specific examples for different subjects and grade levels, the authors lead the reader through all the steps necessary for formulating objectives in each of the three domains and selecting the appropriate media for teacher presentation, student practice, and student evaluation.

Individual learning styles are seen as the primary determiner in media selection by DeNike and Strother (1976). Individuals differ in their disposition to certain types of symbolic forms, in the meanings attached to symbols (a factor of inner- versus other-directedness) and in their manner of reasoning. Individuals also may be primarily visual, auditory, tactile, theoretical, quantitative, etc., in various combinations. Clearly, individual study is more suitable for the inner-directed student, audio components are of less value to the highly visual, and realia, models, and other objects are more suited to the student with tactile orientation. The book outlines detailed procedures for assessing individual styles and prescribing the media indicated.

On the other hand, Topper (1973) contends that "most software formats are interchangeable in use, especially when the audio and visual components are combined." It's the content that matters, although motion picture film clearly is needed to present motion. He does state, however, that, for cognitive learning, objective visuals, cool colors and regular sound are appropriate, whereas for affective results, subjective visuals, hot colors, angle shots, varied sound, and minimal abstraction are needed.

COMMONSENSE MEDIA SELECTION

What is a practical way to go about selecting instructional media that will meet the criteria and accomplish the objectives we have outlined? Which of the many hundreds of guides and reviewing journals described in this work are best to use? No one can master them all, but sophisticated instructional demands of today's schools dictate that judicious use of available guides replace hit-or-miss selection.

Media selectors must use a mix of retrospective and current, critical and descriptive lists. There is no such thing as a complete list—one that is complete in coverage of all media and all suppliers. This should be remembered in the case of distributors' catalogs which, of course, only supply the output of cooperating producers. It should also be remembered in the case of "core" or "starter" collections, which may be quite dated by the time they appear in print.

The prospective user needs to keep in mind the features of workable selection tools (as discussed on page xx) and know how to approach each particular one. If a guide is retrospective—for example, university film library catalogs or *The Elementary School Library Collection* (01-09) (both critical) or a NICEM index (descriptive)—it must be brought up to date. Current critical listings include review columns in the many professional journals cited. Time lag between publication or release of a title and its appearance even in a reviewing column is inevitable. The finest retrospective aid becomes useless if it does not cover what was issued in recent years or lists much that is no longer available. Vendors' catalogs are in the category of current descriptive listings and are best consulted last—after objective sources have provided initial information.

The media selector needs to know whether a guide lists materials actually previewed or used with students or whether it was compiled from catalog or advertising copy. The selector needs to know on what basis selections were made, whether the needed formats are included, and particularly how many titles are listed. An all-inclusive list may overwhelm, while another may be so brief as to be gratuitous.

Adequate subject access, contents synopses, and pricing information help to refine choices.

The annotations for each entry in this book provide these data. (They are more closely described on pages xiii to xv). Subject approaches are stressed throughout.

The time to make choices as to alternate formats is before consulting selection guides. That choice will depend on anticipated use, cost, available space and equipment, and what is already at hand. Tight inventory control over schools' media collections, whether housed in a media center or in departmental offices, certainly is a necessary ingredient of systematic media selection. Without such control, it is easy for a person to order an item that is very similar or identical to one already in the system's possession. Such procedures can be costly. It is preferable to decide whether one wants duplicate copies of a title or would rather spend the money on another format, another topic, or another instructional level.

Some 80 mediagraphies that appear in professional journals are annotated or mentioned in this book, and new ones are published each month. Since they frequently offer an excellent place to start, it is wise to be on the lookout for such articles and to clip or copy them for reference when needed. It also becomes crucial to follow critical reviews when vendors are reluctant to supply preview copies, since these reviews then take the place of previewing before purchase. (Previewing before instructional use is, of course, still a necessity to determine how best to fit the particular medium into the intended instructional design.)

Reviews perform a service by pointing out not only titles of outstanding quality but also those with scientific inaccuracy, misleading contents, technical deficiencies, or limitations of format. Consulting such critiques is vital, since materials found inaccurate or misleading may continue to be offered for sale. (For an example in the sensitive area of drug abuse education, see 09-03).

Word-of-mouth recommendations by persons whose judgment one trusts are important in media as in book selection. Salesmen cannot be objective, but they can refer potential purchasers to others who have used particular materials and who can provide field evaluations.

It is a sad state of affairs—and a waste of public money—when "much of the money schools are spending on nonprint media is wasted on inappropriate materials. Many of these materials are used once and then never taken off the shelf again or are used again only because the teacher doesn't know that there is a more appropriate alternative" (Komoski, 1977).

Improved selection procedures can change the situation. Educators share their findings and experiences with materials in printed reviews and retrospective compilations. It is foolish not to benefit from others' work and, by being better informed, better meet students' needs.

REFERENCES

Allen, William H. "Media Relationships to Instructional Objectives." In *Educational Media Yearbook 1977.* New York, Bowker, 1977. pp. 72-75.

American Association of School Librarians. *Policies and Procedures for Selection of Instructional Materials.* Chicago, 1976.

Anderson, Ronald H. *Selecting and Developing Media for Instruction.* New York, Van Nostrand, 1976.

Armstrong, Jenny R. *A Sourcebook for the Evaluation of Instructional Materials and Media.* Special Education Instructional Materials Center, University of Wisconsin, Madison, WI, 1973. ED 107 050.

Asheim, Lester. *Differentiating the Media.* Chicago, University of Chicago, 1975.

Audiovisual Instruction. April 1975 issue (v.20).

Bergeson, John. *Media in Instruction and Management Manual.* Central Michigan University, Mt. Pleasant, MI, 1976. ED 126 916.

Berry, Dorothea M. *A Bibliographic Guide to Educational Research.* Metuchen, NJ, Scarecrow, 1975.

Boucher, Brian G. *Handbook and Catalog for Instructional Media Selection.* Englewood Cliffs, NJ, Educational Technology, 1973.

Boyle, Deirdre. *Expanding Media.* Phoenix, AZ, Oryx Press, 1977.

Bretz, Rudy. *A Taxonomy of Communication Media.* Englewood Cliffs, NJ, Educational Technology, 1971.

Broadus, Robert N. *Selecting Materials for Libraries.* New York, Wilson, 1973.

Broadus, Robert N. "The Application of Citation Analysis to Library Collection Building." In *Advances in Librarianship* 7:299-335 (1977).

Brown, James W. *A V Instruction.* 5th ed. New York, McGraw-Hill, 1977.

Brown, James W., Kenneth Norbert, and Sara K. Srygley. *Administering Educational Media: Instructional Technology and Library Services.* 2nd ed. New York, McGraw-Hill, 1972.

Brown, R. W. Bill. "Computerized, Objectives-based Media Selection." *Educational Technology* 15:57 (November 1975).

Buckingham, Betty Jo. *Selection Bibliography: A Bibliography of Selection Sources for School Library Media Centers.* Department of Public Instruction, Des Moines, IO, 1976. ED 130 678.

Carter, Mary D., Wallace J. Bonk, and Rose Mary Magrill. *Building Library Collections.* 4th ed. Metuchen, NJ, Scarecrow, 1974.

Catholic Library World. May-June 1976 issue (v.47).

Cavert, C. Edward. *Procedural Guidelines for the Design of Mediated Instruction.* Washington, DC, Association for Educational Communications and Technology, 1974.

Chisholm, Margaret E. *Media Indexes and Review Sources.* College Park, School of Library and Information Services, University of Maryland, 1972.

Coger, Richard M. *The Development of a Selection Model and an Effectiveness Model to Assist Teachers in Monitoring the Levels of Accountability of Educational Media.* Ph.D. thesis, Ohio State University, 1972.

Conover, Craig R. *A Study of the Reported Theory and Practice of Non-Print Software Media Selection.* 1974. ED 099 001.

Coursen, David. *Use of Instructional Media in the Schools.* ERIC Clearinghouse, on Educational Management, Eugene, OR 97403, 1976. ED 123 763.

Davies, Ruth Ann. *The School Library Media Center.* 2nd ed. New York, Bowker, 1974.

Delaney, Jack J. *The Media Program in the Elementary and Middle School.* Hamden, CT, Shoestring, 1976.

DeLuca, Joan. *Materials Selection.* Austin, Texas Educational Agency, 1975. ED 120 986.

DeNike, Lee, and Seldon Strother. *Media Prescription and Utilization as Determined by Educational Cognitive Style.* Line and Color Publishers, 60 E. Stimson Street, Athens, OH 45701, 1976.

Diamond, Robert M. "Piecing Together the Media Selection Jigsaw." *Audiovisual Instruction* 22:50-52 (Jan. 1977).

Educational Products Information Exchange. *Improving Materials Selection Procedures: A Basic "How to" Handbook. EPIE Report No. 54,* New York, 1973.

Erickson, Carlton W. H. *Fundamentals of Teaching with Audiovisual Technology.* 2nd ed. New York, Macmillan, 1972.

Erickson, Carlton W. H. *Administering Instructional Media Programs.* New York, Macmillan, 1968.

Fast, Betty. "Mediacentric." *Wilson Library Bulletin,* 50:370-371 (Jan. 1976); 51: 178-179 (Oct. 1976).

Freeman, Patricia. *Pathfinder: An Operational Guide for the School Librarian.* New York, Harper, 1975.

Froehlich, Robert E. *Film Reviews in Psychiatry, Psychology and Mental Health.* Ann Arbor, MI, Pierian, 1974.

Gerlach, Vernon S., and Donald P. Ely. *Teaching and Media: A Systematic Approach.* Englewood Cliffs, NJ, Prentice-Hall, 1971.

Gillespie, John T., and Diana S. Spirt. *Creating a School Media Program.* New York, Bowker, 1973.

Goodman, R. Irwin. "A Systematic Procedure for Instructional Media Selection." *Audiovisual Instruction* 16:37-38 (Dec. 1971).

Gorman, Don A. *An Instructional Materials Selection/Decision/Prescription Model.* Dubuque, IO, Kendall Hunt Publ., 1976.

Gropper, George L. *Instructional Strategies.* Englewood Cliffs, NJ, Educational Technology, 1974.

Gropper, George L., and others. *Criteria for the Selection and Use of Visuals in Instruction.* Englewood Cliffs, NJ, Educational Technology, 1971.

Haney, John B., and Eldon J. Ullmer. *Educational Communications and Technology.* 2nd ed. Dubuque, IO, Wm. C. Brown, 1975.

Hannigan, Jane Ann. "A Conundrum of Our Time: Access to Media." *School Media Quarterly* 5:253-60 (Summer 1977).

Hicks, Warren B., and Alma M. Tillin. *Managing Multi-Media Libraries.* New York, Bowker, 1977.

Hilliard, Robert L. *Television and the Teacher: A Handbook for Classroom Use.* New York, Hastings House, 1976.

Hostrop, Richard W. *Education Inside the Media Center.* Hamden, CT, Linnet, 1973.

Hug, William E. *Instructional Design and the Media Program.* Chicago, American Library Association, 1975.

Kemp, Jerrold E. *Planning and Producing Audiovisual Materials.* New York, T. Y. Crowell, 1975.

Kinder, James S. *Using Instructional Media.* New York, Van Nostrand, 1973.

Kingston, R. D. "The Selection and Use of Audiovisuals." *American Vocational Journal* 50: 58, 60 (November 1975).

Klasek, Charles B. *Instructional Media in the Modern School.* Lincoln, NE, Professional Educators Publications, 1972.

Komoski, Kenneth. "Evaluating Your Teaching Tools." *Learning* 3:92-101 (March 1975).

Komoski, Kenneth. "Evaluating Nonprint Media." *Today's Education* 66:96-97 (March-April 1977).

Liesener, J. W. *A Systematic Planning Process for School Media Programs.* Chicago, American Library Association, 1976.

Locatis, Craig N., and Francis D. Atkinson. "A Guide to Instructional Media Selection." *Educational Technology* 16:19-21 (Aug. 1976).

Marshall, Faye D. *Managing the Modern School Library.* West Nyack, NY, Parker, 1976.

Merrill, M. David, and R. Irwin Goodman. *Selecting Instructional Strategies and Media: A Place to Begin.* Provo, UT, Division of Instructional Services, Brigham Young University, 1972.

Media Programs: District and School. Chicago, American Association of School Librarians, 1975.

Moses, Kathlyn J., and Lois B. Watt. *Adis to Media Selection for Students and Teachers.* Washington, DC, Superintendent of Documents, 1976. S/N 017-080-01563-3. HE 19.102:M 46/2/976.

National Committee for Citizens in Education. *Fits and Misfits: What You Should Know about Your Child's Learning Materials.* Columbia, MD, 1974.

National Education Association. *Instructional Materials: Selection for Purchase.* Rev. ed. Washington, DC, 1976. ED 130 380.

New York (City). Board of Education. *The School Library Media Center: A Force for Learning.* New York, 1975.

Nickel, Mildred. *Steps to Service: A Handbook of Procedures for the School Library Center.* Chicago, American Library Association, 1975.

Potter, Earl L., and G. Douglas Mayo. "Selection of Media by Media Centers." *Educational Technology* 17:45-48 (April 1977).

Procedures for Textbook and Instructional Materials Selection. Arlington, VA, Educational Research Service, 1976.

Prostano, Emanuel T., and Joyce S. Prostano. *The School Library Media Center.* 2nd ed. Littleton, CO, Libraries Unlimited, 1977.

Romiszowski, A. J. *The Selection and Use of Instructional Media.* New York, Wiley, 1974.

Saunders, Helen E. *The Modern School Library.* 2nd ed. rev. by Nancy Polette. Metuchen, NJ, Scarecrow, 1975.

Selecting Educational Equipment and Materials for School and Home. Association for Childhood Education International, 3615 Wisconsin Avenue, N.W., Washington, DC 20016, 1976.

Selecting Media for Learning: Readings from Audiovisual Instruction. Washington, DC, Association for Educational Communications and Technology, 1974.

Shapiro, Lillian. *Serving Youth—Communication and Commitment in the High School Library.* New York, Bowker, 1975.

Standard Criteria for the Selection and Evaluation of Instructional Material. National Center on Educational Media and Materials for the Handicapped. Columbus, Ohio State University, 1976. ED 132 760.

Stevenson, Gordon. "Standards for Bibliographies of Discographies." *RQ* 15:309-316 (Summer 1976).

Taggart, Dorothy. *A Guide to Sources in Educational Media and Technology.* Metuchen, NJ, Scarecrow, 1975.

Taylor, Kenneth I. "Media in the Context of Instruction." *School Media Quarterly* 4:224-228, 237-241 (Spring 1976).

Topper, Louis. *A-V Technology and Learning.* Englewood Cliffs, NJ, Educational Technology, 1973.

Vandergrift, Kay E. "Are We Selecting for a Generation of Skeptics?" *School Library Journal* 23:41-44 (Feb. 1977).

Wager, Walter. "Media Selection in the Affective Domain: A Further Interpretation of Dale's Cone of Experience for Cognitive and Affective Learning." *Educational Technology* 15:9-12 (July 1975).

Webster, William J. *The Evaluation of Instructional Materials.* Washington, DC, ERIC Clearinghouse on Information Resources, 1976. ED 131 861.

Woodbury, Marda. *A Guide to Sources of Educational Information.* Washington, DC, Information Resources Press, 1976.

Section I
Comprehensive Lists

01–Comprehensive Lists

01-Comprehensive Lists

Multi-media and multi-subject lists make up this chapter. Among them are indexes to media reviews, recommended collections, and journals reviewing media on all subjects and in all formats. Most are serial publications, issued monthly, annually, or on some other regular basis.

Audiovisual Marketplace (Bowker, 1977. $19.95) is a biennial guide to media producers, hardware manufacturers, distributors, educational radio and TV stations, reference books, and related information. "Periodicals and trade journals" list some that have ceased publication.

01-01   **Educators' Purchasing Guide.** 6th ed. North American Publishing Co., 401 N. Broad Street, Philadelphia, PA 19108, 1975. 1v. $29.50. LC 72-9581.

Purpose: comprehensive index to suppliers of equipment and supplies for educational needs, including audio-visual media

Grade level: all

Arrangement: classified subject arrangement for elementary and secondary divisions of audio-visual section and of atlas, globe and map sections

Subjects: all

Entries: name and address of supplier; media symbol

Indexes: alphabetical subject index for each of 3 sections

Period covered: available at time of publication

Revision and updating: supersedes *Educators' Purchasing Master*, 3rd ed. (1971)

Media represented: filmloops, filmstrips, films, graphic materials, maps, microform, simulation games, kits, manipulative materials, audio recordings, slides, transparencies, video recordings

Producers represented: over 2000

Features: Entries are under highly specific subject terms ("game theory," "eggs," "Impeachment," "Jamestown"). Suppliers *not* listed include National Geographic Society, museums, several major producers of simulation games.

Subject terms: all subjects

01-02   **Index to Instructional Media Catalogs: A Multi-Indexed Directory of Materials and Equipment for Use in Instructional Programs.** Bowker, 1974. 272p. $21.50. LC 74-9255.

Purpose: comprehensive index to producers' catalogs

Grade level: all

Arrangement: appr. 140 topical groupings, each subdivided by up to 20 media designations; texts, tests, workbooks, and other print media together with non-print

Subjects: all

Entries: producer listing only

grade level and suitability as basal, supplementary, individualized instructional aid

Indexes: none

Period covered: available at time of publication

Revision and updating:

01-02 (cont'd)

Media represented: filmloops, filmstrips, films, graphic materials, maps, simulation games, kits, audio recordings, video recordings, transparencies, manipulative materials

Producers represented: 631

Features: Similar in purpose to several sections of *Educators' Purchasing Guide* (01-01), but more refined in its grade level and instructional purpose designations and with improved subject access. Among subjects separately entered are: English as a second language, computer mathematics, training, technology, Afro-American history, urban environment, cinematography and television, etc. Among producers not indexed are: Bro-Dart, New York Graphic Society (art reproductions), National Audiovisual Center, National Geographic Society. [See also *Educational Media Catalogs on Microfiche* 01-25).]

Subject terms: all subjects

01-03*   Media Review Digest 1977. (vol. 7). Pierian Press, Ann Arbor, MI 48106, 1977. 542p. $89.50.

Purpose: index to media reviews in 150 periodicals; evaluative

Grade level: all

Arrangement: 4 media groupings: film and videotape, filmstrips, records and tapes, miscellaneous

Subjects: all

Entries: 40,000 citations and cross references, 3200 in DDC listing

> format details, running time, producer, release date; sale/rental price (in most cases); contents note (in some cases); citations and characterization of reviews (+, -, *); excerpts; grade level; subject headings; Dewey Decimal number

Indexes: subject (alphabetical, Dewey Decimal Classification, general subject)

Period covered: 1974-76 (some earlier)

Revision and updating: planned semi-annual supplements between annual volumes

Media represented: audio recordings, films, filmstrips, graphic materials, kits, manipulative materials, simulation games, slides, transparencies, video-recordings

Producers represented: appr. 800

Features: Includes reviews of feature films, listings of film awards and prizes, (including Academy Awards, those of the American Film Festival, and those of several other organizations concerned with non-entertainment film). Mediagraphies locate filmographies and discographies appearing in 1976.

Subject terms: all subjects

01-04   International Index to Multi-Media Information. Audio-Visual Associates, 180 East California Boulevard, Pasadena, CA 91105. Quarterly. $60.00/year. LC 72-621281.

Purpose: index to media reviews in 100 periodicals; evaluative

Grade level: all

Arrangement: alphabetical title

Subjects: all

01-04 (cont'd)
Entries: appr. 9000/year

type of medium; distributor; format; quotes from reviews; release date, price(s), age and grade level not uniformly included

Indexes: subject

Period covered: current releases

Revision and updating: issued quarterly. 1970-1972 cumulative volume published by Bowker (1975; $30.00). December 1975 last issue published

Media represented: filmstrips, films, filmloops, graphic materials, maps, manipulative materials, kits, audio recordings, slides, simulation games, transparencies, video recordings

Producers represented: commercial, academic, institutional, government

Features: Not just an index, this stands by itself as a comprehensive reference to current media production. Review quotes and other data included in entries frequently offer sufficient information to make purchasing decisions. The subject index, even without cross references, is quite workable. Finally, there is access here to releases of organizations, museums, government agencies, and other producers far more numerous than could be known by direct contact. It should be noted that among periodicals *not* indexed are teachers' stand-bys such as *Scholastic Teacher* and *Learning*. An explanation of abbreviations would be a big help!

Subject terms: all subjects

01-05   **Museum Media.** Paul Wasserman and Esther Herman. Gale Research Company, Detroit, MI 48226, 1973. 455p. $62.00. LC 73-16335.

Purpose: comprehensive directory of materials available from museums

Grade level: all

Arrangement: alphabetical by name of institution

Subjects:		
archaeology	horticulture	paleontology
art	monuments and	planetaria
botanical gardens	memorials	zoology
history	natural history	others

Entries: several thousand

bibliographic data, publication date, price (publications); format information, ordering information (media); availability of lists of films, slides, postcards, etc. noted

Indexes: title and keyword index to media, subject and geographic index to institutions

Period covered: available at time of publication

Revision and updating:

Media represented: graphic materials, films, filmstrips, slides, free and inexpensive publications

Producers represented: 732 U.S. and Canadian

Features: Far more than just an aid to art research, this tool also is a key to educational media issuing from institutions such as the Museum of the American Indian, Field Museum of Natural History, Fisher Museum of Forestry (Harvard), Collection of Musical Instruments (Yale), National Museum of Transport, and restorations such as Sturbridge Village, but Williamsburg is

01-05 (cont'd)
Features (cont'd) missing.) Books, booklets and exhibition catalogs constitute
the bulk of the listings. [See also *Sources* (01-22) and *A Guide to Slide and
Photograph Collections of Primitive Art* (20-06).]
Subject terms: all subjects

history	visual arts
science	

01-06 **Media 1974-75.** Purdue University Audio Visual Center, Lafayette,
IN 55907, 1974. 215p. ED 089 722.
Purpose: library catalog; recommendations
Grade level: intermediate, secondary
Arrangement: alphabetical title
Subjects: all
Entries: appr. 2750

type of medium, running time, producer or distributor, release date; rental
price, grade level; contents summary
Indexes: subject, divided by media
Period covered:
Revision and updating:
Media represented: films, slides, kits
Producers represented: various
Features: Slides are particularly well represented.
Subject terms: all subjects

01-07 **Audio-Visual Resource Guide.** 9th ed. National Council of Churches.
Friendship Press, P.O. Box 37844, Cincinnati, OH 45327, 1972.
477p. $8.95. LC 58-13297.
Purpose: recommended media primarily for use in religious education
Grade level: all
Arrangement: alphabetical title

Subjects:	archaeology	the family	the individual
	arts and leisure	health	religion
	community and nation	history	science and
	education		technology

Entries: 2500

format, source, purchase and rental price, release date; audience suitability;
critical review and rating; subject indicators
Indexes: classed subject index
Period covered: 1960s to 1972, some earlier
Revision and updating: previous edition 1970
Media represented: films, filmstrips, graphic materials, kits, slides
Producers represented: religious, educational, government, museums, commercial
Features: Far from being entirely religious in nature, since many titles listed are
suitable for secular settings. Films predominate. Includes 140 "Selected
Feature-Length Films Available in 16mm" (pp. 442-458).

01-07 (cont'd)
Subject terms:

film study

philosophy and

guidance

religion

01-08   Core Media Collection for Secondary Schools. Lucy Gregor Brown.
Bowker, 1975. 221p. $17.50.
Purpose: recommendations "based on favorable reviews in (appr. 50) professional
review journals" and listing in selection guides
Grade level: secondary
Arrangement: by subject (using *Sears List of Subject Headings*)
Subjects: all
Entries: appr. 2000

type of medium, format details, producer, price; grade level; release date;
contents note (not in all cases); recommending source, awards; Dewey
Decimal classification; asterisk marks highly recommended selections
Indexes: title
Period covered: 1960s to February 1974, some earlier
Revision and updating:
Media represented: audio recordings, filmstrips, films, filmloops, kits, transparencies, graphic materials, manipulative materials
Producers represented: appr. 140 commercial, academic, government, institu-
tional, television
Features: Suffers from the shortcomings of *Sears* (e.g., still does not recognize
the USSR, only "Russia"). There also are no entries for film, genetics,
marriage, motion pictures, pregnancy, science fiction, sex education,
venereal disease, and only one (on divorce) under social problems—to
mention just a few current concerns of secondary education.
Subject terms: all subjects

**01-09*   The Elementary School Library Collection; A Guide to Books and
Other Media.** 11th ed. Bro-Dart, Newark, NJ, 1977. 788p. $29.95.
LC 77-11927.
Purpose: recommendations on basis of "literary quality, appeal to children,
excellence in format, authenticity of content and suitability for the range
of reading, listening and viewing abilities" of elementary school children.
"Consideration has been given to materials that have an impact of social
significance" but may not meet all criteria. Audiovisual materials based on
books generally not recommended unless book is recommended.
Grade level: primary, intermediate
Arrangement: Dewey Decimal
Subjects: all
Entries: 1665 (excluding books)

type of medium; format details; producer/distributor, release date, price;
grade level; contents summary; subject terms; asterisk marks titles new to
this edition; availability of Spanish language version
Indexes: author, title, subject
Period covered: available March 1977
Revision and updating: 10th ed. 1976

01-09 (cont'd)

Media represented: audio recordings, filmloops, filmstrips, graphic materials, kits, manipulative materials, slides, transparencies

Producers represented: various

Features: Filmstrips account for over half of non-print entries. Emphasis on titles showing "wholesome attitudes of mutual respect and understanding among all people," poetry recordings, "a full representation of the range of musical literature . . . including modern artists who represent different ethnic groups and their music," creative approaches in art. "Media for Pre-School Children" (p. 777-782) includes over 200 non-print items. *Films for the Elementary Classroom* (32-23) makes a good supplement as films, video programs (as well as maps, pamphlets, and paperback books) are excluded.

Subject terms: all subjects
      early childhood education

01-10*   **A Catalog of United States Government Produced Audiovisual Materials 1974.** National Audiovisual Center, Washington, DC 20409, 1974. 356p. free. ED 101 752.

Purpose: comprehensive catalog of sales and rental films available from National Audiovisual Center

Grade level: all

Arrangement: alphabetical title

Subjects:

aviation	electronics	rehabilitation
business and economics	industrial arts	safety
civics and government	marine	space programs
education	medicine	others

Entries: 4500

    running time, producer, release date; sale and rental price, if any; ordering information; contents note; asterisk marks new entries
        omitted: grade level

Indexes: subject (indicates type of medium if other than 16mm film)

Period covered: 1942-1973

Revision and updating: *Price Change List* (1976); *Select List*; subject listings; also direct inquiry

Media represented: films, filmloops, audio recordings, filmstrips, slides

Producers represented: appr. 70 federal agencies

Features: The Center offers to supply filmographies on request and make referrals to appropriate commercial or government agency handling free-loan films. Sales and free rentals through the Center. Many agencies issue their own lists of films and other media, including *US Navy Films for the Public* (Department of the Navy, Washington, DC 20350) and *Index of Army Motion Pictures for Public Non-Profit Use* (Department of the Army, 2800 Eastern Boulevard, Baltimore, MD 21220). Others are mentioned in appropriate chapters in Section II. Similar list: *Guide to Government-Loan Films* (01-23).

Subject terms: all subjects

01-11* **Previews.** Bowker. $15/year.
Purpose: evaluations
Grade level: all
Arrangement: 5 or more media groupings in each issue, subdivided by subject
Subjects: all subjects

art	guidance	religion
computers	health	safety
consumer education	language arts	sex education
driver education	literature & drama	social studies
early childhood	mathematics	sociology
environment/ecology	music	sports
family living	nutrition	venereal disease
filmmaking	psychology	women's studies

Entries: appr. 1500/year

running time, format details, producer, price, release date; rental price (films); availability of teacher's guide; grade level; signed critical review
Indexes: indexed in *Media Review Digest* (01-03)
Period covered: current releases
Revision and updating: published 9x/year
Media represented: audio recordings, films, filmstrips, graphic materials, kits, slides, transparencies
Producers represented:
Features: Annual "Filmstrips and Slides Round-up" (33-04); "Audiovisual Guide" (01-31).
Subject terms: all subjects

01-12 **Booklist.** Chicago, American Library Association. $20.00/year.
Purpose: recommendations on the basis of authenticity, content, medium utilization, technical quality "to provide a current guide to materials worthy of consideration for purchase by . . . school media centers"
Grade level: all
Arrangement: by media categories
Subjects: all
Entries: appr. 800/year excluding government publications

format, producer, release date, rental and purchase prices; age level; critical reviews
Indexes: title index to reviews in each issue and annual index in August issue; indexed in *Media Review Digest* (01-03)
Period covered: current releases
Revision and updating: published 23x/year
Media represented: films, filmstrips, audio recordings, slides, video recordings (cassettes), government publications, manipulative materials, kits
Producers represented: various
Features: Reviews of films and filmstrips are published in each issue and make up about one-half the total number. Other categories appear at various intervals. Reviews of recordings emphasize the non-musical. See separate description of "Government Publications" column (35-06).
Subject terms: all subjects

01-13   The Seed Catalog; A Guide to Teaching/Learning Materials. Jeffrey
Schrank. Beacon Press, 1974. 374p. illus. $12.95; $5.95pa. LC 73-16888.
Purpose: recommendations "for those in any situation who believe that learning
takes place through involvement with a great variety of viewpoints and
opinions"; "biased in favor of [the] provocative, creative, and controversial"
Grade level: secondary
Arrangement: chapters on various media as well as other publications, periodicals,
organizations; randomly arranged by publisher or issuing organization within
chapters
Subjects: all
Entries: over 300

ordering information; facsimile reprints from publishers' catalogs for some;
some contents notes; critical reviews of appr. 200 films
Indexes: combined author, title, subject index includes media symbols
Period covered: 1960s-1970s
Revision and updating: Schrank also edits *Media Mix* (01-28) where some of
this material first appeared
Media represented: free and inexpensive publications, audio recordings, simula-
tion games, films, video recordings, slides, filmstrips, graphic materials
Producers represented: small presses, organizations, standard educational
suppliers
Features: A guide to what is topical in the counterculture, to "radical software,"
and to novel approaches to current concerns such as drug and sex education,
population, feminism. The film section is the most valuable.
Subject terms:

        film study   contemporary issues
        health and safety education

01-14   Media Evaluations 1974. Indiana Association for Educational
Communications and Technology. School of Education, Indiana
State University, Terre, Haute, IN 56909, 1974. 40p. ED 090 952.
Purpose: evaluations by an Association committee; copy of evaluation forms
supplied
Grade level: all
Arrangement: general Dewey Decimal order within media groupings
Subjects: all
Entries: appr. 150

running time, producer, sale price, release date; signed critical review and
rating
        omitted: grade level
Indexes: combined subject and title
Period covered: 1969-1973
Revision and updating:
Media represented: audio recordings, films, filmstrips, filmloops, kits, graphic
materials, slides
Producers represented: appr. 40
Features: Films are largest single group.
Subject terms: all subjects

01-15*   **Curriculum Review.** Curriculum Advisory Service, 500 S. Clinton St., Chicago, IL 60607. $35/year.
Purpose: evaluations
Grade level: all
Arrangement: subject
Subjects: all
Entries: appr. 25/year (excluding print & curriculum materials)

      producer, release date; price; grade level; signed critical review
Indexes:
Period covered: released up to two years prior to publication
Revision and updating: published 5x/year
Media: filmstrips, simulation games, kits
Producers: various commercial, institutional
Features: Primarily evaluations of curriculum materials, supplementary books and professional references plus feature articles.
Subject terms: all subjects

01-16*   **Teacher.** Macmillan Professional Magazines, Greenwich, CT 06830. $8.00/year.
Purpose: "Keeping Up" column recommends instructional materials
Grade level: primary, intermediate
Arrangement: by subject
Subjects: all
Entries: appr. 60/year

      format, producer, price; grade level
         omitted: release date; running time (films)
Indexes: indexed in *Media Review Digest* (01-03)
Period covered: current and recent releases
Revision and updating: published 9x/year
Media represented: audio recordings, films, filmstrips
Producers represented: various
Features: Includes free-loan films. Also books.
Subject terms: all subjects

01-17*   "The *Learning A-V* Awards." Bruce Raskin. *Learning*, v.5, December 1976, p. 53-62.
Purpose: "the best of the most recently released"; recommendations by panels of teachers, AV librarians, subject specialists, media creators and technicians on basis of prescribed evaluation criteria (available from magazine at 530 University Avenue, Palo Alto, CA 94301. $0.50 & ssae)
Grade level: all
Arrangement: by subject

Subjects:	art/humanities	math	social studies
	language arts	science	miscellaneous

Entries: 71

      running time (films), producer, purchase and rental price; grade level; synopsis, comments and teaching suggestions
Indexes:
Period covered: 1975/76 releases

01-17 (cont'd)
Revision and updating: annually in December issues; 12/75 issue recommended 67
Media represented: films, filmstrips
Producers represented: appr. 40
Features: 31 films, 40 individual filmstrips and sets. Little for senior high.
Subject terms: all subjects

01-18*   **Instructor**. 7 Bank Street, Danville, NY 14437. $14.00/year.
Purpose: "Reviews" column in most issues
Grade level: primary, intermediate
Arrangement: by subject and media
Subjects: all
Entries: appr. 25/year (excluding books)

> format data, price, producer/distributor; grade level; signed critical review
>   omitted: release date

Indexes: indexed in *Media Review Digest* (01-03)
Period covered: current and recent releases
Revision and updating: published 10x/year
Media represented: filmstrips, kits, manipulative materials
Producers represented: various
Features: Mostly books, professional books and curriculum sets.
Subject terms: all subjects

01-19*   **Media and Methods**. North American Publishing Co., 401 North
     Broad Street, Philadelphia, PA 19108. $9.00/year.
Purpose: "Mediabag" (announcements) and "Recommended" columns appear
     4-5x/year
Grade level: secondary
Arrangement: random
Subjects: language arts, social studies
Entries: appr. 75/year

> running time, producer/distributor; ("Recommended") release date, price;
>   signed critical review

Indexes: indexed in *Media Review Digest* (01-03)
Period covered: current releases
Revision and updating: published 9x/year
Media represented: audio recordings, films, filmstrips, graphic materials, slides,
     television, video recordings
Producers represented: various commercial
Features: Focus on "now" methods and subjects. October issue on television,
     December issue on film, and selection of year's best filmstrips in April
     issue (33-05) are annual features. Frequent filmographies (see 11-20, 32-24,
     and 07-01, 07-11, 11-16, 17-25 "Features"; see also introductions to 15—
     Psychology and Guidance, 17—Social Studies and 22—Women's Studies).
     Prime Time School Television (43-08) is published as an insert.
Subject terms:
       film study   social studies
       language arts

01-20* **Films and Other Media for Projection.** Library of Congress, Washington, DC 20541. $60.00/year.

Purpose: comprehensive; part of *National Union Catalog*
Grade level: all
Arrangement: alphabetical title
Subjects: all
Entries: appr. 10,000/year

> format data, running time, producer, release date; contents summary; subject headings; Dewey Decimal and Library of Congress classification numbers

Indexes: subject index in each issue; cross reference from name of producer
Period covered: current and recent releases
Revision and updating: published 4x/year; last issue is annual cumulation; *Motion Pictures and Filmstrips*, 1968-1972 (4v. 1973). $125.
Media represented: films, filmstrips, slides, transparencies
Producers represented: appr. 600 in U.S. and Canada
Features:
Subject terms: all subjects

01-21* **Alternatives in Print 77-78: Catalog of Social Change Publications.** 5th ed. New Glide Publications, 330 Ellis Street, San Francisco, CA 94102, 1977. 198p. $12.95; $8.95pa. LC 76-54384.

Purpose: comprehensive "access to publications and productions of the counter-culture, the Third World, the small press, and the dissident press" compiled by a task force of American Library Association-Social Responsibilities Round Table members.
Grade level: secondary
Arrangement: alphabetical by publisher
Subjects: representative subject headings:

Africa	directories	peace movement
alternative lifestyle	ecology	poetry
arts	education	radical
Black liberation	feminism	professionalism
movement	health	sexism
children's books	imperialism	Women's liberation
community	literature	movement
development	Marxism	others

Entries: over 10,000

> titles and prices only
> omitted: date of publication

Indexes: subject
Period covered: material in print at time of publication
Revision and updating: previous editions 1973, 1975
Media represented: audio recordings, films, free and inexpensive publications, graphic materials, video recordings
Producers represented: appr. 1500 small presses and organizations, including some in Canada, Europe and other countries

01-21 (cont'd)

Features: The "alternative press" output can serve as source material for study of contemporary issues and related subjects. As with all non-evaluative listings, preview and examination of the material before classroom use are a must. Films, posters, radio, tapes and videotapes are retrieved through the subject index. [Similar lists: *International Directory of Little Magazines and Small Presses* (Dustbooks, P.O. Box 1056, Paradise, CA 95969. $8.95; $5.95pa.); "Alternative Periodicals" column appears 2-3x/year in *Wilson Library Bulletin*.]

Subject terms:

contemporary issues	ethnic studies	international
economics	health and safety	education
	education	poetry

01-22*   Sources: A Guide to Print and Nonprint Materials Available from Organizations, Industry, Government Agencies, and Specialized Publishers. Gaylord Professional Publications, P.O. Box 61, Syracuse, NY 13201. $60/year.

Purpose: comprehensive; "a continuing constantly building, compendium of information about nontraditional sources", aiming at "characterization of specific sources, rather than complete bibliographic listings"

Grade level: all

Arrangement: alphabetical by publisher

Subjects: all

Entries: over 4000

(print) title, price (if any); (non-print) title, format data, running time omitted: publication or release date

Indexes: title; free & inexpensive; subject

Revision and updating: published 3x/year

Media represented: audio recordings, films, filmloops, filmstrips, free and inexpensive publications, graphic materials, kits, manipulative materials, slides, video recordings

Producers represented: appr. 600 in first issue

Features: Information that was previously unavailable in published form or had to be pieced together from *Encyclopedia of Associations, Directory of Research Centers*, and other reference works. A necessary supplement to school-oriented guides to free materials, which generally omit sources that by any stretch of the imagination could be considered "anti-establishment." Very little duplication with *Alternatives in Print* (01-21).

Subject terms: all subjects

01-23*   Guide to Government-Loan Films. Serina Press, Alexandria, VA 22305, 1976. 2v. $19.90.

Purpose: comprehensive; v.1 The Civilian Agencies; v.2 The Defense Agencies

Grade level: all

Arrangement: by issuing agency, v.1 also by media

Subjects: all

01-23 (cont'd)
Entries: several thousand

running time, release date (not in all cases), summary; distributors
separately listed
omitted: audience suitability
Indexes: subject
Period covered: 1960s-1970s, also earlier
Revision and updating: previous edition 1969
Media represented: films, filmstrips, slides
Producers represented: U.S. government
Features:
Subject terms: all subjects

**01-24*   Nonprint Materials on Communication; An Annotated Directory
of Select Films, Videotapes, Videocassettes, Simulations and
Games.** June D. Buteau. Scarecrow Press, Metuchen, NJ 08840,
1976. 444p. $16.00. LC 76-21857.

Purpose: recommendations; "relevant, recent, timely, provocative, authoritative,
or rare" items and primary source materials
Grade level: secondary
Arrangement: 3 media groupings, each divided topically

Subjects:		
animal (films only)	information systems	parliamentary
argument	the interview	procedure
business/organizational	intrapersonal	perception
cross cultural	language	persuasion
delivery	learning theory	political
dyadic	listening	process/theory
educational technology	mass media	public speaking
family	movements (civil rights,	rhetorical topics
freedoms	peace, Women's)	therapy
group discussion	nonverbal	

Entries: 2236 (including adult and professional use)

running time, producer/distributor, release date (not in all cases); audience
level; contents summary; (simulation games) time and number of players
required
omitted: price
Indexes: "cross-category"
Period covered: available at time of writing
Revision and updating:
Media represented: over 1000
Features: Over 1700 films, appr. 250 each simulation games and video recordings.
Index shows categories a particular title is pertinent to rather than titles
listed in various categories pertinent to a given topic—which would have
been more useful.
Subject terms:

language arts	social studies
mass media	

01-25*   **Educational Media Catalogs on Microfiche.** Olympic Media Information, 71 West 23rd Street, New York, NY 10010. $87.50/year.
Purpose: comprehensive collection of catalogs of audiovisual software distributors
Grade level: all
Arrangement: by producer
Subjects: all
Entries: entire distributor's catalog
Indexes: hard copy listing of producers, giving fiche numbers and grid coordinates of entry and of catalog index location
Period covered: catalogs issued during preceding six months
Revision and updating: semi-annual updates
Media represented: filmloops, filmstrips, films, graphic materials, kits, audio-recordings, transparencies, manipulative materials, maps, slides, video recordings
Producers represented: appr. 275
Features:
Subject terms: all subjects

01-26*   **Children's Book & Music Center 1978/79.** 5373 W. Pico Blvd., Los Angeles, CA 90019, 1977. 178p. free.
Purpose: distributor's catalog; recommendations
Grade level: all
Arrangement: 10 subject categories
Subjects: American heritage, U.S. history   emotional and social growth
basic skills in reading, math,   multi-cultural education
and science   non-sexist materials
creative arts (art, dance, music)   physical education & movement
earliest years   others
Entries: appr. 200 (excluding books)

order number, price; contents note; "First Choice" titles starred (*); symbols mark early childhood materials
Indexes: subject
Period covered: available at time of publication
Revision and updating: annual
Media represented: audio recordings, filmstrips, graphic materials, kits
Producers represented: not known
Features: primarily books, including books for parents and teachers
Subject terms:
American history   ethnic studies
biography   language arts
dance   music
early childhood   women's studies
education

01-27*   **AV Guide.** 434 S. Wabash, Chicago, IL 60605. $8.00/year.
Purpose: descriptive
Grade level: all
Arrangement: by media
Subjects: all

01-27 (cont'd)
Entries: appr. 175/year

> running time, format data, producer; contents note
>> omitted: release date, price, grade level

Indexes:
Period covered: not known
Revision and updating: published 12x/year
Media represented: films, filmstrips, free and inexpensive publications, kits, transparencies
Producers represented: various
Features: Each issue, consisting of four pages, also carries feature stories and equipment announcements.
Subject terms: all subjects

01-28* **Media Mix.** Claretian Publications, 221 West Madison Street, Chicago, IL 60606. $9.00/year.

Purpose: evaluations and announcements
Grade level: secondary
Arrangement: by media
Subjects: all
Entries: appr. 100/year

> format, rental and sales price; production date; critical review with teaching suggestions for films
>> omitted: grade level

Indexes: title index in each issue; indexed in *Media Review Digest* (01-03)
Period covered: current and recent
Revision and updating: published 8x/year
Media represented: films, television, free and inexpensive publications, simulation games
Producers represented: several
Features: The editor, Jeffrey Schrank, is the author of *Deception Detection* (04-06 "Features"), other books on consumer problems and of *The Seed Catalog* (01-13).
Subject terms: all subjects

01-29* **Teacher's Choice; Catalogue of Curriculum Materials.** Institute of Open Education, 133 Mt. Auburn Street, Cambridge, MA 02138, 1976. 168p. $4.00pa. illus.

Purpose: recommendations by teachers
Grade level: all
Arrangement: by subject
Subjects: affective reading
early childhood science
English/language arts social studies
math miscellaneous
Entries: appr. 100 (including print)

> publisher or producer, price; grade level, instructional suggestions; contents description, full review
>> omitted: release date

01-29 (cont'd)
Indexes: title
Period covered: available at time of publication
Revision and updating:
Media represented: manipulative materials, graphic materials, filmstrips, kits, free and inexpensive publications
Producers represented: appr. 60 producers and publishers
Features: Published as "an alternative to publisher's catalogues", this is a profusely illustrated, attractive guide to selected materials. Also includes directions for teacher-made activities.
Subject terms: all subjects
early childhood education

01-30* **Children's House.** P.O. Box 111, Caldwell, NJ 07006. $5.70/year.
Purpose: "Sights and Sounds" column by Carol Emmens recommends films and other materials
Grade level: primary, intermediate
Arrangement: random
Subjects: all
Entries: appr. 45/year

running time, producer/distributor; contents summary and critical review omitted: price, release date, grade level
Indexes:
Period covered: current releases
Revision and updating: published 4x/year
Media represented: audio recordings, films, filmstrips
Producers represented: various commercial and independent producers, including foreign
Features: The magazine serves Montessori schools.
Subject terms: all subjects

01-31 **"Audiovisual Guide."** *Previews*, October 1977.
Purpose: "a cross-media listing of new and forthcoming materials"
Grade level: all
Arrangement: by media within 60-70 subject groupings

Subjects:	anthropology	library and study	radio programs
	archaeology	skills	(old time)
	driver education	literature and drama	sex education
	early childhood	medicine and nursing	and marriage
	feature films	psychology	vocational
	first aid	religion	training
	government and law		others

Entries: appr. 1400

format, producer/distributor, sale/rental price; grade level; contents summary
Indexes: none
Period covered: May 1977-April 1978
Revision and updating: previous edition September 1976

01-31 (cont'd)

Media represented: films, filmloops, filmstrips, audio recordings, graphic materials, simulation games, kits, maps, slides, transparencies, manipulative materials, video recordings, radio

Producers represented: appr. 150

Features: Taken from producers' announcements, this is the only comprehensive source of information on coming releases.

Subject terms: all subjects

Section II
Lists by Subjects

02—Bilingual Education
03—Career Education
04—Consumer Education
05—Early Childhood Education
06—Energy and Environment Education
07—Film Study
08—Health and Safety Education
09—Drug Abuse Education
10—Sex Education
11—Language Arts
12—Mathematics and Metric Education
13—Music
14—Physical Education
15—Psychology and Guidance
16—Science
17—Social Studies
18—Ethnic Studies
19—World Cultures and International Education
20—Visual Arts
21—Vocational Education
22—Women's Studies

Note: 23-29 reserved for future expansion.

02-Bilingual Education

Several other terms in the Subject Index will yield additional suggestions and may be particularly useful for bilingual education for other than the Spanish-speaking: "Ethnic studies," "Foreign language," "History," "World cultures," and "World literature." See also 18—Ethnic Studies and 19—World Cultures and International Education.

The Elementary School Library Collection (01-09) notes availability of Spanish and other language versions of filmstrips and *Films 1977-1978* (32-05) indexes foreign language films. The catalog of the *Children's Book and Music Center* (01-26) offers Spanish language recordings.

Información para el consumidor (see 04-01 "Features") is a catalog of government consumer publications in Spanish; Spanish language materials are issued by the Departments of Agriculture and of Health, Education and Welfare, and by the Food and Drug Administration (see 08—Health and Safety Education, introduction) and other agencies. See also 08-04.

Only lists for Spanish bilingual education were found for inclusion here. Lists for instruction in foreign languages and English as a second language are found in 11—Language Arts.

02-01*   **Spanish Language Film Catalog.** Gerry Mandell. Dissemination and Assessment Center for Bilingual Education, 7703 North Lamar Boulevard, Austin, TX 78752, 1975. 315p. $4.50pa.
Purpose: comprehensive list of films with Spanish sound-track
Grade level: all
Arrangement: alphabetical by English title
Subjects: all
Entries: over 1900

     running time, producer/distributor, release date; grade level; contents summary
         omitted: price
Indexes: subject, producer/distributor
Period covered: bulk are from 1960s
Revision and updating:
Media represented: films
Producers represented: over 400 commercial, academic, government, including foreign
Features:
Subject terms: all subjects
         bilingual education

02-02*   **Selector's Guide for Bilingual Education Materials** (EPIE Report #73-74). Educational Products Information Exchange, 475 Riverside Drive, New York, NY 10027, 1976. 2v. $20.00ea.
Purpose: evaluations; "supplementary instructional materials" v.1, p. 102-120, v.2, p. 106-137

02-02 (cont'd)
Grade level: all
Arrangement: each section by title
Subjects: Spanish language arts
             Spanish "branch programs" (contents subjects)
Entries: appr. 20 (excluding print)

    format, producer, release date; grade level; contents, methodology,
    critical evaluation
             omitted: price
Indexes: none
Period covered: 1969-1976
Media represented: films, filmstrips, graphic materials
Producers represented: various, including foreign
Features: Other sections evaluate basic instructional programs and professional
    materials.
Subject terms: all subjects
             bilingual education

02-03*   **Cartel; Annotations and Analyses of Bilingual Multicultural Materials.**
             Dissemination and Assessment Center for Bilingual Education, 7703
             North Lamar Blvd., Austin, TX 78752. $6.50/year; $1.75/issue
             (occasional issues published as ED documents, e.g., #37 (January
             1976) ED 120 288).
Purpose: comprehensive; some evaluations
Grade level: all
Arrangement: alphabetical title
Subjects: all
Entries: appr. 90/year (excluding print)

    format data, producer, release date; price; grade level; summary and
    evaluation
Indexes: subject
Period covered: current and recent releases
Revision and updating: published 4x/year
Media represented: audio recordings, filmloops, films, filmstrips, graphic materials,
    kits, manipulative materials
Producers represented: various
Features: Primarily a bibliography of curricula and professional books. Cumula-
    tive issues 1973-75 $3.70 each. Center also publishes its own materials and
    Spanish Language Film Catalog (02-01).
Subject terms:
             bilingual education
             ethnic studies

02-04*   **"Spanish English Nonprint Materials."** Robert A. Gilman, *Booklist*,
             v.74, September 1, 1977, pp. 47-50.
Purpose: recommendations of "reliable materials", selected on basis of intelli-
    gibility, clarity, accuracy, avoidance of stereotyping, currency, visual
    attractiveness, integration of basic components with supplemental materials
Grade level: all

02-04 (cont'd)
Arrangement: by media
Subjects: bilingual, bicultural education
Entries: 36
  running time, format data, producer/distributor, release date, sale/rental
  price; grade level; critical summary
Indexes:
Period covered: 1973-1977
Revision and updating:
Media represented: audio recordings, films, filmstrips, kits
Producers represented: 17
Features: "Majority of items ... evaluated failed to meet ... criteria." Excludes
  dubbed materials.
Subject terms: all subjects
  bilingual education

03—Career Education

Media lists dealing with broader aspects of guidance are found in 15—Psychology and Guidance, those on training for specific jobs in 21—Vocational Education. Specific subject sections (music, science, health and safety education, etc.) will help locate materials dealing with careers in specific fields, as will the term "biography" in the Subject Index. See also 34—Free and Inexpensive Publications, particularly 34-02 and 34-07.

Training Film Profiles (Olympic Media Information, 71 West 23rd Street, New York, NY 10010. $150/year) evaluates 240 films and other visuals in six issues per year. Though most are intended for management training programs, some are suitable for career education.

03-01   **Career Development Resources; A Guide to Audiovisual and Printed Materials for Grades K-12.** Harry N. Drier, Jr. Charles A. Jones Publ. Co., Worthington, OH 43085, 1973. 301p. $11.95. LC 73-80353.
Purpose: comprehensive; not previewed by editors
Grade level: all
Arrangement: 4 graded sections; media listings for 3 areas of career education
  within each
Subjects: career planning and preparation, self-understanding, the world of work
Entries: 2200 (including print)
  type of medium, producer; format detail, price, release date and contents
  notes (not in all cases)
Indexes: none
Period covered: not known
Revision and updating: rev. ed. of *K-12 Guide for Integrating Career Development
  into Local Curriculum* (1972)
Media represented: films, filmstrips, audio recordings, kits, transparencies, slides,
  microform, simulation games

03-01 (cont'd)
Producers represented: various commercial, academic, institutional
Features: The purchasing information included is often insufficient.
Subject terms: career education

03-02* **Career Index 1976-7.** Chronicle Guidance Publications, Inc., Moravia,
NY 13118. $7.50. LC 74-26726.
Purpose: comprehensive
Grade level: secondary
Arrangement: alphabetical by publisher
Subjects: career education
Entries: 1500/year (including books)

format, ordering information, rental price for films; publication date;
asterisks mark free materials
Indexes: occupations; subject
Period covered: available at time of publication
Revision and updating: published annually
Media represented: free and inexpensive publications, films
Producers represented: 700, including professional and trade associations,
government agencies, film libraries
Features: Includes many hardcover and paperback books.
Subject terms:
career education
vocational education

03-03* **Vocational Guidance Quarterly.** American Personnel Guidance
Association, 1607 New Hampshire Ave., N.W., Washington, DC
20009. $10.00/year.
Purpose: "Current Career Literature" column in each issue; evaluations
Grade level: all
Arrangement: by occupation
Subjects: vocational guidance
Entries: appr. 400/year

source, price; rating (highly recommended, recommended, useful); contents
note
Indexes: film reviews indexed in *Media Review Digest* (01-03)
Period covered: current publications
Revision and updating: published 4x/year
Media represented: films, free and inexpensive publications, government
publications
Producers represented: various institutional
Features: Ten films rated in September 1976 issue. The Association and its
divisions also publish *Inform* (03-12) and *Career Guidance Films I & II*
($1.50), "an annotated listing of more than 240 films" from over
60 producers.
Subject terms: career education

03-04   **Bibliography of K-6 Career Education Materials for the Enrichment of Teacher and Counselor Competencies.** Marla Peterson. Eastern Illinois University, School of Education, Center for Educational Studies, Charleston, IL 61920, 1972. 201p. ED 073 287.

Purpose: "resources to aid local school system personnel in developing elementary school career education programs"; recommendations

Grade level: primary, intermediate

Arrangement: by publisher or producer

Subjects: career education

Entries: appr. 300

> format, price; grade level; release date; availability of teacher's guide; brief annotations supplemented by symbols indicating concepts developed, occupational area, curriculum area

Indexes: media; occupations

Period covered: 1969-1972

Revision and updating:

Media represented: films, filmstrips, filmloops, kits, audio recordings, graphic materials, manipulative materials

Producers represented: over 50, U.S. only

Features: Thorough attention is given to developing concepts of self-worth and of the world of work. Each entry is keyed to that purpose as well as to integrating career education into all subject areas. Organized for easy use.

Subject terms: career education

03-05*   **Guide to Federal Career Literature: 1976.** Civil Service Commission. Superintendent of Documents, Washington, DC 20402, 1976. 35p. $1.05pa. S/N 006-000-00906-9. ED 126 262.

Purpose: comprehensive guide to federal recruiting literature

Grade level: secondary

Arrangement: 30 issuing agencies

Subjects: careers

Entries: 205

> format, pagination, date of publication; contents summary

Indexes: by college majors

Period covered: 1970-76, some earlier

Revision and updating: previous edition 1972

Media represented: government publications

Producers represented: U.S. government

Features: Lists federal job information centers and recruiting offices. SB110 from the Superintendent of Documents lists a large number of government pamphlets for career education.

Subject terms: career education

03-06*   **Elementary Resource Guide.** Business and Office Career Education Curriculum Project, National Business Education Association, 1906 Association Drive, Reston, VA 22091, 1975. 215p. $7.50pa.

Purpose: "Student materials" pp. 199-215

Grade level: primary, intermediate

Arrangement: by publisher

03-06 (cont'd)
Subjects: career education
Entries: appr. 80 (excluding print)

running time (films), producer; sale/rental price; contents summary; grade
level; appropriate curriculum area
omitted: number of frames, other format data
Indexes: none
Period covered: listed in producers' 1971-1973 catalogs
Revision and updating:
Media represented: kits, films, filmstrips, graphic materials, manipulative
materials, filmloops
Producers represented: 23 commercial
Features: Bulk of book described career development activities suitable for
different curriculum areas and grade levels.
Subject terms: career education

03-07   **Grades 7, 8 & 9 Learning Resources for Career Education.** Edwin
York. New Jersey Occupational Resource Center, Edison, NJ 08817,
1973. 28p. ED 080 712.
Purpose: recommendations for media center acquisition
Grade level: secondary
Arrangement: 9 media groupings, including print
Subjects: career education
Entries: appr. 100

running time, producer, price; number of players and required time for
simulation games; contents note
omitted: release date
Indexes: subjects (specific jobs and fields)
Period covered: not known
Revision and updating:
Media represented: kits, filmstrips, audio recordings (tapes), films, simulation
games
Producers represented: appr. 50
Features: [See also York's article "A Career Education Media Mix" (03-17).]
Subject terms: career education

03-08   **Senior High Learning Resources for Career Education.** Edwin York.
New Jersey Occupational Education Resource Center, Edison, NJ
08817, 1973. 32p. ED 080 711.
Purpose: materials recommended for high school media centers
Grade level: secondary
Arrangement: by media
Subjects: career education
Entries: appr. 75

ordering information; full annotations including reports on field tests in
some cases
omitted: release date

03-08 (cont'd)
Indexes: subject (specific jobs and fields)
Period covered: late 1960s-1971
Revision and updating:
Media represented: filmstrips, films, simulation games, kits, audio recordings
(cassette), slides, transparencies
Producers represented: various, including industrial
Features: A checklist geared to USOE's 15 career clusters, including books for
students and teachers as well. Some of the listed materials are available
to New Jersey schools only. [See also 03-17.]
Subject terms: career education

03-09 **Elementary School Learning Resources for Career Education.** Edwin
York. New Jersey Occupational Resource Center, Edison, NJ 08817,
1973. 28p. ED 080 713.
Purpose: recommendations; "provide a record of current resources available for
school media centers"
Grade level: primary, intermediate
Arrangement: by media
Subjects: career education
Entries: appr. 50

running time, producer, price; number of players and time required for
games; contents note
omitted: release date
Indexes: subject (specific jobs)
Period covered: not known
Revision and updating:
Media represented: filmstrips, films
Producers represented: appr. 50, chiefly commercial
Features: [See also 03-17.]
Subject terms: career education

03-10* **Career Education Pamphlets; A Library of 1200 Free and Inexpensive
Sources.** Dale E. Shaffer, 437 Jennings Avenue, Salem, OH 44460,
1976. 68p. ED 130 090.
Purpose: "a basic collection of occupational booklets and paperbacks suitable
for any library or school"; recommendations
Grade level: intermediate, secondary
Arrangement: 217 career field and topics
Subjects:
Entries: 1216

title, source, price (if any)
omitted: date of publication, number of pages (in most cases)
Indexes: none
Period covered: available at time of publication
Revision and updating:
Media represented: free and inexpensive publications
Producers represented: 403 sources

03-10 (cont'd)
Features: Half of titles listed are free, none over $3.00.
Subject terms:
>   career education
>   vocational education

03-11*   A Bibliography of Free Loan Materials for Career Education. 3rd ed.
>   Roger H. Lambert & others. Wisconsin Vocational Studies Center,
>   University of Wisconsin, Madison, WI 53706, 1976. 47p. ED 132 278.

Purpose: catalog of materials available on free loan within state; descriptive
Grade level: secondary
Arrangement: 12 topical groupings

Subjects:	career exploration	career preparation
	career orientation	others

Entries: appr. 1100 (including books)

>   title, publication date, pagination, price (if any)

Indexes: "disadvantaged materials"
Period covered: 1970s
Revision and updating: annual
Media represented: free and inexpensive publications, government publications
Producers represented: academic, institutional, departments of education
Features: also books
Subject terms: career education

03-12*   Inform. National Career Information Center, 1607 New Hampshire
>   Avenue, Washington, DC 20009. $25/year.

Purpose: "Career Resource Bibliography" comprehensive listing of free pamphlets
>   on a different occupation or career cluster each month; "Films and Film-
>   strips" (descriptive)

Grade level: intermediate, secondary
Arrangement: by career cluster (free and inexpensive publications); random
>   (others)

Subjects: career education
Entries: several hundred

>   publisher & publication date (publications), running time, producer/distributor,
>   sale price (visuals)

Indexes:
Period covered: recent and current materials; 1970-76 (Career Resource
>   Bibliographies)

Revision and updating: published 10x/year
Media represented: films, filmstrips, free and inexpensive publications, government
>   publications

Producers represented: various commercial, institutional, government
Features: Also listings of other free and inexpensive government publications,
>   by source, and of books. [See also 03-03, "Features."]

Subject terms: career education

03-13*   **Counselor's Information Service.** B'nai B'rith Career and Counseling
           Services, 1640 Rhode Island Avenue, NW, Washington, DC 20036.
           $9/year. (occasional issues published as ED documents, e.g., September
           1976 (ED 132 486), December 1975 (ED 119 080).
Purpose: comprehensive
Grade level: secondary
Arrangement: subject
Subjects: adult education and the aging   guidance materials
             aids for the teacher   handicapped and rehabilitation
             counselor's bookshelf   counseling
             guidance administration and   occupational information
               procedures   student aids
Entries: appr. 700/year (excluding hardcover books)

           publisher, address, publication date, price; number of pages
Indexes: none
Period covered: current and recent publications
Revision and updating: published 4x/year
Media represented: free and inexpensive publications
Producers represented: various
Features: A 59-page, 117-item *"Starter" File of Free Occupational Literature*
           was published by the same organization in 1975 ($1.50), covering 1970-74
           publications.
Subject terms:
           career education
           guidance

03-14*   **Career Education Resource Guide.** Michigan State Department of
           Education, Lansing, MI 1975. 407p. ED 118 951.
Purpose: recommendations on basis of classroom use in one district
Grade level: all
Arrangement: by media and grade level within 4 subject groupings
Subjects: career awareness and exploration   career planning and placement
             career decision-making   self awareness and assessment
Entries: appr. 600 (excluding print)

           running time, producer, release date; price, grade level; applicable curriculum
           area; contents summary and evaluation; applicable career concepts
Indexes: title index for each section
Period covered: 1967-1975
Revision and updating:
Media represented: audio recordings, filmloops, films, filmstrips, graphic materials,
           kits, microforms, simulation games, slides, transparencies
Producers represented: appr. 100 commercial
Features: Listings are duplicated in more than one section, if applicable. Other
           1975 career education resource guides compiled by educational agencies
           include: *A Selected Annotated Bibliography of Resource Materials for the
           Implementation of Career Education Grades K through 3* (Rutgers), which
           lists nothing published later than 1972 (ED 110 747); *Career Education: An
           Annotated Instructional Materials List K-12* (Montgomery County, MD,

03-14 (cont'd)
Public Schools), comprising 225 recommended media, the largest single group
being filmstrips (ED 118 756); *Resources for Career Development* (Indiana
Career Resource Center, 1209 South Greenlawn, South Bend, IN 46615,
$4.00pa.), a comprehensive list of some 200 a-v as well as 400 printed
materials, including professional materials; *Career Development Resources:
A Bibliography of Audio-Visual and Printed Materials K-12* (Minnesota State
Department of Education), approximately 150 items (ED 117 292);
Instructional Materials for Career Education (Cornell), some 150 items
(ED 122 069); *Annotated Bibliography of Commercially Produced Audio,
Printed, and Visual Career Education Materials* (Marshall University,
Huntington, WV), approximately 75 items (ED 109 430); *Materials Catalogue;
Career Services & Industrial Arts* (Alabama State Department of Education),
approximately 90 filmstrips, films, and other materials suitable for secondary
level (ED 117 536); *An Annotated Bibliography of Instructional Materials
Which Emphasize Positive Work Ethics*. Charles Curry. Virginia Polytechnic
Institute and State University, Blacksburg, VA 24061, 1975. 122p. (ED 115 766).
Subject terms: career education

03-15*   EPIE Career Education Set. Educational Products Information
Exchange, 475 Riverside Drive, New York, NY 10027. 1975. 2v.
$31.00.
Purpose: volume II analyzes and evaluates materials
Grade level: all
Arrangement: by media
Subjects: career education
Entries: appr. 500 (excluding texts, curriculum sets, books, etc.)

format, producer, release date; price; target audience, curriculum applications,
contents; producers' evaluation measures
Indexes: title
Period covered: available at time of preparation
Revision and updating:
Media represented: audio recordings, filmloops, films, filmstrips, graphic materials,
kits, transparencies
Producers represented: appr. 200 academic, commercial, government
Features: Films and filmstrips predominate (in addition to print). Volume I
presents selection and evaluation guidelines, including useful hints on
how to detect racist and sexist biases. [Note critique in 03-17.]
Subject terms: career education

03-16*   Films for Business and Industrial Organization and Management.
4th ed. Pennsylvania State University Audio-Visual Services, Willard
Building, University Park, PA 16802, 1976. 46p. free.
Purpose: film library catalog; recommendations
Grade level: secondary
Arrangement: alphabetical title

03-16 (cont'd)
Subjects: longer index listings include:

automation and technology	economics
communications	labor relations
	management

Entries: 450-500

running time, release date, producer, grade level, rental price; contents summary
Indexes: subject
Period covered: 1960s to 1974; some from 1940s and 50s
Revision and updating: *Newsletter*
Media represented: films
Producers represented: various commercial, academic, government, institutional
Features: Though not primarily intended for school use, this has some titles pertinent to career education and vocational guidance.
Subject terms:

career education
economics

03-17* **"A Career Education Media Mix."** Edwin G. York. *Previews*, v.5, October 1976, p. 10-17.
Purpose: recommendations on basis of topical suitability, currency, user feedback, producer reputation, adequacy of technical format out of 327
Grade level: all
Arrangement: 7 topical groupings
Subjects:

career awareness	self-awareness
decision-making process	socio-economic and tech-
educational and occupational	nological understandings
skills	teacher preparation
	work attitudes and habits

Entries: 97

format, producer, release date; grade level; running time (films); contents note
Indexes:
Period covered: January 1974-August 1976
Revision and updating:
Media represented: films, filmstrips, kits
Producers represented: various
Features: An antidote to the massive EPIE compilation (03-15), here termed "an impressive effort at non-help." York is Director of the New Jersey Educational Department Occupational Resource Centers and the author of earlier lists of career education resources recommended for media centers (03-07 to 03-09).
Subject terms: career education

04-Consumer Education

Practical how-to-shop suggestions are more frequently dealt with in materials indexed under the subject term "home economics," social and political aspects of consumerism in those under "contemporary issues" and "economics." For games simulating consumer situations, see the "Practical Economics" chapter in *The Guide to Simulations/Games for Education and Training* (41-01). Guides to Free and Inexpensive Publications (34) offer many suggestions, but the teacher must consider the source and possible bias of free goods and must balance various points of view.

Federal, state, and local governments issue many helpful teaching aids. The appropriate agencies are listed in *Reference Guide for Consumers* (04-06). The Consumer Products Safety Commission, Washington, DC 20207 has issued a catalog of *Publications, Radio, Films, Slides, Fact Sheets, TV*. Publications of the Food and Drug Administration are referred to in 08–Health and Safety Education.

04-01*   The Consumer Information Catalog; A Catalog of Selected Federal Publications of Consumer Interest. Consumer Information Center, Pueblo, CO 81009. free.

Purpose: comprehensive
Grade level: all
Arrangement: topical
Subjects: (vary from issue to issue)

automobiles	food	money management
children	health	recreation, travel,
diet and nutrition	housing	leisure activities
employment and	landscaping, gardening,	retirement years
education	pest control	

Entries: appr. 900/year

title, number of pages, publication date, price (if any), order number; contents note
omitted: audience suitability
Indexes: none
Period covered: available at time of publication
Revision and updating: published 4x/year
Media represented: government publications
Producers represented: U.S. government
Features: Most are free. Order blank included. *Información para el consumidor* is a "catalog of [appr. 100] consumer publications in Spanish" issued by the same office. The Center also publishes *Consumer News* (semi-monthly; $4/year) and annual *Guide to Federal Consumer Services* (free).
Subject terms:

bilingual education	health and safety education
consumer education	home economics
energy and environment education	nutrition

04-02   Changing Times. 1927 H Street, NW, Washington, DC 20006.
$9.00/year.
Purpose: "Things to Write For" is a regular one-page feature, alternating with
"Paperback Bookshelf"
Grade level: intermediate, secondary
Arrangement: random
Subjects: economics
Entries: appr. 60/year

contents note; ordering information
omitted: grade level
Indexes:
Period covered: material currently released
Revision and updating: published 12x/year
Media represented: free and inexpensive publications, government publications
Producers represented: various
Features:
Subject terms:
consumer education   home economics
health and safety education

04-03   "Consumer Education." Hayden Green. *Booklist*. v.69, June 1, 1973,
pp. 933-938.
Purpose: recommendations
Grade level: secondary
Arrangement: 5 media categories
Subjects: as listed in Illinois State Superintendent of Public Instruction Guidelines
Entries: appr. 40

running time, format, producer, price, release date; contents summary
Indexes:
Period covered: available at time of publication
Revision and updating:
Media represented: filmstrips, kits, slides, audio recordings, transparencies
Producers represented: commercial, institutional, government
Features: Chiefly filmstrips.
Subject terms: consumer education

04-04*   Resources for Consumer Education; 16mm Films. Nancy B. Greenspan.
Center for Consumer Education Services, Plainfield Avenue, Edison,
NJ 08817, 1976. 24p. free.
Purpose: comprehensive
Grade level: all
Arrangement: alphabetical title
Subjects: advertising   economic influences—   food/shopping
automobiles   government   protection
consumer behavior   economic understanding   shoplifting
credit   financial management   social philosophy

04-04 (cont'd)
Entries: 75

running time, producer/distributor, sale/rental price, release date; synopsis;
grade level (separate chart); availability of Spanish language version
Indexes: subject (chart)
Period covered: 1962-1976
Revision and updating: replaces *Selected Audio-Visual Materials for Consumer
Education* (1974)
Media represented: films
Producers represented: various
Features: Companion volume on filmstrips and slides scheduled for 1978
publication.
Subject terms:
bilingual education
consumer education

04-05*   A Guide to Free and Inexpensive Consumer Education Resources.
Home Economics Department, Marshall University, Huntington, WV
25701, 1976. 330p. ED 130 949.
Purpose: comprehensive; "Audiovisuals, Multi-Media Bibliographies" pp. 53-62;
"Games, Simulations" p. 97; Main Listing pp. 109-330
Grade level: secondary
Arrangement: by 3 media and 20 topical groupings

Subjects:	clothing	energy conservation	investment and
	consumer in the	food	savings
	economy	furniture, appliances,	money
	consumer in the market	equipment	management
	credit	housing	services
Entries: several thousand (incl. print)			others

(pamphlets): number of pages, publication date, price; reading level; contents
note; (audiovisuals); source, price; contents note; (simulation games): source,
price
omitted: release date, format details, intended audience (audiovisuals
and simulation games)
Indexes: none
Period covered: 1970s-1976
Revision and updating:
Media represented: films, filmstrips, free and inexpensive publications, graphic
materials, simulation games, transparencies
Producers represented: appr. 300
Features: Also lists books, curriculum guides, lesson plans, periodical articles.
Audiovisuals not necessarily inexpensive.
Subject terms:
consumer education   home economics
energy and environment education

04-06* **Reference Guide for Consumers.** Nina David. Bowker, 1975. 327p. $15.50. LC 75-12912.
Purpose: "Multimedia materials" pp. 1-190; evaluations
Grade level: secondary
Arrangement: topical
Subjects:

automobiles	food	motorcycles
bicycles	fraud	phonograph
consumer complaints	houses	recordings
consumer education	insurance	photographic
consumer protection	medical care	equipment
credit	mobile homes	product safety
debt	money management	savings & thrift
		others

Entries: 519

title, publisher, publication date, price, pagination; full evaluative description
Indexes: subject, title, author
Period covered: 1960s-1974
Revision and updating:
Media represented: films, free and inexpensive publications, government publications
Producers represented: various commercial, institutional, government
Features: Federal, state, and local government agencies listed pp. 191-202,
212-259. Minimal number of films. [Similar list: *Deception Detection; An
Educator's Guide to the Art of Insight* by Jeffrey Schrank (Beacon, 1975.
$8.95) recommends appr. 25 films, filmstrips and other materials.]
Subject terms: consumer education

04-07* **Consumer Education Resources.** Michigan Consumer Education Center,
University Library, Eastern Michigan University, Ypsilanti, MI 48197,
1976. 85p. ED 135 972.
Purpose: comprehensive
Grade level: intermediate, secondary
Arrangement: by media
Subjects:

basic economics in the market place	factors affecting consumer behavior
buying and using goods and services	money management & credit rights and responsibilities

Entries: appr. 400 (excluding books, periodicals, etc.)

format, producer, release date (not in all cases): (films); running time, grade
level
Indexes: subject
Period covered: 1965-76
Revision and updating:
Media represented: audio recordings, films, filmstrips, kits, simulation games,
transparencies, video recordings
Producers represented: various
Features: Also curriculum guides, case studies, text, bibliographies, periodicals.
Subject terms: consumer education

04-08*   **A Resource Directory of Selected Consumer Education Materials for Grades K-8.** Illinois Office of Education. Program Planning and Development Section, Springfield, IL 62777, 1976. free. ED 135 721.
Purpose: descriptive
Grade level: all
Arrangement: by media
Subjects: consumer education
Entries: appr. 75

    running time, producer, release date; sale price; grade level; contents summary
Indexes: none
Period covered: 1969-1976
Revision and updating:
Media represented: films, filmstrips, kits
Producers represented: various, including government
Features: Also books and periodicals. Bibliographies and catalogs included under "kits."
Subject terms: consumer education

05–Early Childhood Education

    The listing under "early childhood education" in the Subject Index and the classification "primary" in the Instructional Level Index lead to more general tools with special applicability to this age group. *The Elementary School Library Collection* (01-09) recommends over 200 "Media for Pre-school Children." *Films for Children Ages 3 to 5* (Instructional Laboratories, Department of Education, University of California, Berkeley, CA 94720, 1976. $6.00) offers reviews by children of some 60 films. *Early Years* (P.O. Box 1223, Darien, CT 06820; $9.50/year) in several issues each year recommends a small number of audiovisual titles on the basis of field tests.

05-01*   **Free and Inexpensive Materials for Preschool and Early Childhood.** 2nd ed. Robert Monahan. Fearon Publishers, Inc., Belmont, CA 94002, 1977. 118p. $3.00pa.
Purpose: recommendations
Grade level: primary
Arrangement: topical
Subjects: animals and pets   dental health   recreation and
         art   foods and recipes   physical education
         audiovisual   health   safety
         citizenship and   holidays   transportation
          community   nutrition   others
Entries: appr. 600 (including professional)

    running time (films), pagination (print), source, ordering information; contents note; items for use with children marked with asterisk (*)
      omitted: publication or release date

05-01 (cont'd)
Indexes: none
Period covered: available at time of publication
Revision and updating: previous edition 1973
Media represented: films, free and inexpensive publications, kits
Producers represented: various
Features: Bulk of entries are teachers' materials.
Subject terms: early childhood education

05-02 "**Early Childhood Education.**" Dave Ziegler. *Booklist.* v.70, September
15, 1973, pp. 90-105.
Purpose: recommended multi-media list prepared by media specialist and
kindergarten teachers
Grade level: primary
Arrangement: 7 subject groupings
Subjects: all
Entries: appr. 150

format; distributor, sale and rental price; release date; evaluations
Indexes:
Period covered: 1961-1972
Revision and updating:
Media represented: films, filmstrips, audio recordings, graphic materials, kits
Producers represented: various commercial
Features: Language arts account for one-half the entries, art and health and
safety for the fewest. 16mm films constitute almost half the total.
Subject terms: early childhood education

05-03* **Play and Learn with Toys and Games; A Bibliography of Toys and
Games that Teach Institutionalized Children.** South Dakota State
Library, Pierre, SD 57501, 1976. 45p. ED 127 924.
Purpose: comprehensive
Grade level: primary
Arrangement: subject
Subjects: communication skills   motor skills   sensory skills
          concepts   music therapy   social studies
          life skills   reading readiness   skills
          math readiness skills   skills
Entries: appr. 280

format date, producer; contents note
Indexes: none
Period covered: available at time of publication
Revision and updating:
Media represented: manipulative materials
Producers represented: appr. 35 commercial, also Montessori toys

05-03 (cont'd)
Features: Though intended for use with special children, this list of many
standard children's toys and games can be used to teach the same skills
to children in the primary grades.
Subject terms:
early childhood education
language arts

06–Energy and Environment Education

The scope of this section has been expanded to encompass rapidly emerging concerns with energy education. The term "environment education" is used here in its broadest sense, as education in all subject areas that creates awareness of our total relationship with the environment. Outdoor education is considered an aspect of physical education; ecology is one of the life sciences. A short guide on population education resources is also included in this chapter.

Pertinent references in other chapters include "Films on noise pollution and deafness" (08-12) and listings of simulation games (17-27, 17-28, and 41-01). The Agency for Instructional Television (43-05) has a new series on the Landsat earth resources information satellite.

Recommended selections from the large number of media produced during the years 1968 to 1974 that were the high points of environmental concern may be found in *Project I-C-E Catalog of Media Resources* (Instruction-Curriculum-Environment Center, 1927 Main Street, Green Bay, WI 54301, 1975. 63p. $1.50pa.) and *Guide to Ecology Information and Organizations* by John G. Burke (H. W. Wilson, 1976. $12.50. pp. 156-168).

Government at all levels can be successfully mined for a vast array of materials. A few from federal agencies are:

Energy Research and Development Administration, Technical Information Center, P.O. Box 62, Oak Ridge, TN 37830

The Environmental Impact of Electrical Power Generation: Nuclear and Fossil (1975; including teacher's guide); *12 Energy Films*; Publications Order Form

Federal Energy Administration, Washington, DC 20461
Energy Conservation, Understanding and Activities for Young People

Department of the Interior, Washington, DC 20240
Film Catalog

Forest Service, Washington, DC 20013
Investigating Your Environment; Forest Service Films

Bureau of Mines, 4800 Forbes Avenue, Pittsburgh, PA 15213
Films; Publications and Articles; New Publications (monthly)

Environmental Protection Agency, Washington, DC 20460
   ABC's of Human Ecology; Resource Recovery; Needed: Clean Air; Needed: Clean Water

Bureau of Reclamation, Engineering and Research Center, P.O. Box 25007, Denver, CO 80225
   Publications (including maps); *Film Catalog*

Soil Conservation Service, Washington, DC 20250
   Soil Conservation (monthly; $5.65/year)

   Selected U.S. Government Publications (35-01) in 1977 featured many publications on solar energy and the energy problem in general.
   Each state has departments and agencies dealing with natural resources, environmental conservation and quality, pollution, wildlife management, and the like. They are listed in the state legislative manual (found in many public libraries) and in the telephone directory for the state capital. The *Book of the States 1976-77* (Council of State Governments, Lexington, KY 40511) lists state energy offices, their functions and responsibilities. Many of these agencies publish illustrated booklets, posters, maps, and other free goods and have free-loan films for schools. A request on school letterhead to the Public Information Office should bring forth a list of materials and ordering instructions.
   Contact with local public health, environmental management, planning agencies and Extension Service offices may also prove fruitful.
   The usual guides to free and inexpensive materials locate publications of many organizations active in this field, and the usual caveats regarding free goods apply. Guides compiled for school use do not often help locate the pro-environmentalist point of view represented by organizations such as the National Audubon Society, Public Interest Research Groups and the Sierra Club (see 34—Free and Inexpensive Publications, introduction).

06-01*   **Index to Environmental Studies (Multi-Media).** National Information Center for Educational Media, University of Southern California, University Park, Los Angeles, CA 90007, 1977. 1113p. $34.50; $18.50 (microfiche). LC 76-1414.

Purpose: comprehensive
Grade level: all
Arrangement: alphabetical title

Subjects:	agriculture	engineering	physical science
	botany	food supply	pollution
	conservation of	fuels	resources
	natural resources	geography	sanitation
	earth science	life science	others
	ecology	outdoor life	

Entries: 26,000 (including adult)
         type of medium, format data, producer, distributor, release date (generally); grade level; contents note; out-of-print titles so noted
                  omitted: price
Indexes: classed subject
Period covered: 1950s-1970s

06-01 (cont'd)

Revision and updating: replaces *Index to Ecology (Multi-Media)*, 2nd ed. 1973; *Update of Nonbook Media*

Media represented: audio recordings, filmloops, films, filmstrips, transparencies, video recordings

Producers represented: various

Features: Energy education materials are scattered among subject headings such as "basic physical science–energy and matter," "ore deposits–U.S.," "resources," and others. Science sections represented bulk of entries.

Subject terms:

      energy and environment education   science

      geography

06-02   **Environment Film Review.** Environment Information Center, Inc., 292 Madison Ave., New York, NY 10017, 1972. 155p. $20.00pa.

Purpose: "a critical guide to ecology films"

Grade level: all

Arrangement: 21 topical categories

Subjects:

air pollution	food and drugs	radiological
chemical and biological	land use	contamination
contamination	noise pollution	renewable resources
energy	non-renewable	solid waste
environmental	resources	transportation
education	oceans and estuaries	water pollution
environmental design	population planning	weather
and urban ecology	and control	modification
		wildlife

Entries: 627

    running time, release date, producer, distributor, sale and rental price; grade level; critical review

Indexes: subject, industry, title

Period covered: available at time of publication

Revision and updating: 06-09

Media represented: films

Producers represented: over 100, including government, industry, commercial and public television

Features: Largest number of entries in "General" category and in chapters on environmental design, land use, resources and pollution.

Subject terms: energy and environment education

06-03   **Films: Man and the Environment.** 2nd ed. Pennsylvania State University Audio-Visual Services, Willard Building, University Park, PA 16802, 1974. 18p. free.

Purpose: film library catalog; recommendations

Grade level: all

Arrangement: alphabetical by subject

Subjects:

environmental design and urban	renewable resources
ecology	wildlife
environmental education	others

06-03 (cont'd)
Entries: appr. 200

> running time, producer, release date; rental price; grade level; contents summary

Indexes: subject
Period covered: 1960s-1973; many in the 1970s
Revision and updating: *Newsletter*
Media represented: films
Producers represented: various
Features: Subject index uses the categories of *Environment Film Review* (06-02). Very little overlap with that list.
Subject terms:
> energy and environment education
> urban studies

06-04*   **Man in His Environment; Film Bibliography.** Carolyn Blackmon. Field Museum of Natural History, Chicago, IL 60605, 1975. 36p. $1.00pa.
Purpose: recommendations on basis of "accuracy of content, conceptual development, instructional usefulness, and topical significance" out of 300 screened
Grade level: all
Arrangement: alphabetical title
Subjects: ecological problems and alternatives
Entries: appr. 100

> running time, producer/distributor; grade level; evaluative summary; awards won
>> omitted: price, release date

Indexes: none
Period covered: not known
Revision and updating:
Media represented: films
Producers represented: appr. 40 distributors
Features:
Subject terms:
> energy and environment education
> life science

06-05   **Aids to Environmental Education: Grades 7-9, 10-14; Update I.** Massachusetts Audubon Society, Lincoln, MA 01773, 1974. 115p. $1.60. ED 093 764.
Purpose: recommendations
Grade level: secondary
Arrangement: by media in each grade level section
Subjects: environmental education
Entries: appr. 60
> producer, release date; evaluative annotation
>> omitted: running time, price
Indexes: none

06-05 (cont'd)
Period covered: available at time of publication
Revision and updating:
Media represented: films, filmloops, filmstrips, graphic materials
Features: This is primarily a listing of books (for students and teachers), periodicals, and curriculum materials. [Similar list: A recommended list for all grades, *A Beginning*, was issued by the Sierra Club in 1973 (ED 113 143).]
Subject terms: energy and environment education

06-06   Aids to Environmental Education: Preschool-Grade 3; Grades 4-6; Update I. Massachusetts Audubon Society, Lincoln, MA 01773. 1974. 69p. $1.20. ED 093 763.
Purpose: recommendations
Grade level: primary, intermediate
Arrangement: by media in each grade level section
Subjects: environmental education
Entries: appr. 40

      producer, release date (in a few cases); evaluative annotation
            omitted: running time, price
Indexes: none
Period covered: mostly 1970-1972
Revision and updating:
Media represented: filmstrips, graphic materials
Producers represented: various
Features: Primarily a listing of books (for students and teachers), periodicals, and curriculum materials. [Similar list: A recommended list for all grades, *A Beginning*, was issued by the Sierra Club in 1973 (ED 113 143).]
Subject terms: energy and environment education

06-07*   Energy Education Materials Inventory. Federal Energy Administration. 5v., 1976. ED 133 912-196.
Purpose: comprehensive inventory done under government contract; v,I, Print materials ("pamphlets" pp. 79-83; "posters" pp. 84-85); v.II, Non-print; v.III, Films; v.IV, Kits, Games, etc.; v.V, Reference Sources
Grade level: all
Arrangement: by media
Subjects: energy
Entries: over 1000

      source, release date, price, if any (not in all cases); grade level
            omitted: contents
Indexes: v.VI projected
Period covered: 1960s-1975
Revision and updating:
Media represented: audio recordings, filmloops, films, filmstrips, government publications, free and inexpensive publications, graphic materials, kits, slides, transparencies, video recordings, simulation games
Producers represented: various commercial, government, television

06-07 (cont'd)

Features: In hard-to-read computer print-out style, this compilation includes out-of-print materials along with current ones. Some items listed as simulation games actually are kits and/or handbooks.

Subject terms: energy and environment education

06-08* **Energy Films Catalog.** U.S. Energy Research and Development Administration, Washington, DC 20545, 1976. 71p. illus. free. ED 129 602.

Purpose: comprehensive producer's catalog

Grade level: all

Arrangement: alphabetical title

Subjects: longer listings include:

accelerator	nuclear power
atomic elements	personalities
atomic energy	radiation
biology	radioisotopes
medicine	research
national laboratories	safety
and energy centers	

Entries: 188

running time, release date; TV clearance; full contents description; awards won; grade level, producers, sponsors and sales sources in separate listing omitted: sale price

Indexes: subject

Period covered: 1960s-1975, some earlier

Revision and updating: loose insert pages

Media represented: films

Producers represented: U.S. government, academic institutional, television

Features: All fre-loan in continental U.S. from ERDA Film Library, P.O. Box 62, Oak Ridge, TN 37830.

Subject terms:

energy and environment education	physical science
life science	

06-09* **Environment Index 76.** Environment Information Center, Inc., 292 Madison Avenue, New York, NY 10017, 1976. 794p. $85.00.

Purpose: "Films" pp. 75-78; comprehensive

Grade level: all

Arrangement: 21 topical categories

Subjects:

air pollution	general	radiological
chemical and biological	international	contamination
contamination	land use	renewable resources
energy	noise pollution	solid waste
environmental education	non-renewable	transportation
environmental design	resources	water pollution
and urban ecology	oceans and estuaries	weather
food and drugs	population planning	modification
	and control	wildlife

06-09 (cont'd)
Entries: appr. 140
  running time, producer/distributor, sale/rental price; release date
   omitted: contents note, grade level
Indexes: none
Period covered: 1975-76 releases
Revision and updating: published annually; *Environment Abstracts* (monthly)
Media represented: films
Producers represented: various
Features:
Subject terms:

energy and environment education	earth science life science	nutrition oceanography urban studies

06-10*   **Energy-Environment Materials Guide.** Kathryn Mervine and Rebecca
  Cawley. National Science Teachers Association, 1742 Connecticut
  Avenue NW, Washington, DC 20009, 1975. 1v. $2.00pa.
Purpose: a sampling of current materials that are "interesting, informative, and
 likely to be available in your school or public library"
Grade level: all
Arrangement: by subject and grade level
Subjects: energy fundamentals   supply and demand   future energy
    energy resources   nuclear power   sources
    electric power   environmental   energy conservation
    energy into power   effects   energy policy
Entries: 80

  running time, source, grade level; one-line summaries in a very few cases
   omitted: price
Indexes: none
Period covered:
Revision and updating:
Media represented: audio recordings, films, filmstrips
Producers represented: various, including institutional, government
Features: Includes free films. Bulk of *Guide* consists of lists of curriculum
 materials, readings for teachers and students, sources of materials and
 information
Subject terms:
  energy and environment education
  physical science

06-11*   **"The Matter of Energy: A Film Perspective."** David O. Weber, *Lifelong
  Learning, EMC One-76.* University of California Extension Media
  Center, Berkeley, CA 94720, 1976.
Purpose: recommendations by author and staff members of the Lawrence Berkeley
 Laboratory of the University of California
Grade level: all
Arrangement: topical

06-11 (cont'd)

Subjects:	alternatives	nuclear-fission reactors
	background	oil and natural gas
	coal	problem-oriented overviews
	energy conservation	solar energy
	fusion	water

Entries: appr. 45

    contents summary and critique; EMC order #
    omitted: running time, release date, producer, price, grade level
Indexes:
Period covered: available at time of publication
Revision and updating: *Films 1977-1978* (32-05)
Media represented: films
Producers represented: not known
Features: Running text outlines energy problem. Chiefly for secondary level.
Subject terms: energy and environment education

06-12*   Population Education: Sources and Resources. Judith Seltzer and
    JoAnn Robinson. Population Reference Bureau, Inc., 1754 N Street,
    NW, Washington, DC 20036, 1975. 32p. single copies free. ED 113 230.
Purpose: recommended "Audio-Visual Aids and Activities" pp. 18-22
Grade level: intermediate, secondary
Arrangement: by media
Subjects: family planning, food supply, population trends
Entries: 43
    running time, producer, release date, sale/rental price; grade level, contents
    note
Indexes: title
Period covered: 1967-1975
Revision and updating:
Media represented: films, graphic materials, simulation games
Producers represented: various
Features: Films predominate. Also lists organizations and other information
    sources, reference guides, curriculum and study guides, periodicals, readings
    [Similar list: *Multimedia Materials for Studies on World Peace* (19-19), in
    part deals with population pressures and their role in international conflict.
    See also 10-01.]
Subject terms:
    energy and environment education
    futures

07–Film Study

The study of filmmaking and of the film as a communications tool cuts across the lines separating traditional disciplines of art, language arts, and industrial arts. The term "film study" in the Subject Index and 32–Films will yield many references in addition to those cited in this chapter.

Film News (32-18), *Media Review Digest* (01-03) and *Superfilms* (32-22) serve as references for award-winning films as does *Educational Media Yearbook* (Bowker, 1977. $19.95. pp. 76-98). For a study of the role of the popular film in myth-making, several books by Richard A. Maynard offer filmographies (see 07-07 and 19-10, "Features," and 17–American History, introduction). Filmographies of films in every genre abound. Examples in addition to those cited in this chapter are *The Fabulous Fantasy Films*, by Jeff Rovin (A. S. Barnes & Co., Cranbury, NJ 08512, 1977. $19.95) and *The Great Gangster Pictures*, by James R. Parish and Michael R. Pitts (Scarecrow Press, Metuchen, NJ 08840, 1976. $15.00).

07-01*   **Films for Filmstudy.** 3rd ed. Pennsylvania State University Audio-Visual Services, Willard Building, University Park, PA 16802, 1976. 46p. free.

Purpose: film library catalog; recommendations
Grade level: secondary
Arrangement: alphabetical title

Subjects:
animation	films about filmmaking
comedies	films about the arts
documentaries	interviews with filmmakers and
experimental films	directors
feature film excerpts	production techniques–film
film history	and tv
	serials

Entries: over 500

running time, producer, release date, rental price; contents summary and comments on technique

Indexes: subject
Period covered: 1912-1975
Revision and updating: previous edition 1973; *Newsletter*
Media represented: films
Producers represented: various
Features: [Similar list: See also *Films for Communications and Language Arts* (11-03) and "Films on Film: A Checklist" by Judith Trojan (*Take One*, v.5, March 1977, p. 30; May 1977), describing 40-50 "films that aim to enlighten, entertain, and educate in the history, aesthetics and personalities of world cinema"; "Feature Film Feast–New Releases and Sleepers," *Media and Methods*, v.13, December 1976, pp. 22-29, 61-65, recommends 30 "works that share a common significance as film art." See also 07-12.]

07-01 (cont'd)
Subject terms:
>   the arts
>   film study
>   social studies

07-02*   Themes Two: One Hundred Short Films for Discussion. William
>   Kuhns. Pflaum CEBCO, Fairfield, NJ 07006, 1974. 193p. illus. $7.95pa.
Purpose: recommendations selected from over 200 short films
Grade level: secondary
Arrangement: alphabetical title
Subjects: allegorical, animation and abstract graphic films
Entries: 100

>   running time, producer, distributor, release date; country of origin;
>   director; 1-2 page synopsis and critical review;
>   omitted: price
Indexes: thematic
Period covered: 1964-73 (a few earlier)
Revision and updating: previous edition 1971
Media represented: films
Producers represented: U.S. and foreign
Features:
Subject terms:
>   film study
>   social studies
>   values education

07-03*   Hal in the Classroom: Science Fiction Films. Ralph J. Amelio. Pflaum
>   CEBCO, Fairfield, NJ 07006, 1974. 153p. $4.95pa. LC 74-84007.
Purpose: "Filmography," pp. 114-136; recommendations
Grade level: secondary
Arrangement: short films, feature films
Subjects: "man and his humanistic concerns, especially in regard to the future";
>   fantasy films
Entries: appr. 150

>   running time, distributor, release date (feature films only); sale and rental
>   price; contents summary
>   omitted: grade level
Indexes: none
Period covered: 1929-1973
Revision and updating:
Media represented: films
Producers represented: 30 distributors
Features: [See also "Fantasy in Film" in *Films 1977-1978* (32-05), *The Great*
>   *Science Fiction Pictures* by James Robert Parish and Michael R. Pitts
>   (Scarecrow, 1977. 382p. $15), a checklist of close to 600 films, plus
>   radio and television series, *Films on the Future* (17-20) and (11-13),
>   "Features."]

07-03 (cont'd)
Subject terms:
 film study
 futures
 science fiction

07-04* **Discovery in Film Book Two.** Malcolm W. Gordon. Paulist Press, Paramus, NJ 07652, 1973. 162p. $5.95.
Purpose: recommendations
Grade level: secondary
Arrangement: topical
Subjects: communication love
 freedom peace
 happiness
Entries: 81
 running time, producer, sale/rental price; critical review; audience suitability and suggestions for use
 omitted: release date
Indexes: title
Period covered: available at time of writing
Revision and updating:
Media represented: films
Producers represented: various, including independent filmmakers, religious, TV documentaries
Features: No evident sectarian bias despite being published by a religious publishing house.
Subject terms:
 film study
 guidance

07-05* **Film; The Museum of Modern Art Department of Film Circulating Programs.** Museum of Modern Art, 11 West 53rd Street, New York, NY 10019, 1973. 56p. free.
 Supplement. 1976. 15p. free.
Purpose: rental library catalog; recommendations
Grade level: secondary
Arrangement: by subject, country of origin and chronology
Subjects: the art of filmmaking fiction films narrative films
 early cinema history independent films, study films
 experimental films documentaries,
 factual films films on the arts
Entries: over 600 (including *Supplement*)
 running time, director, credits, release date; contents summary and critique; rental price
Indexes: title, filmmakers
Period covered: 1890s-1976
Revision and updating: loose-leaf flyers
Media represented: films, graphic materials
Producers represented: various commercial, government, independent

07-05 (cont'd)
Features: The Museum also maintains archives of film stills. Subscribing educational institutions may purchase copies.
Subject terms:
the arts
film study

07-06*   A Filmography of Films about Movies and Movie-Making. Eastman Kodak Company, Rochester, NY 14650, 1974. 18p. free.
Purpose: recommendations
Grade level: intermediate, secondary
Arrangement: alphabetical title
Subjects: filmmaking
Entries: appr. 300

running time, producer, credits, release date (in most cases); contents description with some notes on techniques
omitted: prices
Indexes: none
Period covered: 1907-1973
Revision and updating: previous edition 1971
Media represented: films
Producers represented: various, including television
Features: "Films listed are in Kodak Supermatic Cassettes, unless otherwise noted." Kodak also has both sale and free-loan films and slide sets on photographic and darkroom techniques among other topics. They are listed in *Your Programs from Kodak* (free-loan), *Visual Communications Programs from Kodak*, and *Catalog of Kodak Educational Materials.*
Subject terms: film study

07-07*   The Great Western Pictures. James R. Parish and Michael R. Pitts. Scarecrow Press, Metuchen, NJ 08840, 1976. 477p. illus. $16.50.
Purpose: "to offer . . . a broad spectrum of the Western motion picture as produced in the United States"; comprehensive
Grade level: intermediate, secondary
Arrangement: alphabetical title
Subjects: film study
Entries: appr. 300

producing studio, production date, credits, running time; full synopsis and critique
Indexes: none
Period covered: 1911-1975
Revision and updating:
Media represented: films
Producers represented: various
Features: Also lists of Western shows on radio and television. [Similar lists: *The Western*. Allen Eyles. Barnes, 1975. 207p. $9.95, includes film index; *The American West on Film: Myth and Reality*. Richard A. Maynard.

07-07 (cont'd)
Features (cont'd): Hayden Book Company, Rochelle Park, NJ 07662, 1975.
144p. $4.95, includes filmography of 26 titles.]
Subject terms:
American history
film study

07-08* **From "A" to "Yellow Jack"; A Film-Study Film Collection.** Indiana
University Audio-Visual Center, Bloomington, IN 47401, 1975. 88p.
free. ED 111 332.
Purpose: recommended films available from the Indiana rental film library
Grade level: secondary
Arrangement: alphabetical title
Subjects: animated   filmmaking techniques
documentary   literature
experimental   non-narrative
feature film excerpts   others
Entries: 250

running time, producer, release date, rental fee; contents summary
Indexes: subject, directors
Period covered: 1920s-1970s
Revision and updating:
Media represented: films
Producers represented: appr. 25, including television
Features: "[E]xperimental films, film classics, historically interesting films,
works of recognized directors and films which are models of film techniques." [Similar list: *Viewfinders Newsletter* No. 8 (Viewfinders, P.O. Box
1665, Evanston, IL 60204) lists 25 "Films about Filmmaking and Television Production" handled by that distributor (and others). See also other
lists mentioned in 07-01, "Features" and 07-12.]
Subject terms:
film study
literature

07-09* **New American Filmmakers; Selections from the Whitney Museum of
American Art Film Program.** American Federation of Arts, 41 East
65th Street, New York, NY 10021, 1976. 95p. illus. free.
Purpose: rental library catalog; films shown at the Whitney Museum of American
Art 1970-1974
Grade level: secondary
Arrangement: by subject
Subjects: animation and film graphics   expanded forms
documentary film   narrative film
Entries: appr. 230

running time, producer, release date, sale and rental price; contents note,
information about filmmaker; quotes from reviews
Indexes: title, filmmakers
Period covered: 1940s-1974

07-09 (cont'd)
Revision and updating:
Media represented: films
Producers represented: appr. 180 independent filmmakers
Features: Each entry illustrated by a still.
Subject terms:
> contemporary issues
> film study

07-10*   **Wilson Library Bulletin.** New York, NY, H. W. Wilson Co., $14.00/year.
Purpose: "Cine-Opsis," by Jane Varlejs, recommends films "that go beyond the normal 'classroom films' in stimulating response and discussion, while also serving as examples of excellence in cinematic achievements," each month on a different current topic.
Grade level: all
Arrangement: random
Subjects: all
Entries: 75-85/year

> running time, release date, rental price, distributor
> omitted: grade level
Indexes: indexed in *Media Review Digest* (01-03)
Period covered: currently distributed, some older ones
Revision and updating: 12x/year
Media represented: films
Producers represented: various
Features: *Wilson Library Bulletin* is almost universally subscribed to by school and public libraries.
Subject terms:
> contemporary issues
> film study

07-11*   **"Animated Films: A History and Filmography."** Philip Segal. *Previews*, v.5, November 1976, p. 8-11.
Purpose: recommendations
Grade level: all
Arrangement: by producer; also computer films, early animation, experimental films, European
Subjects: animated films
Entries: appr. 50

> titles and distributors only
Indexes:
Period covered: early 1900s-1970s
Revision and updating:
Media represented: films
Producers represented: 12 distributors
Features: Filmography is incidental to text, which details history of animation.
> [Similar lists: "Beyond Disney: Choice Animated Films" (*Media and Methods*, v.12, December 1975, pp. 28-32); "Animation: Alive and Well"

07-11 (cont'd)
Features (cont'd): (v.13, April 1977, pp. 42-44); "Satirical Shorts and Spoofs" (v.12, April 1976, pp. 36-38; 42). 16 prizewinners at the Ottawa 1976 Animated Film Festival are featured in *Film News*, v.34, January-February 1977, pp. 8-10, 12-15, 17.]
Subject terms: film study

07-12* **Movies about Movies/Chicago '77.** Film Center, School of the Art Institute of Chicago, Columbus Drive & Jackson Boulevard, Chicago, IL 60603, 1977. 62p. illus. $2.50pa.
Purpose: Films shown at the Center's film festival
Grade level: all
Arrangement: topical
Subjects: comedians in movies about movies   shorts
            inside Hollywood   the star phenomenon
            outside Hollywood
Entries: 42

    release date, studio, running time; credits; lengthy signed summary and review
Indexes: title
Period covered: 1924-1976
Revision and updating:
Media represented: films
Producers: U.S. and foreign studios
Features: "Movies about Movies Filmography" (pp. 59-61), a chronological listing of over 300 titles, released 1908-1976, including the 42 singled out in this catalog.
Subject terms:
        film study
        mass media

08–Health and Safety Education

Lists detailed in here are concerned with all aspects of health and safety education. Those dealing only with drug abuse education (including alcohol and tobacco) and sex education are referred to in 09–Drug Abuse Education and 10–Sex Education. Materials useful for driver education may be located under that term in the Subject Index. Alcohol education materials also frequently deal with traffic safety. For items on nutrition, see the sub-head Home Economics in 21–Vocational Education, and employ the subject term "nutrition."

Catalogs of university film libraries (e.g., 32-05 and 32-23) and of instructional and public television libraries (43–Television) suggest many quality films and video recordings.

Relevant government sources include:

Food and Drug Administration, Office of Public Affairs, 5600 Fishers Lane, Rockville, MD 20852

> *FDA Informational Materials for the Food and Cosmetic Industries* (pamphlets and visuals, including Spanish language publications and narrations)
>
> *FDA Consumer* ($8.55/year from Consumer Information Center, Pueblo, CO 81009)

National Institute for Occupational Safety and Health, 4676 Columbia Parkway, Cincinnati, OH 45226

> *Publications List* (biennial); *Free-Loan Films and Filmstrips*

National Highway Traffic Safety Administration, 400 Seventh Street, SW, Washington, DC 20591

> *Safety Belt Activity Book: A Guide for Teachers of Grades K-6* (1977)

National Audiovisual Center, Washington, DC 20409

> *Safety: Selected U.S. Government Audiovisuals* (1977)

Selected U.S. Government Publications (35-01) and *The Consumer Information Catalog* (04-01) announce new government publications.

The guides listed in 34–Free and Inexpensive Publications suggest sources for much free and inexpensive material. To these may be added the Health Research Group, 2000 P Street, NW, Washington, DC 20036.

08-01* **Index to Health and Safety Education.** 3rd ed. National Information Center for Educational Media, University of Southern California, University Park, Los Angeles, CA 90007, 1977. 1141p. $47.00; $23.50 (microfiche). LC 76-1621.

Purpose: comprehensive
Grade level: all
Arrangement: alphabetical title

Subjects:
consumer education	home economics
driver education	human body
drug abuse	physical education
health and safety education	sex education

Entries: over 33,000 (including adult)

> type of medium, format data, producer, distributor, release date (generally); grade level; contents note; out-of-print titles so noted
>> omitted: price

Indexes: classed subject
Period covered: 1909-1970s
Revision and updating: *Update of Nonbook Media*
Media represented: audio recordings, filmloops, films, filmstrips, slides, transparencies, video recordings
Producers represented: several thousand

08-01 (cont'd)
Features:
Subject terms:

consumer education
driver education
health and safety education

home economics
life science
physical education

08-02 **National Directory of Safety Films.** National Safety Council, 444 N.
Michigan Avenue, Chicago, IL 60611, 1973. $4.95pa.
Purpose: comprehensive listing of films available from various sources
Grade level: all
Arrangement: topical
Subjects: safety
Entries: appr. 1000

running time, release date, distributor; contents summary
omitted: price, grade level
Indexes: title
Period covered: available at time of publication
Revision and updating: biennial
Media represented: films, slides, filmstrips
Producers represented: over 200 commercial, academic, institutional, government
Features: Films and slide shows for sale or rental from the Council are listed
in the 1977-78 *Catalog.*
Subject terms:

driver education
health and safety education

industrial arts

08-03 **Films for Health, Recreation, and Physical Education.** 3rd ed.
Pennsylvania State University, Audio-Visual Services, Willard
Building, University Park, PA 16802, 1974. 42p. free.
Purpose: film library catalog; recommendations
Grade level: intermediate, secondary
Arrangement: alphabetical by subject
Subjects: health
human development
physiology

sports
others

Entries: appr. 480

running time, producer, release date; rental price; grade level; contents
summary
Indexes: subject
Period covered: mainly 1960s
Revision and updating: *Newsletter*; 32-23 for elementary grades
Media represented: films
Producers represented: various commercial, academic, government
Features:
Subject terms:

health and safety education
physical education

08-04   **Guide to Audio-Visual Aids for Spanish-Speaking Americans.**
U.S. Public Health Service, Health Services Administration,
5600 Fishers Lane, Rockville, MD 20852, 1973. 37p. free.
DHEW Publication No. (HSA) 74-30.
Purpose: comprehensive; lists materials with Spanish language sound tracks
Grade level: intermediate, secondary
Arrangement: 15 major topics
Subjects: health
Entries: appr. 180

running time, release date, producer, distributor; purchase and rental
price; contents summaries and audience suggestions "are those of the
distributors"
Indexes: none
Period covered: 1960s-1973
Revision and updating:
Media represented: films, filmstrips, slides
Producers represented: commercial, institutional, government, including foreign
Features: All but a very few listings are films. Materials have not been previewed,
references to awards are omitted, and no independent evaluations are
attempted.
Subject terms:
health and safety education
home economics

08-05   **Films for Safety and First Aid.** 2nd ed. Pennsylvania State University,
Audio-Visual Services, Willard Building, University Park, PA 16802,
1974. 15p. free.
Purpose: film library catalog; recommendations
Grade level: all
Arrangement: alphabetical title
Subjects: safety
Entries: appr. 125

running time, producer, rental price, release date; contents summary;
grade level
Indexes: subject
Period covered: 1943-1972
Revision and updating: *Newsletter*; 32-23 for elementary grades
Media represented: films
Producers represented: various
Features:
Subject terms:
driver education   industrial arts
health and safety education

08-06*   **Drug and Health Mediagraphy; Personal Health.** Ralph R. Dykstra.
R&D Complex, Faculty of Professional Studies, SUNY at Buffalo,
1300 Elmwood Avenue, Buffalo, NY 14222, 1974. 87p. ED 106 992.

08-06 (cont'd)
Purpose: recommendations by teachers
Grade level: all
Arrangement: by media in four topical sections
Subjects: dental health   nutrition
            first aid and survival   safety education
Entries: over 300 (excluding print)

    running time, producer, release date (generally); contents summary;
    reading, chronological age and mental age level
        omitted: price
Indexes: none
Period covered: 1950s-1960s
Revision and updating:
Media represented: audio recordings, films, filmstrips, free and inexpensive
    publications, graphic materials, kits, manipulative materials, slides
Producers represented: various commercial and institutional
Features: Films account for appr. half.
Subject terms:
        health and safety education
        nutrition

08-07   **A Catalogue of Some Health Films.** Pan American Health Organization,
        Regional Office of the World Health Organization, 525 23rd Street,
        NW, Washington, DC 20037, 1973. 28p. free.
Purpose: free-loan WHO films; comprehensive
Grade level: secondary
Arrangement: alphabetical title, plus supplement
Subjects: health
Entries: 28

    running time, producer, release date; summary
Indexes: none
Period covered: 1955-1973
Revision and updating:
Media represented: films
Producers represented: U.N. and its agencies; governments; private and academic
    producers in various countries
Features: The films generally deal with various diseases, and with public and
    environmental health.
Subject terms: health and safety education

08-08*   **Health: A Multimedia Source Guide.** Joan Ash & Michael Stevenson.
        Bowker, 1976. 185p. $16.50. LC 76-28297.
Purpose: comprehensive
Grade level: all
Arrangement: by type of source (associations, audiovisual producers, government
    agencies, pharmaceutical companies, research institutes)
Subjects: physical and mental health

08-08 (cont'd)
Entries: several hundred sources

name, address and purpose of organization; types of materials issued, including specific titles

Indexes: subject, free and inexpensive materials
Period covered: available at time of writing
Revision and updating:
Media represented: free and inexpensive publications, government publications, films, filmstrips, slides, transparencies, video recordings
Producers: various
Features:
Subject terms:
        health and safety education
        psychology

08-09*   **8mm Films in Medicine and Health Sciences.** 3rd ed. Reba Ann Benschoten. University of Nebraska Medical Center, 42nd Davey Ave., Omaha, NE 08105, 1977. 507p. $9.00pa. LC 77-7874.
Purpose: comprehensive
Grade level: secondary
Arrangement: subject
Subjects: anatomy   nursing care
                bandages   oral hygiene
                drug abuse   physiology
                genetics   sex education
                movement   others
Entries: several hundred (excluding professional)

format, running time, producer, release date; price, contents summary; audience level

Indexes: title
Period covered: 1960s-1976
Revision and updating: previous editions 1969 and 1972
Media represented: films, filmloops
Producers represented: appr. 1200
Features: Most of the 3850 listings are for college and professional use; a very few are for elementary schools
Subject terms:
        health and safety education   physical education
        health services

08-10*   **The Health Sciences Video Directory 1977.** Lawrence Eidelberg. Shelter Books, Inc., 218 East 19th Street, New York, NY 10003, 1977. 270p. $27.50. LC 76-29480.
Purpose: comprehensive; intended for "undergraduate, continuing, in-service and patient health education"
Grade level: secondary
Arrangement: alphabetical title
Subjects: dentistry, medicine, nursing

08-10 (cont'd)
Entries: over 300 (excluding professional)
    running time, format details, release date (not in all cases), producer/distributor;
    sale/rental price; audience suitability; contents summary
Indexes: subject
Period covered: 1960s-1976
Revision and updating:
Media represented: video recordings
Producers represented: 120 producers and distributors including commercial
    and institutional
Features: Uses medical subject headings system of National Library of Medicine.
    Titles found under "patient education" in the subject index and others rated
    suitable for allied health specialists and students preparing for such careers,
    hospital support staff, nursing students and community health groups deserve
    consideration in appropriate secondary settings.
Subject terms:
    health and safety education   nutrition
    health services   vocational education

08-11*   Hospital/Health Care Training Media Profiles. Olympic Media Informa-
    tion, 71 West 23rd Street, New York, NY 10010. $75/year.
Purpose: evaluations
Grade level: secondary
Arrangement: alphabetical title in each issue
Subjects: health care
Entries: 240/year
    running time, distributor, release date; sale and rental prices; synopsis,
    evaluation, audience suitability; related materials
Indexes: subject, title
Period covered: current releases, some older
Revision and updating: published 6x/year
Media represented: audio recordings, filmloops, films, filmstrips, kits, slides,
    video recordings
Producers represented: various
Features: Primarily intended for training of nursing and allied health care profes-
    sionals and the general public, some of the selections are suitable for health
    and career education.
Subject terms:
    health and safety education
    health services

08-12*   "Films on Noise Pollution and Deafness." Salvatore J. Parlato, Jr.
    Lifelong Learning EMC One-76, University of California Extension
    Media Center, Berkeley, CA 94720, March 1976.
Purpose: recommendations
Grade level: intermediate, secondary
Arrangement: topical

08-12 (cont'd)
Subjects: basics   noise pollution
     deafness   nonverbal films
     institutional programs sponsored films
     mime
Entries: appr. 30

   EMC order # or producer; contents and critique
     omitted: running time, release date, purchase price, producer (most
      cases), grade level
Indexes:
Period covered: available at time of publication
Revision and updating:
Media represented: films
Producers represented: not known
Features: Parlato is also the author of *Superfilms* (32-22) and *Films Too Good Good for Words* (32-09).
Subject terms:
    energy and environment education
    health and safety education

09–Drug Abuse Education

   Films and other media on drug abuse education proliferated during the 1960s and early 1970s when such abuse first became a national concern. So did guides to such media. During the more recent period the focus is on alcoholism. Additional material will be found in *A Selective Guide to Materials for Mental Health and Family Life Education* (15-12), *The MHMC Guide to Recent Mental Health Films* (15-13) and the sub-headings "alcoholism," "drug abuse," and "drug dependence" under "Patient Education" in *Health Sciences Video Directory* (08-10).
   The National Clearinghouse for Drug Abuse Information, P.O. Box 1635, Rockville, MD 20850 supplies a list of *Publications for Researchers, Community Workers, Educators, Concerned Public* that are available from it and from the Superintendent of Documents. The National Clearinghouse for Alcohol Information, P.O. Box 2345, Rockville, MD 20852 has free pamphlets and posters. The Superintendent of Documents, Washington, DC 20402 publishes free subject bibliographies SB 015 (*Smoking*), SB 163 (*Drug Education*) and SB 175 (*Alcoholism*).

09-01   **Drug Education: A Bibliography of Available Inexpensive Materials.**
     Dorothy P. Wells. Scarecrow Press, Metuchen, NJ 08840, 1972. 111p.
     $6.00. LC 72-317.
Purpose: comprehensive
Grade level: secondary
Arrangement: by publisher in 3 sections (general, late additions, reprints); by title
   in government documents section

09-01 (cont'd)
Subjects: drug education
Entries: 394

pagination, publication date, publisher, price; intended audience; synopsis
Indexes: author, title, subject
Period covered: available at time of publication
Revision and updating:
Media represented: free and inexpensive publication, government publications
Producers represented: appr. 100 institutional, government
Features: Important for the names of agencies issuing materials even though
specific titles may no longer be in print. Alcohol and tobacco are excluded
from consideration.
Subject terms: drug abuse education

09-02* In Focus: Alcohol and Alcoholism Media. National Clearinghouse for
Alcohol Information, P.O. Box 2345, Rockville, MD 20852, 1977.
73p. free.
Purpose: descriptive
Grade level: intermediate, secondary
Arrangement: alphabetical title
Subjects: alcoholic personality physiology
attitudes prevention
case histories rehabilitation and treatment
drinking and driving social forces
occupational alcoholism youth
others
Entries: over 300

running time, producer/distributor, sale/rental price; release date; grade
level; synopsis
Indexes: subject
Period covered: 1970-76, some earlier
Revision and updating: monthly announcement service by subscription
Media represented: films, filmstrips, slides, video recordings
Producers represented: commercial, institutional, government, academic, tele-
vision, including Canadian
Features: Primarily films.
Subject terms:
drug abuse education
driver education

09-03 Drug Abuse Films. 3rd ed. National Coordinating Council on Drug
Education, 1601 Connecticut Ave., NW, Washington, DC 20009,
1973. 117p. $5.00pa.
Purpose: evaluations based on scientific accuracy and conceptual integrity
Grade level: all
Arrangement: 4 sections: Recommended; Restricted; Unacceptable; Materials
aimed at minority groups
Subjects: drug abuse

09-03 (cont'd)
Entries: over 200

> type of medium; running time, sale and rental price; producer, distributor, release date; audience suitability; very full synopsis and evaluation

Indexes: title
Period covered: late 1960s-1972
Revision and updating:
Media represented: films, filmstrips, audio recordings, slides, transparencies
Producers represented: various, including NIMH
Features: Only 32 titles receive full recommendation, chiefly films, and another hundred are rated for "restricted" use only. The "unacceptable" category contains a large proportion of smaller media. Materials dealing with tobacco and alcohol are not considered. Selection guidelines are on page 9. A further critique in *Social Education*, v.38, March 1974, pp. 303-308, 314), finds that only 12 of the films recommended here stimulate critical thinking and are appropriate for elementary and secondary school.
Subject terms: drug abuse education

09-04*   Alcohol Education Materials; An Annotated Bibliography. Gail Gleason Milgram. Rutgers Center of Alcohol Studies, New Brunswick, NJ 08903, 1975. 304p. $12.50. LC 74-620158.
Purpose: comprehensive
Grade level: intermediate, secondary
Arrangement: alphabetical by author
Subjects:

alcohol education	alcoholics	effects of alcohol on
alcohol and highway	Alcoholics Anonymous	the human body
safety	alcoholism: disease	intoxication
alcohol and life	alcoholism: treatment	sociology of drinking
alcohol: nature	controls: individual	habits
and history	controls: social	teen-age drinking

Entries: appr. 500 (excluding books)

> publisher, date, price; intended audience; contents summary

Indexes: title, audience level, type of publication, subject
Period covered: 1950-May 1973
Revision and updating:
Media represented: free and inexpensive publications
Producers represented: over 600
Features: Also books and curriculum guides.
Subject terms:
> drug abuse education
> driver education

10-Sex Education

Reference is made to 22–Women's Studies, 15–Psychology and Guidance, particularly *Family Life* (15-11) and 08–Health and Safety Education. The *Health Sciences Video Directory* (08-10) uses subheadings "contraception and family planning" and "sex behavior and disorders" under "Patient Education." Recorded public television programs on sex education, parenthood, and related topics are found in *Video Program Catalogue 1976-77* and *Supplement* (43-02).

10-01* **Film Resources for Sex Education.** Derek L. Burleson. Sex Information Council of the U.S. Human Sciences Press, 72 Fifth Avenue, New York, NY 10001, 1976. 52p. $4.95pa.

Purpose: reviews of "material (that) can be used effectively in an educational setting" originally appeared in *SIECUS Newsletter* v.I-VII and *SIECUS Report* v.I-III.

Grade level: all

Arrangement: alphabetical title

Subjects:
childbirth	out-of-wedlock	sexual development
emotional aspects	pregnancy	teenage marriage
family planning &	premarital sex	venereal disease
population education	reproduction	others
marriage and family life	sex roles	

Entries: appr. 200

format, running time, producer, release date; sale/rental price; grade level; evaluation

Indexes: subject

Period covered: 1960s-1975

Revision and updating: previous edition 1973; *SIECUS Report.* Sex Information and Education Council of the U.S., 137 N. Franklin Street, Hempstead, NY 11550. $9.95/year.

Media represented: audio recordings, filmloops, films, filmstrips, kits, slides, transparencies, video recordings

Producers represented: appr. 80 commercial, institutional, religious

Features: Includes a few films suitable for adult and professional audiences only. Few media other than films.

Subject terms:
> guidance
> sex education

10-02 **"Venereal Disease."** Dorothy P. Wells. *Library Journal.* v.99, September 15, 1974, pp. 2126-2131.

Purpose: recommendations for pamphlet collection

Grade level: secondary

Arrangement: by issuing organization

Subjects: venereal disease

10-02 (cont'd)
Entries: appr. 90

format details, ordering information, publication date; contents note
Indexes:
Period covered: 1960s-1973
Revision and updating:
Media represented: free and inexpensive publications, government publications
Producers represented: 46 commercial, institutional, state and local governments, World Health Organization
Features:
Subject terms: sex education

10-03 "Feature Films for Sex Education." Richard Maynard. "Sex Education—Who Needs It?" Sandra Soehngen. *Media and Methods.* v.9, November 1972, pp. 43-46, 48-49.
Purpose: "previewed by *Media and Methods* staff . . . the best of what we saw"
Grade level: secondary
Arrangement: by media
Subjects: sex education
Entries: 22

running time (films), producer or distributor; critical evaluation
omitted: price, release date, format details for filmstrips
Indexes:
Period covered: not known
Revision and updating:
Media represented: films, filmstrips
Producers represented: various commercial
Features: Only four filmstrips are included.
Subject terms: sex education

10-04* **Pregnancy and Nutrition.** Society for Nutrition Education, 2140 Shattuck Avenue, Berkeley, CA 94704, 1975. 11p. $2.50pa.
Purpose: recommendations; "Each listing has been evaluated by qualified nutritionists and is considered to be reliable and accurate"
Grade level: secondary
Arrangement: by media
Subjects: diet planning   others
fetal development
Entries: 28 (excluding professional)

format data, producer or publisher, date, price; descriptors
Indexes: author, title
Period covered: 1965-1975
Revision and updating: *Journal of Nutrition Education* (21-25)
Media represented: filmstrips, films, free and inexpensive publications, graphic materials, manipulative materials
Producers represented: various institutional, government

10-04 (cont'd)
Features: Includes Spanish language and bilingual titles.
Subject terms:
> nutrition
> sex education

10-05*   Annotated Guide to Venereal Disease Instructional Materials Available in Canada. Department of National Health and Welfare, Ottawa, 1975. 43p. ED 131 018.

Purpose: recommendations; to "assist all educators and health workers in presenting a complete range of up-to-date instructional and informational materials"
Grade level: all
Arrangement: by media
Subjects: venereal disease
Entries: appr. 60 (excluding adult materials and materials available to Canadian residents only)
> running time, producers, release date, sale & rental prices; contents summary; grade level
Indexes: none
Period covered: 1970-75, some earlier
Revision and updating:
Media represented: audio recordings, films, filmstrips, kits, transparencies
Features: Most are films and filmstrips. Also includes English and French publications, charts, posters, video and audio tapes from Canadian federal and provincial governments.
Subject terms: sex education

11-Language Arts

This term and its narrower ones, including "reading and language," "poetry," "world literature" and others, will yield lists of media in addition to those cited in this chapter. Materials referenced in 05—Early Childhood Education are relevant; for film as literature, see 07—Film Study.

The *Directory of Spoken-Voice Audio-Cassettes* (30-07) gives sources for recordings of adult literature while *The Elementary School Library Collection* (01-09) is a starting point for media on children's literature. In addition, audio-tapes of the Extension Media Center of the University of California, Berkeley, CA 94720 include a number of poetry recordings, and the Library of Congress Music Division, Recorded Sound Section, Washington, DC 20540, has poetry recordings for sale (request *Spoken Recordings* price list). The University of Michigan Audio-visual Education Center, 416 Fourth Street, Ann Arbor, MI 48103 supplies audio tapes of interviews with children's authors.

Superfilms (32-22) lists many award-winning films on literature, poetry, reading, and language development for all grades. "Audio-visual aids for English history" (19-22) has suggestions of interest to the English literature classroom.

Good Reading for the Disadvantaged Reader; Multi-Ethnic Resources (George D. Spache. Garrard, 1975. $5.75pa.) includes a chapter on audiovisual resources.

Foreign Language

In addition to the three references listed in this chapter, *The Elementary School Library Collection* (01-09) contains foreign language recordings, and the listing of foreign language films in *Films 1977-1978* (32-05) should.be noted. Media on the culture of various countries may be located using the term "world cultures" in the Subject Index. For instruction in Spanish, 02—Bilingual Education and 18—Ethnic Studies suggest Spanish language media in all formats, including government publications.

The guides listed in Free and Inexpensive Publications (34) give official sources supplying information about other countries.

Directory of Spoken-Voice Audio-Cassettes (30-07) lists sources of foreign language instructional recordings. The National Audiovisual Center (01-10) distributes foreign language instruction tapes of the Foreign Service Institute of the Department of State. Corresponding books are sold by the Superintendent of Documents, Washington, DC 20402 (request SB 82). SB 130 lists Spanish language government publications.

English as a Second Language

While sources outside the United States generally are not encompassed by this work, it should be noted that some of the work of the English Teaching Information Centre, The British Council, 10 Spring Gardens, London SW 1A2BN is placed in the *ERIC* data bank (ED 111 220, 111 221).

11-01*   **Language Arts; Audio Visual Quick List.** Baker and Taylor Co., P.O. Box 230, Momence, IL 60954, 1977. 52p. free.
Purpose: distributor's catalog; comprehensive
Grade level: all
Arrangement: by grade level and media
Subjects: language arts, library skills
Entries: appr. 400

> type of medium, producer, price; grade level; contents note; occasional quotes from reviews
> > omitted: release date

Indexes: none
Period covered: available at time of publication
Revision and updating:
Media represented: audio recordings, filmstrips, kits
Producers represented: appr. 200

11-01 (cont'd)
Features: This is the only catalog listing audio-visual media still available
from a major wholesaler.
Subject terms:

literature   reading and language
poetry

11-02*   **Xedia Micromedia Classroom Libraries.** Xerox Education Publications,
1250 Fairwood Avenue, P.O. Box 444, Columbus, OH 43216, 1976.
32p. free.
Purpose: publisher's catalog; comprehensive
Grade level: all
Arrangement: by grade level and subject
Subjects: adventure, mystery &   fantasy   picture books
science fiction   history   science
animals   humor   sports
the arts   mathematics   starter
career education   multi-ethnic life   collections
classic tales
Entries: 1915

author, title, price; reading and interest levels
Indexes: none
Period covered: available at time of publication
Revision and updating: annual
Media represented: microform
Producers represented:
Features: Books for grades K-9 from various publishers reproduced on microfiche.
Subject terms:

American history   literature
career education   reading and language
ethnic studies   science

11-03*   **Films for Communication and Language Arts.** 3rd ed. Pennsylvania
State University, Audio-Visual Services, Willard Building, University
Park, PA 16802, 1976. 76p. free.
Purpose: film library catalog; recommendations
Grade level: secondary
Arrangement: alphabetical title
Subjects: communication   poetry
film study   reading
French   speech
literature   theatre arts
others
Entries: appr. 750

running time, distributor, release date, rental price; grade level; contents
summary
Indexes: subject
Period covered: 1960s-1974, some earlier

11-03 (cont'd)
Revision and updating: 2nd ed. 1973; *Newsletter*
Media represented: films
Producers represented: various commercial and academic
Features: Includes a very few titles for the elementary level.
Subject terms:
film study   performing arts
language arts

11-04   Chicorel Index to Poetry: Poetry on Discs, Tapes, and Cassettes.
Chicorel Pub. Co., 275 Central Park West, New York, NY 10024,
1972. 443p. $60.00. LC 71-106198.
Purpose: comprehensive
Grade level: secondary
Arrangement: alphabetical by title of collection
Subjects: poetry
Entries: 700 collections
label and number, price, release date; contents listing; subject terms
Indexes: author/title and first line (interfiled with main title entries); performer
Period covered: retrospective
Revision and updating:
Media represented: audio recordings, filmloops
Producers represented: various commercial and institutional, including foreign
Features:
Subject terms: poetry

11-05   A Multi-Media Approach to Children's Literature. Ellin Greene and
Madalynne Schoenfeld. American Library Association, 50 East Huron
Street, Chicago, IL 60611, 1972. $3.75. 262p. LC 72-1376.
Purpose: recommendations "based on first-hand evaluation and use with children.
The response of children . . . was a deciding factor"; a list of media based on
children's books
Grade level: primary, intermediate
Arrangement: by title of book, followed by AV media
Subjects: children's literature
Entries: 650

type of medium, producer, price; grade level; synopsis
Indexes: author, title, subject
Period covered: 1950s-1972
Revision and updating: 2nd ed. 1977
Media represented: films, filmstrips, audio recordings, graphic materials, mani-
pulative materials
Producers represented: appr. 60
Features: Index leads to media (and books) relating to "American life," "ethnic
groups," "foreign countries," etc., and also to media about or presented by
authors and illustrators. [Similar list: 11-19.]
Subject terms:
literature   reading and language

11-06 "Selected Filmstrips and Recordings for the English Classroom." John R. Searles. *English Journal*. v.62, Jan. 1973, pp. 109-115.
Purpose: an index to reviews published in the journal from 1967 to 1972
Grade level: secondary
Arrangement: by subject and media (5 groupings)
Subjects: English
Entries: appr. 175

    citations to reviews only
Indexes:
Period covered: 1967-1972
Revision and updating: earlier list published December 1966
Media represented: filmstrips, audio recordings
Producers represented: various
Features:
Subject terms:
      literature   reading and language

11-07 Selected List of Instructional Materials for English As a Second Language: Audio-Visual Aids. Center for Applied Linguistics, 1611 North Kent Street, Arlington, VA 22209, 1974. 8p. free. ED 090 797.
Purpose: comprehensive
Grade level: primary
Arrangement: by media
Subjects: English as a second language
Entries: appr. 75

    producer, price
        omitted: release date, grade level
Indexes: none
Period covered: not known
Revisions and updating:
Media represented: audio recordings, graphic materials, manipulative materials
Producers represented: various commercial
Features: Also lists films, filmstrips, and transparencies instructing teachers in media production.
Subject terms: English as a second language

11-08 Shakespeare on Film. Peter Morris. Canadian Film Institute, 1762 Carling Ave., Ottawa, Ontario K1J 6N5, 1972. 39p. illus. $3.50.
Purpose: comprehensive list of Shakespeare plays made into feature length films
Grade level: secondary
Arrangement: chronological
Subjects: Shakespeare
Entries: appr. 70

    running time, cast, director, distributor, production date; country and language in which film produced; critical review
Indexes: title (of plays)
Period covered: 1929-1971
Revision and updating:

11-08 (cont'd)
Media represented: films
Producers represented: various U.S. and foreign
Features: Includes foreign language films. [Similar lists: "Putting the bard on the small screen" (*Sightlines*, v.11, Fall 1977, p. 8-13); *Shakespeare on Film*, by Jack J. Jorgens (Indiana University Press, 1977. $15.00) offers critiques of 16 feature film adaptations.]
Subject terms:
> literature
> performing arts

11-09 **"A-V Aids for Teaching Sixteenth Century English History: A Critical Review."** Frederic A. Youngs, Jr. *History Teacher.* v.7, May 1974, pp. 374-393.
Purpose: critical guide
Grade level: secondary
Arrangement: subject
Subjects: English history
Entries: 50-60
> running time, producer, distributor, release date, purchase and rental price; candid evaluations in text of article
Indexes:
Period covered: available at time of publication
Revision and updating:
Media represented: films, filmstrips, slides, transparencies, audio recordings, kits, maps, graphic materials
Producers represented: several, including British
Features: Suitable for a unit on the Elizabethan era. [See also 19-22.]
Subject terms:
> history
> literature

11-10* **English Journal.** National Council of Teachers of English, 1111 Kenyon Road, Urbana, IL 61801. $20/year.
Purpose: "The Short Film" column by Rebecca Fulginiti appears irregularly; recommendations
Grade level: secondary
Arrangement: random
Subjects: English
Entries: appr. 60/year
> running time, producer, sale/rental price (not always); full critical summary including teaching suggestions
> > omitted: release date
Indexes: indexed in *Media Review Digest* (01-03)
Period covered: current releases
Revision and updating: published 9x/year
Media represented: films
Producers represented: various

11-10 (cont'd)
Features: January issue features "Multi-Media," "More Sources of Free and Inexpensive Materials (mostly professional), and "Films/Visuals/Media" (publishers' announcements). [See also 11-13 and 11-16 "Features" and 11-06.]

11-11* **The Reading Teacher.** International Reading Association, Newark, DE 19711. $15.00/year.
Purpose: "Critically Speaking" reviewing column; "New Materials on the Market" annual feature in February issue
Grade level: primary, intermediate
Arrangement: by media (column), alphabetical title (annual)
Subjects: reading
Entries: appr. 25/year (excluding books, professional materials, curriculum sets)

format data, price, producer; release date; signed critical review in most cases, some "briefly noted" (column); title, producer, reading difficulty, interest level, skills developed; information supplied by publishers (annual)
omitted: format data, price (annual)
Indexes: title index to reviews in May issue indicates type of medium; indexed in *Media Review Digest* (01-03)
Period covered: current and recent releases
Revision and updating: published 8x/year
Media represented: audio recordings, films, filmstrips, kits, graphic materials
Producers represented: commercial and institutional
Features: *Journal of Reading* (same publisher, same price), for secondary level, also has a "Reviews" column that evaluates 15-20 audio-visual titles per year.
Subject terms: reading and language

11-12 **"Films to Liven a Language Arts Program."** Carol Emmens. *Previews,* v.3, February 1975, pp. 5-9.
Purpose: "the year's best for elementary grade children" judged on content, technical quality, usefulness and authenticity
Grade level: primary, intermediate
Arrangement: alphabetical title
Subjects: language arts
Entries: 34

running time, producer or distributor, sale and rental price; grade level; critical annotation
Indexes:
Period covered: November 1973-November 1974 releases
Revision and updating:
Media represented: films
Producers represented: 19
Features: [See also 01-30 and 15-10 for other works by the same author.]
Subject terms: language arts

11-13* **Filmed Books and Plays.** Rev. ed. A. G. S. Enser. Academic Press, New York, 1975. 549p. $24.00.

11-13 (cont'd)
Purpose: "a list of books and plays from which (English language) films have
    been made"; comprehensive
Grade level: all
Arrangement: alphabetical film title, author
Subjects: literature on film
Entries: over 3500

    producer, release date, author, original title (if different), publisher
Indexes: original title
Period covered: 1928-1974
Revision and updating: previous editions 1968, 1971
Media represented: films
Producers represented: 37 British and American studios
Features: Availability of films in 8 or 16 mm format may be checked in 32-02.
    [Similar lists: *Feature Films 1961-1970* (32-21) contains a "literary and
    dramatic source index" of novels and plays made into movies during that
    period. Two small books provide briefer lists: *Films in the Language Arts
    Class* (John Aquino. National Education Association, Saw Mill Road, West
    Haven, CT 06516, 1977. $2.50. ED 130 330) lists 34 film adaptations of
    works often taught. *Science Fiction as Literature* (same author and publisher.
    1976. ED 127 313) lists 15 film adaptations of science fiction works. See
    also "Hollywood and American Literature: The American Novel on the
    Screen" (*English Journal*, v.66, January 1977, pp. 82-86) and 42 films listed
    in *From "A" to "Yellowjack"* (07-08).]
Subject terms:
        film study   world literature
        literature

11-14*   **A Title Guide to the Talkies: 1964 through 1974.** Andrew A. Aros.
        Scarecrow Press, Metuchen, NJ, 1977. 335p. $12.50. LC 76-40451.
Purpose: comprehensive list "to which readers can go to read a novel, play, or
    non-fiction work that served as the source materials of a motion picture"
Grade level: all
Arrangement: alphabetical title
Subjects:
Entries: 3429

    film title, original title, author, publisher, release date
Index: author
Period covered: films exhibited 1964-1974
Revision and upating: continuation of *A Title Guide to the Talkies.* 1965
Media represented: films
Producers represented: American, British and other studios
Features: Serves the opposite function of 11-13 and similar works cited there.
Subject terms:
        film study   world literature
        literature

11-15*   Selected Sound Recordings of American, British and European Literature in English. Homer E. Salley. Technological Media Center, University of Toledo, 2801 W. Bancroft Street, Toledo, OH 43606, 1976. 144p. $10.00. ED 130 631.

Purpose: comprehensive
Grade level: secondary
Arrangement: 12 topical groupings
Subjects: American literature   Greek classics
            detective literature   speech dialects
            English literature   others
            European drama
Entries: 1365

     author, title, label & number, playing time, release date
         omitted: price
Indexes: none
Period covered: not known
Revision and updating:
Media represented: audio recordings
Producers represented: 53, including National Council Teachers of English, Library of Congress, National Center for Audiotapes, commercial
Features: Includes dramatizations, readings, criticism, also sound tracks from films. [Similar list: "Sound Recordings of Fiction and Drama." *Media and Methods*, v.12, March 1976, pp. 44-46, 48.]
Subject terms:
         film study   performing arts
         literature   world literature

11-16*   Available Recordings of American Poetry and Poets. Homer E. Salley. University of Toledo, Toledo, OH 43606, 1975. 46p. ED 114 059.

Purpose: comprehensive
Grade level: intermediate, secondary
Arrangement: alphabetical by poet
Subjects: poetry
Entries: appr. 350

     name of album, producer and order number; contents listing.
         omitted: price
Indexes: none
Period covered: available at time of publication
Revision and updating:
Media represented: audio recordings
Producers represented: 14, including Library of Congress, National Council of Teachers of English
Features: [Similar lists: "Poets and Poetry on Film" (*Media and Methods*, v.13 May/June 1977, pp. 42-44) has 15 examples of "successful blending of poetry and film"); "Poetry and Film for the Classroom" (*English Journal*, v.66, January 1977, pp. 88-91) lists 21 "of the best films made from poems."]
Subject terms: poetry

11-17* **Bible-Related Curriculum Materials: A Bibliography.** Thayer S. Warshaw and Betty Lou Miller. Abingdon Press, 1976. 168p. $5.95pa.
Purpose: recommendations by teachers attending Indiana University Institute on Teaching the Bible in Secondary English
Grade level: secondary
Arrangement: 30 chapters based on biblical passages
Subjects: The Bible as Literature (including recordings)
The Bible in Literautre (including recordings)
The Bible in Film and Other Media
Entries: over 300 (excluding books)

running time, producer, release date; contents summary
omitted: price
Indexes: none
Period covered:
Revision and updating:
Media represented: audio recordings, films
Producers represented: various commercial, institutional
Features: A near-comprehensive listing of even remotely Bible-related literary selections (fiction, poetry, plays) in books and on records, including materials recommended for teachers only.
Subject terms:

literature	philosophy and religion
poetry	world literature

11-18* **Master Locator Booklet for Classroom Materials in TESOL.** Adolf Hieke. 3rd ed. Indiana University Linguistics Club, 310 Lindley Hall, Indiana University, Bloomington, IN 47401, 1975. 119p. $4.05. ED 123 929.
Purpose: comprehensive; "supplementary classroom aids and devices" pp. 75-79
Grade level: all
Arrangement: by media
Subjects: English as a foreign or second language
Entries: over 200 (excluding books)

author, title, publisher, date (audio); producer, price (others);
omitted: format details, grade level; running time, price (audio);
running time, release date (visual)
Indexes: author
Period covered: not known
Revision and updating:
Media represented: audio recordings, films, filmstrips, graphic materials, manipulative materials
Producers represented: various, including British
Features: Also texts and other books, including materials for TEUP (Teaching English to the Underprivileged). Over a third of media listed are audio tapes, with a few discs.
Subject terms: English as a second language

11-19*   **Reading Guidance in a Media Age.** Nancy Polette. Scarecrow, 1975. 267p. $10.00.
Purpose: "Children's Literature in Media: A Basic Collection" pp. 181-197; recommendations after classroom use
Grade level: primary, intermediate
Arrangement: topical
Subjects: fiction   literature and poetry
         folk tales and fairy tales   mythology
Entries: appr. 135

    format, producer; grade level; contents note
    omitted: release date, price
Indexes: none
Period covered: not known
Revision and updating:
Media represented: audio recordings, filmstrips
Producers: 14
Features: [Similar list: 15 "Notable children's filmstrips of 1976" (Booklist, v.74, October 1, 1977, p. 304-305).]
Subject terms:
    literature   reading and language
    poetry

11-20*   **"Feature Films That Work."** Barbara Bologha and Edwin Blesch, Jr. *Media and Methods*, v.12, December 1975, p. 14-18, 20, 44-51
Purpose: "films that have worked in classrooms like ours where teachers are concerned with human values"; recommendations to stimulate students to think, write, react
Grade level: secondary
Arrangement: alphabetical title
Subjects: various
Entries: appr. 120

    running time, release date, distributors, rental price; signed reviews for 23
    of the films
Indexes:
Period covered: 1922-1974
Revision and updating: "Feature Film Feast–New Releases and Sleepers." v.13, December 1976, p. 22-29, 61-65
Media represented: films
Producers represented: various commercial
Features: Films of over 50 min. available on 16mm. [Similar lists: "Short Films: The Pick of the Flicks." (same issue, pp. 22-26, 61-73).]
Subject terms:
    film study
    language arts

11-21*   **Non-Print Media and the Teaching of English.** Ken Donelson. (*Arizona English Bulletin*, v.18, October 1975). National Council of Teachers of English, 1111 Kenyon Road, Urbana, IL 61801. 168p. $3.50. ED 128 812.

11-21 (cont'd)
Purpose: "101 Short Films: A Basic Film Library," pp. 94-100; recommendations
Grade level: secondary
Arrangement: alphabetical title
Subjects: language arts
Entries: 101

> running time, source, rental price; contents note
> > omitted: release date

Indexes:
Period covered: not known
Revision and updating:
Media represented: films
Producers represented: various
Features: [See 11-22, "Purpose," for a shorter list by the same author.]
Subject terms:
> film study
> language arts

11-22*   **Focus: Film in the English and Language Arts Classroom.** James S.
          Mullican. (*Indiana English Journal*, v.10, Winter 1975/76). Indiana
          Council of Teachers of English, Indiana State University, Terre
          Haute, IN 47809. 49p. ED 132 582.
Purpose: recommendations, "Films for Children" (Jill P. May, pp. 28-31); "A
          Basic Library of Short Films" (Ken Donelson, pp. 32-37)
Grade level: all
Arrangement: alphabetical title in each article
Subjects: language arts
Entries: appr. 70

> running time, producer, sale or rental price; grade level (May); evaluative
> summary
> > omitted: release date

Indexes:
Period covered: not known
Revision and updating:
Media represented: films
Producers represented: various
Features: "Films for Children" includes a number that are based on titles well
          known in children's literature.
Subject terms:
> film study
> language arts

11-23*   **Selected Print and Nonprint Resources in Speech Communication;
          An Annotated Bibliography K-12.** Jerry D. Feezel and others. Speech
          Communication Association, 5205 Leesburg Pike, Falls Church, VA
          22041; Clearinghouse on Reading and Communication Skills, 1111
          Kenyon Road, Urbana, IL 61801, 1976. 68p. $2.50pa. ED 120 892.

11-23 (cont'd)
Purpose: recommends "worthy instructional resources"; "nonprint-students" and
    "multimedia," pp. 27-44
Grade level: all
Arrangement: random
Subjects: argumentation and   interpersonal   oral interpretation
             forensics   communication   of literature
           drama and theatre   language development   public speaking
           film study   mass media   radio-TV
           group discussion   nonverbal   production
                                      communication   general
Entries: 57 (excluding print and professional materials)

    running time, producer, price, rental price (films); grade level; subject
    terms; contents summary
         omitted: release date (in most cases)
Indexes: detailed subject index
Period covered: available at time of publication
Revision and updating:
Media represented: films, manipulative materials, graphic materilas, filmstrips, audio
    recordings, simulation games, kits
Producers represented: various commercial
Features: Over half are films.
Subject terms:
         film study   performing arts
         mass media   reading and language

11-24*   **Bibliography of Audiovisual Instructional Materials for the Teaching of
         Spanish.** California State Department of Education, 721 Capitol Mall,
         Sacramento, CA 95814, 1975. 129p. $0.75. ED 119 508.
Purpose: evaluative
Grade level: all
Arrangement: 16 curricular areas, games and puzzles
Subjects: all
Entries: appr. 400 (excluding supplementary materials)

    running time, producer, price, release date; grade level, language proficiency
    level; contents summary
Indexes: media
Period covered: 1960s-70s, some earlier
Revision and updating:
Media represented: audio recordings, films, filmstrips, graphic materials, kits,
    manipulative materials, slides
Producers represented: appr. 50, including commercial, government, institutional
Features: Supplements bibliographies of printed materials published 1971 and 1972.
Subject terms: foreign language

11-25*   **Catalog of Instructional Materials.** Defense Language Institute, Monterey,
         CA 93940, 1975. 225p. ED 112 652.

11-25 (cont'd)
Purpose: sales catalog
Grade level: secondary
Arrangement: by language
Subjects: 37 foreign languages and dialects
Entries: over 300
    release date, price; detailed contents description
Indexes: none
Period covered: available at time of publication
Revision and updating: 1978 edition indicates materials available to DOD
    personnel only
Media represented: audio recordings, transparencies
Producers represented: U.S. government
Features: Prices quoted are for Department of Defense personnel; prices for
    other purchasers on request.
Subject terms: foreign language

11-26*   **Bibliography of Instructional Materials for the Teaching of German.**
    California State Department of Education, 721 Capitol Mall, Sacramento,
    CA 95814, 1975. 85p. ED 112 611.
Purpose: comprehensive
Grade level: all
Arrangement: 7 subject categories
Subjects: art   science and mathematics
              language arts   social sciences
              literature   others
              music
Entries: appr. 200 (excluding books)
    running time, distributor (films); label and number (records); release date
    (not in all cases); contents synopsis, subject category, language competency
    and maturity level
Indexes: title, series
Period covered: available at time of publication
Revision and updating:
Media represented: audio recordings, films, filmstrips, free and inexpensive
    publications, graphic materials, maps, slides
Producers represented: various, including foreign
Features: Also lists basal programs, readers, grammars, dictionaries, etc.
Subject terms: foreign language

12–Mathematics and Metric Education

    That metric education is a major concern of mathematics instruction at the
time of writing is reflected in the fact that almost all new entries in this chapter deal
with it.

Films for Mathematics and Physical Sciences (16-12) annotates some 140 films on mathematics, including 19 on computers. *The Guide to Simulations/Games for Education and Training* (41-01) includes a chapter on games requiring computer facilities.

12-01* **Mathematics Teacher.** National Council of Teachers of Mathematics, 1906 Association Drive, Reston, VA 22091. $14.00/year.
Purpose: "New Products" column; evaluations
Grade level: secondary
Arrangement: by media
Subjects: mathematics
Entries: appr. 50/year
    producer, format details, price; grade level; release date; signed reviews
Indexes: indexed in *Media Review Digest* (01-03)
Period covered: current releases
Revision and updating: published 9x/year
Media represented: audio recordings, filmloops, films, filmstrips, kits, manipulative materials, slides, transparencies, video recordings
Producers represented: various
Features: Almost half of reviews are for films.
Subject terms: mathematics

12-02 **"Metric System."** Edna Grimes. *Booklist.* v.71, October 15, 1974. pp. 224-230.
Purpose: recommendations based on evaluations by teachers of various disciplines
Grade level: all
Arrangement: 10 media groupings
Subject: metric system
Entries: over 50 (excluding books, periodical articles)
    producer, release date, sale and rental price; grade level; contents summary
Indexes:
Period covered: 1966-1974
Revision and updating:
Media represented: kits, manipulative materials, filmloops, filmstrips, films, government publications
Producers represented: 40
Features: Note the 29 "realia" items (including measuring tapes, weights, scales, balances, etc.) and eight films. [Similar list: "Metric System: A Bibliography" (*Catholic Library World*, v.48, April 1977, p. 397) recommends 14 media in various formats (no films) for all grades.]
Subject terms: metric education

12-03 **"Primary Mathematics."** John MacDonald. *Booklist.* v.70, March 15, 1974, pp. 783-785.
Purpose: recommendations based upon evaluations by teachers in classroom use; emphasis on "materials to meet the special mathematics development needs of children in small groups or with a volunteer aid"
Grade level: primary
Arrangement: by media

12-03 (cont'd)
Subjects: mathematics
Entries: 23 sets
    producer, price; grade level; contents summary
        omitted: release date
Indexes:
Period covered: not known
Revision and updating:
Media represented: filmstrips, audio recordings, manipulative materials, graphic
    materials, transparencies, kits
Producers represented: 11
Features:
Subject terms: mathematics

12-04   Some References on Metric Information. National Bureau of Standards.
        Superintendent of Documents, Washington, DC 20402, 1973. 12p.
        $0.25. S/N 0303-01219. LC 73-600344.
Purpose: list of National Bureau of Standards publications
Grade level: intermediate, secondary
Arrangement: random
Subjects: metric system
Entries: 22
    price, date of publication, ordering information
Indexes: none
Period covered: 1970-1972
Revision and updating:
Media represented: graphic materials, government publications
Producers represented: U.S. government
Features: Three charts, lists of publishers and organizations also included. "Sources
    and Resources: The Metric System," *Social Education*, v.38, March 1974,
    pp. 269-272 is a reprint of this pamphlet.
Subject terms: metric education

12-05*   Arithmetic Teacher. National Council of Teachers of Mathematics,
        1906 Association Drive, Reston, VA 22091. $14.00/year.
Purpose: "Metric Materials" and "Etcetera" evaluate media
Grade level: primary, intermediate
Arrangement: random
Subjects: mathematics
Entries: appr. 55/year (excluding professional and books)
    format data, producer, release date, sale/rental price; signed critical review
    including suggested instructional uses; rating (good, questionable)
Indexes: index in May issue; indexed in *Media Review Digest* (01-03)
Period covered: current releases
Revision and updating: published 8x/year
Media represented: audio recordings, films, filmstrips, graphic materials, kits,
    manipulative materials
Producers represented: various

12-05 (cont'd)
Features: Brief announcements of new media with no details as to price, exact
format, grade level, etc., also appear in "Books and Materials" column
(appr. 150/year)
Subject terms: mathematics

12-06   A Catalog of Nonprint Material Useful in Computer Related Instruction.
Ben Jones. Lane County School District, Eugene, OR 97405, 1973. 66p.
ED 096 976.
Purpose: recommendations
Grade level: secondary
Arrangement: alphabetical title
Subjects: computer science
Entries: appr. 200
running time, type of medium, source, rental price; grade level, evaluative
summary
Indexes: subject
Period covered: not known
Revision and updating:
Media represented: films, filmloops, audio recordings, manipulative materials
Producers represented: 48, including government
Features: All but a few of the listings are films, including many free-loan.
Subject terms: computer studies

12-07*   The Metric System: A Bibliography of Instructional Materials.
Karen G. Beam. 2d ed. Indiana Department of Public Instruction,
Indianapolis, IN 46208, 1975. 31p. ED 104 718.
Purpose: comprehensive
Grade level: all
Arrangement: by media
Subjects: metric system
Entries: appr. 200
format data, producer, release date; price; grade level; contents note (not in
all cases)
Indexes: none
Period covered: 1960s-1974
Revision and updating:
Media represented: audio recordings, filmloops, films, filmstrips, government
publications, graphic materials, kits, manipulative materials, slides, trans-
parencies, video recordings
Producers represented: various
Features: One-quarter of listings are games, realia, and other manipulative materials;
government publications identified by classification, not stock numbers (S/N).
Subject terms: metric education

**12-08*   Metric Education: An Annotated Bibliography for Vocational, Technical
and Adult Education.** Center for Vocational Education, The Ohio State
University, Columbus, OH 43210, 1974. 154p. ED 115 953.

12-08 (cont'd)
Purpose: comprehensive
Grade level: secondary
Arrangement: by media
Subjects: metric system
Entries: 369
    running time, producer, release date; sale and rental price; audience level; contents note
Indexes: author, title, occupational cluster, audience level
Period covered: 1969-1974 (bulk are 1974)
Revision and updating:
Media represented: audio recordings, filmloops, films, filmstrips, graphic materials, kits, manipulative materials, slides, transparencies, video recordings, free and inexpensive publications, government publications
Producers represented: appr. 100, including foreign
Features: Includes 20 instructional television programs on video.
Subject terms:
    metric education
    vocational education

12-09*   **Materials for Metric Instruction.** Gary G. Bitter. Center for Science and Mathematics Education, Ohio State University, Columbus OH 43210, 1975. 85p. $2.00. ED 115 488 (also available from National Council of Teachers of Mathematics, 1906 Association Drive, Reston, VA 22091)
Purpose: comprehensive
Grade level: all
Arrangement: by media
Subjects: metric system
Entries: appr. 115
    running time (films), format, producer, release date, sale price; contents of kits; grade level; detailed contents notes and comments
        omitted: film rental price
Indexes: none
Period covered: 1970-1975
Revision and updating:
Media represented: audio recordings, films, filmstrips, graphic materials, kits, manipulative materials, slides
Producers represented: various commercial, academic, institutional
Features: [Similar lists: *An Effort to Produce a Recommended List of Elementary Metric Materials* (1975. ED 118 425); 2 . . . *To Get Set* (American Association of School Librarians, 1201 16th Street, NW, Washington, DC 20036, 1975. $0.60).]
Subject terms: metric education

13-Music

Guides to ethnomusicology are included here; additional ones may be found using terms such as "ethnic studies," "world cultures," and their narrower terms in the Subject Index. Dance is covered in 14–Physical Education. Audio Recordings (30), comprised of listings of both spoken and musical recordings, is of course relevant.

The Elementary School Library Collection (01-09) emphasizes "artists who represent different ethnic groups and their music" as well as the range of Western musical literature including popular music "of historical significance." The catalog of the *Children's Books and Music Center* (01-26) recommends children's recordings and filmstrips about classical composers, recordings of music for listening and relaxation, jazz, pop, rock, and soul.

Consult *American Folklore Films and Videotapes* (18-13) for films on American folk music and *Applachian Books and Media* (18-20) for recordings of folk and bluegrass music. *Folk Recordings* lists items for sale by the Library of Congress Music Division, Recorded Sound Section, Washington, DC 20540. *American Dance Band Discography* (Arlington House, 1975. $35.00) compiles information on 50,000 78rpm records of over 2000 bands. *The Best Musicals*, Arthur Jackson (Crown, 1977. $15.95) supplies both discographies and filmographies of Broadway and Off-Broadway shows.

Many video recordings of televised music programs are found in the Public Television Library *Video Program Catalogue* and *Supplement* (43-02) and several short series on music in *Index to College Television Courseware* (43-10).

Musica (Box 1266, Edison, NJ 08817, 1977. $3.50pa.) gives program data on 750 radio stations that play classical music.

Music Educators Journal (Music Educators National Conference, 1902 Association Drive, Reston, VA 22091. $6.00/year) announces some media in its "Professional Materials" column. See also 13-12 and 13-13.

Schwann Artist Catalog (1976. 300p. $4.50) lists some 25,000 classical recordings, arranging them under the name of the performing artist.

13-01* **Annual Index to Popular Music Record Reviews 1975.** Andrew D. Armitage and Dean Tudor. Scarecrow Press. Metuchen, NJ 08840, 1976. 552p. $20.00. LC 73-8909.
Purpose: index to reviews in 65 periodicals
Grade level: intermediate, secondary
Arrangement: 13 sections (rock, country, folk, ethnic, jazz, blues, soul, stage and show band, humor, religious, mood-pop)
Subjects: musical recordings
Entries: 5084

label, number; name of periodical, date, page, length of review; reviewer's rating on scale 0-5
Indexes: artist, anthology
Period covered: 1975 reviews
Revision and updating: annual
Media represented: audio recordings
Producers represented: various U.S., Canadian, English

13-01 (cont'd)
Features: *Rocking Chair* (Cupola Productions, Box 27, Philadelphia, PA 19105. $9.85/year) reviews 30-40 popular recordings each month, rating them for artistic quality and potential demand by public library users. [Similar list: "Best Popular Records of 1975," *Previews*, v.4, May 1976, pp. 10-15, by same authors.]
Subject terms: music

13-02   Record and Tape Reviews Index 1973. Antoinette O. Maleady. Scarecrow Press, Metuchen, NJ 08840, 1974. 683p. $20.00. LC 72-3355.
Purpose: index reviews appearing in 18 periodicals, including *American Record, American Record Guide, Gramophone, High Fidelity, Library Journal, Music Journal, Music Quarterly, New Records, New York Times, Opera News, Saturday Review, Stereo Review,* and others.
Grade level: all
Arrangement: 3 sections: composers (alphabetical), music in collection (by recording company), spoken recordings (by author or title)
Subjects: recordings
Entries: over 2000

label and number; review citation; symbol indicating rating, if any, given by reviewer
Indexes: performer index to Sections I and II
Period covered: 1973 reviews
Revision and updating: published annually
Media represented: audio recordings
Producers represented: various
Features: Spoken recordings represent minimal proportion; emphasis is on classical music. Four annual issues were published 1972-1975, covering 1971-1974 reviews.
Subject terms: music

13-03   The White House Record Library. White House Historical Association, 726 Jackson Place, NW, Washington, DC 20506, 1973. 105p. price not known.
Purpose: recommendations by specially appointed committee
Grade level: all
Arrangement: by composer or recording artist in genre categories
Subjects: classical   jazz
            country   popular
            folk   spoken
            gospel
Entries: appr. 2000

label and number
    omitted: date
Indexes: record labels
Period covered: not known
Revision and updating:

13-03 (cont'd)
Media represented: audio recordings (discs)
Producers represented: various commercial, Library of Congress
Features: Emphasis is on American music and twentieth century. [Similar list:
 A Basic Record Library (W. Schwann, Inc., 137 Newbury Street, Boston,
 Mass. 02116) recommends 500 selections representing diverse historical
 periods, including 150 marked for first purchase.]
Subject terms: music

13-04* **Records in Review.** Wyeth Press, Great Barrington, MA 01230, 1977.
 472p. $14.95. LC 55-10600.
Purpose: reviews previously published in *High Fidelity* (13-05)
Grade level: intermediate, secondary
Arrangement: alphabetically by composer; collections by type

Subjects:	chamber music	miscellaneous	string collections
	collections	collections	vocal collections
	choral collections	orchestral	woodwind & brass
	Medieval and	collections	collections
	Renaissance collections	piano collections	

Entries: over 1000

 format details, label and number; full signed review; month review appeared
 omitted: price, release date
 Indexes: performer
Period covered: current and recent releases; 1976 reviews
Revision and updating: published annually
Media represented: audio recordings
Producers represented: various
Features:
Subject terms: music

13-05* **High Fidelity.** ABC Leisure Magazines, Inc., Great Barrington, MA 01230.
 $18.00/year.
Purpose: portion of magazine devoted to record reviews
Grade level: intermediate, secondary
Arrangement: by type

Subjects:	classical	popular
	jazz	others

Entries: appr. 1000/year

 label and number, price; symbols indicating re-issues, budget recordings, etc.;
 signed critical reviews
Indexes:
Period covered: current releases
Revision and updating: published 12x/year; *Records in Review* (13-04) is annual
 compilation
Media represented: audio recordings
Producers represented: various
Features: "Critics' choice: the best classical records reviewed in recent months" in
 most issues; also "Best of the year" in December issue; also "Critics'

13-05 (cont'd)
Features: (cont'd) Choice–Pop" (January 1977). Occasional discographies–e.g., Gilbert & Sullivan (v.27, May 1977, pp. 52-58). Also 13-14, 13-23. [Similar list: *American Record Guide* (Box 812, Melville, NY 11746. $7.50/year) each month offers in-depth reviews of some 40-50 new recordings, chiefly of classical and serious contemporary music.]
Subject terms: music

13-06*   **Stereo Review.** Ziff-Davis Pub. Co., 1 Park Ave., New York, NY 10016. $7.98/year.
Purpose: 3 columns review recordings
Grade level: intermediate, secondary
Arrangement: by type
Subjects: best recordings of the month, classical, popular
Entries: 900-1000/year

> label and number, price, format details (cassette, cartridge, reel, mono, stereo, quadrophonic, etc.); signed critical reviews evaluating quality of performance and of recording

Indexes:
Period covered: current releases
Revision and updating: published 12x/year
Media represented: audio recordings
Features: "Record of the Year Awards" annually in February issue; "A Beginner's Guide to Chamber Music," by Irving Kolodin (v.39, May 1977, pp. 70-74) recommends appr. 30 recordings; See also 13-09. [Similar list: *American Record Guide* (see 13-05, "Features").]
Subject terms: music

13-07   **The Musician's Guide.** 5th ed. Music Information Service, Inc., 310 Madison Ave., New York, NY 10017, 1972. 1013p. $39.50.
Purpose: "Classical Record Library," pp. 584-598; "Jazz Record Library," pp. 599-604; "Basic Rock Library," pp. 605-606; recommendations based on performance, sound, availability, historical significance
Grade level: secondary
Arrangement: by musical type, artist, composer (varies)
Subjects: music
Entries: 400 classical, 250 jazz, 65 rock

> label and number; conductor, performer, etc.
>   omitted: price, release date

Indexes:
Period covered: available at time of publication
Revision and upating:
Media represented: audio recordings
Producers represented: various
Features: This is an authoritative selective listing. [Similar list: *A Basic Record Library of Jazz* (W. Schwann, Inc., 1975. $0.75pa.) is a "selective list of (250) especially important recordings." See also 13-03, 13-09 and 13-15. For jazz and rock recordings, see 13-20 and 13-26.]

13-07 (cont'd)
Subject terms: music

13-08   **The New Listener's Companion and Record Guide.** 4th ed. B. H. Haggin.
Horizon Press, 1974. 399p. $10.00; $4.95pa.
Purpose: recommendations
Grade level: all
Arrangement: "Great Recorded Performances of the Past" (by performer);
"Best Recorded Performances of Today" (by composer)
Subjects: classical music
Entries: appr. 700

label and number; critical review
Indexes: producers, composers, performers (does not cover 4th ed. supplement)
Period covered: releases through 1973
Revision and updating: 5th ed. 1977
Media represented: audio recordings (discs)
Producers represented: various
Features: The 4th edition is a reprint of the 3rd, with addition of pp. 365-399
containing approximately 175 new releases. Valuable for performer listings.
Subject terms: music

13-09   **"Best Recordings of the Centenary."** David Hall. *Stereo Review*, v.39,
July 1977, p. 76-79.
Purpose: recommendations
Grade level: all
Arrangement: alphabetical by composer
Subjects: classical and 20th century serious music
Entries: appr. 50

label and number; performers; date of recording (not in all cases); critical
review
Indexes:
Period covered: 1907-1970's, available at time of writing
Revision and updating:
Media represented: audio recordings
Producers represented: various, including foreign
Features: Includes 78rpm recordings and reissues on LP of earlier recordings:
[Similar lists: *Discovering Music: Where to Start on Records and Tapes.*
Roy Hemming. (Four Winds Press, 1974. $14.95) recommends first choice
and budget-label recordings for each of 70 composers and 160 performers
of classical music.
Subject terms: music

13-10*   **"Leonard Bernstein, a Composer Discography."** J. F. Weber. *Journal of
the Association for Recorded Sound Collections*, v.6, no. 1, 1974.
pp. 30-39.
Purpose: comprehensive, excluding "single songs from Broadway shows and
arrangement for band, piano, etc."
Grade level: all

13-10 (cont'd)
Arrangement: chronological by date of composition
Subjects: Leonard Bernstein
Entries: appr. 90
   date, label and number; performing orchestra and artists
Indexes:
Period covered: 1945-1973
Revision and updating:
Media represented: audio recordings
Producers represented: various
Features: The *Journal* (Fine Arts Library, University of New Mexico, Albuquerque, NM 87131. $10/year. 3x/year) publishes an annual "Bibliography of discographies" of several hundred items covering blues, classical, country, gospel, jazz, rock, etc. that appeared in some 45 journals, as well as individual discographies.
Subject terms: music

13-11   **A Teacher's Guide to Folk Singing.** New York State Education Department, Bureau of Secondary Curriculum Development, Albany, NY 12234, 1972. 33p. ED 073 036.
Purpose: teaching and resource recommendations for a minicourse
Grade level: secondary
Arrangement: by media; records listed by performers, filmstrips by producers
Subject: folk singing
Entries: over 250
   (tapes) running time, release date, listing only; (films) running time, producer, release date, synopsis, (records) label and number
Indexes: none
Period covered: available at time of publication
Revision and updating:
Media represented: films, filmstrips, audio recordings
Producers represented: various; tapes from National Center for Audio Tapes (30-06)
Features: Includes listing of ballets, musicals, operas, symphonies, etc., based on folk songs. Emphasis is on the United States.
Subject terms: music

13-12   **"Music in World Cultures."** *Music Educators Journal.* October 1972. Reprint available from Music Educators National Conference, 8150 Leesburg Pike, Vienna, VA 22180. $3.50.
Purpose: entire issue devoted to topic; "Bibliography and Discography," pp. 134, 177, 179-180, 184-190, 192, 194-196, 198-199; "Filmography," pp. 136, 201-204, 207-209-210; recommendations
Grade level: all
Arrangement: by region
Subjects: Africa   Asia
            Americas   Europe

13-12 (cont'd)
Entries: discography: over 100; filmography: 67
    label and number (recordings); running time, producer, grade level, contents
    (films)
        omitted: release date
Indexes:
Period covered: not known
Revision and updating:
Media represented: audio recordings (discs), films
Producers represented: various
Features: Particularly strong in coverage of various regions of Asia; only a few
    entries for black or white American folk music.
Subject terms:
        music   world cultures
        Native Americans

13-13   **"The Charles Ives Centennial."** *Music Educators Journal.* October 1974.
Purpose: "Ives in Sound and Print" one of eight articles on pp. 71, 103-104, 106,
    108-109
Grade level: all
Arrangement: alphabetical by label
Subjects: Charles Ives
Entries: appr. 80

    label and number, orchestra, conductor; contents note
        omitted: release date
Indexes:
Period covered: not known
Revision and updating:
Media represented: audio recordings (discs)
Producers represented: various
Features:
Subject terms: music

13-14   **"Sousa on Disc and Tape."** R. D. Darrell. *High Fidelity.* v.23, November
    1973, pp. 61-62.
Purpose: recommended as the "best interpretively, technically, programmatically"
Grade level: all
Arrangement: by performing band
Subject: John Philip Sousa
Entries: 19

    label and number, performing band, U.S. release date; key to contents;
    availability in open reel, cartridge, cassette format; critical review
        omitted: price
Indexes:
Period covered: some out-of-print recordings included
Revision and updating:
Media represented: audio recordings
Producers represented: various

13-14 (cont'd)
Features:
Subject terms: music

13-15*   Classical Music Recordings for Home and Library. Richard S. Halsey,
American Library Association, 50 E. Huron Street, Chicago, IL 60611,
1976. 340p. $15.00.
Purpose: recommendations; "composer-title list," pp. 45-150
Grade level: all
Arrangement: by genre
Subjects: chamber music   concerti   operas
             choral music   early music   other orchestral
             complete songs and   keyboard instruments   works
               works scored for voice new & experimental popular arias
               & accompaniment   music   symphonies
Entries: 4101

composer, title, label and number; ratings "derived from a comprehensive
statistical analysis" (1 or 2 stars or none); "aesthetic significance" and
"access" rating (1 to 5); minimum age level
Indexes: title, composer, subject (to text), performer
Period covered: 1961-1975 releases
Revision and updating:
Media represented: audio recordings
Producers represented: various
Features: Also recommendations for listening programs, collection building, and
discussion of reviewing journals and chapter on buying sound recordings
(including non-musical).
Subject terms: music

13-16*   All Together Now; The First Complete Beatles Discography, 1961-1975.
Harry Castleman and Walter J. Podrzik. Pierian Press, Ann Arbor, MI
48104, 1976. 368p. illus. $14.95.
Purpose: comprehensive
Grade level: all
Arrangement: chronological
Subject: Beatles
Entries: appr. 1000

release date, recording date, label and number; contents
Indexes: title
Period covered: 1961-975
Revision and updating:
Media represented: audio recordings, films
Producers represented: British and U.S. releases
Features: In addition to main listing of the Beatles' own recordings, there are
lists of recordings that influenced them musically, recordings of live concerts,
radio and TV appearances, alleged Beatle recordings, songs about them, Apple
releases, 22 films in which the Beatles appeared, books, and others.
Subject terms: music

13-17* **Folk Music Sourcebook.** Larry Sandberg and Dick Weissman. Knopf, 1976. 260p. illus. $15.00. $8.95pa. LC 75-34472.
Purpose: Bibliographies and discographies for each chapter
Grade level: all
Arrangement: topical
Subjects: Anglo-American music / Black American music / Cajun music / Canadian folk music / Caribbean (including Puerto Rico) / Chicano music / contemporary music and the folksong revival — England, Scotland, Ireland / folk songs for children / folk tales / general folk anthologies & folk festival recordings / instructional (guitar & other instruments) — music of the world / North American Indian music / social and historical documentaries and anthologies / Western swing, Nashville
Entries: several hundred

label and number; some contents annotations
omitted: price, release date
Indexes: name-subject
Period covered: not known
Revision and updating:
Media represented: audio recordings, films, video recordings
Producers represented: various
Features: "Films" (pp. 244-247) attempts a comprehensive listing of some 120 titles released 1941-1970; videotapes of one producer noted (pp. 247-248).
Subject terms:
ethnic studies   world cultures
music

13-18* **Opera Recordings; A Critical Guide.** Kenn Harris. Drake Publishers, Inc., 381 Park Avenue South, New York, NY 10016, 1973. 328p. $8.95. LC 72-3224.
Purpose: comprehensive listing, with author's evaluations
Grade level: all
Arrangement: alphabetical title
Subjects: 76 operas
Entries: several hundred

label and number, conductor, orchestra, performers; number of discs; critical review
Indexes: names of individuals and orchestras
Period covered: available at time of writing
Revision and updating:
Media represented: audio recordings
Producers represented: various U.S. and European
Features:
Subject terms:
music
performing arts

13-19*   **Rolling Stone.** 745 Fifth Avenue, New York, NY 10022. $14.00/year.
Purpose: "Records" reviewing column
Grade level: secondary
Arrangement: random
Subjects: popular music
Entries: appr. 500/year

     label and number; full signed review; a few in each issue briefly listed ("new and noted")
Indexes: indexed in *Popular Periodical Index* (semi-annual)
Period covered: current releases
Revision and updating: published 26x/year
Media represented: audio recordings
Producers represented: U.S. and foreign
Features:
Subject terms: music

13-20*   **The Rolling Stone Illustrated History of Rock & Roll.** Rolling Stone
     Press and Random, 1976. 382p. illus. $19.95; $9.95pa. LC 76-14190.
Purpose: discographies at end of each of about 70 articles, "Rock Films,"
     pp. 350-357
Grade level: all
Arrangement: topical
Subjects: blues   rock & roll
                  folk rock   soul
                  rhythm & gospel
Entries: several hundred

     title, label, number
Indexes: name
Period covered: 1950s-1970s
Revision and updating:
Media represented: audio recordings, films
Producers represented: various
Features: [Similar lists: *The Illustrated Encyclopedia of Rock* (Nick Logan and
     Bob Woffinden. Harmony: Crown, 1977. 256p. $17.95; $7.95pa.) features
     briefer discographies; "A Rock and Roll Discography" (Jim O'Connor.
     School Library Journal, v.22, September 1975, pp. 21-24) recommends appr.
     200 albums from the 1950s and '60s.]
Subject terms: music

13-21*   **Audio.** North American Publishing Co., 401 North Broad Street,
     Philadelphia, PA 19108. $8.00/year.
Purpose: "Record Reviews" in each issue
Grade level: intermediate, secondary
Arrangement: by genre
Subjects: classical   jazz & blues
                  folk   theater music
                  European records (not in each issue)

13-21 (cont'd)
Entries: appr. 400/year

label, number, price, signed critical review with ratings on sound and performance (not for classical / theater music); European records column discusses recordings in text only
Indexes:
Period covered: current releases
Revision and updating: published 12x/year
Media represented: audio recordings
Producers represented: various U.S. and European
Features:
Subject terms: music

13-22* **African Music; A People's Art.** Francis Bebey. Independent Publisher's Group, 14 Vanderventer Avenue, Port Washington, NY 11050, 1975. 184p. $10.00.
Purpose: "Selective Discography," pp. 149-173; "Recent Recordings," pp. 174-176
Grade level: all
Arrangement: by country, theme, instrument
Subjects: birth   lullabies
           celebrations   others
           love songs
Entries: appr. 350

label and number; detailed synopses in country listings only
    omitted: release date
Indexes: none
Period covered: not known
Revision and updating:
Media represented: audio recordings
Producers represented: various
Features: Some 200 recordings are listed thematically. [Similar list: The chapter on "Afro-American Music" in *The Black American Reference Book* (Prentice-Hall, 1976. $29.95) lists approximately 40 selections with labels and numbers.]
Subject terms:
           Africa   music
           Black studies

13-23* **"Record Riches of a Quarter-Century: Great Recordings of 1951-76 Selected by the Editors."** *High Fidelity*, v.26, April 1976, pp. 85-87.
Purpose: recommendations
Grade level: all
Arrangement: by type
Subjects: classical, popular
Entries: appr. 125

(classical) orchestra, conductor, label & number; date of review in magazine
    (popular) label & number only
Indexes:
Period covered: "recordings first issued" 1951-1976

13-23 (cont'd)
Revision and updating:
Media represented: audio recordings
Producers represented: U.S. and foreign labels
Features: Includes out-of-print recordings. [Similar list: 13-09.]
Subject terms: music

13-24*   Directory of Selected Opera Films Available from American Distributors.
Central Opera Service Bulletin, Metropolitan Opera, Lincoln Center,
New York, NY 10023, 1977 (*Bulletin*, v.19, Winter 1976/77). 42p.
$6.00pa.
Purpose: comprehensive
Grade level: all
Arrangement: 4 topical groupings
Subjects: composers & operas (including films about composers); arias & ensembles
    in concerts and festivals (i.e., collections); biographical films exclusive of
    composers; educational films (i.e., films about opera)
Entries: appr. 120
    running time, producer, language, conductor, orchestra, etc.; release date,
    rental source
Indexes: title, series
Period covered: 1950s-1975
Revision and updating:
Media represented: films
Producers represented: various
Features:
Subject terms:
    music
    performing arts

13-25*   Instrumentalist. 1418 Lake Street, Evanston, IL 60204. $9.00/year.
Purpose: "Free for the Asking" (descriptive) and "New Recordings" (evaluations)
    columns
Grade level: intermediate, secondary
Arrangement: random
Subjects: instrumental music
Entries: appr. 100/year
    producer or label, price; critical review ("New Recordings")
Indexes:
Period covered: recent releases
Revision and updating: published 11x/year
Media represented: audio recordings, free & inexpensive publications
Producers represented: various
Features:
Subject terms: music

13-26*   "A Basic Jazz Discography." Procter Lippincott. *School Library
Journal*, v.22, November 1975, pp. 20-24.

13-26 (cont'd)
Purpose: recommended basic collection on $1000 budget of "musicians who made original, developmental and far reaching contributions"
Grade level: secondary
Arrangement: collections, styles and eras

Subjects: blues   New Orleans
           Chicago   New York
           gospel   ragtime
           Kansas City   swing

Entries: over 100

> label and number, number of discs in album; contents note (collections); comments about musicians or recordings (in some cases)
> omitted: release date

Indexes:
Period covered: available at time of writing
Revision and updating:
Media represented: audio recordings
Producers represented: various commercial
Features:
Subject terms: music

14–Physical Education

The guides referred to in 34—Free and Inexpensive Publications offer access to the many give-away and low-cost materials available in this subject area. The Public Television Library (43-02) can supply taped series on a number of individual sports.

Superfilms (32-22) lists about 50 award-winning sports films, and 18 films on women in sports may be found in *Positive Images: Non-Sexist Films for Young People* (22-03).

Minicourses (Wm. Ray Heitzmann. National Education Association, Saw Mill Road, West Haven, CT 06516, 1977) outlines a minicourse on sports literature, suggesting a number of supporting visuals.

See also *Films for Arts and Crafts* (20-02) and *American Folklore Films and Videotapes* (18-13) for films on both art and ethnic dancing.

14-01*   Educators Guide to Free Health, Physical Education and Recreation Materials. 9th ed. Educators Progress Service, Randolph, WI 53956, 1976. 521p. $11.00pa. LC 68-57948.
Purpose: free materials for classroom use; comprehensive
Grade level: all
Arrangement: 12 groupings by media and subject

14-01 (cont'd)

Subjects:
accident prevention and safety	foods and nutrition	sanitation and environmental control
career opportunities in health fields	individual and dual sports	sex education and family living
diseases, handicaps, and mental health	personal health and hygiene	team sports
first aid	physical fitness	
	public health	

Entries: appr. 2500

ordering information, release date for films
omitted: grade level

Indexes: title, subject
Period covered: available at time of publication
Revision and updating: annual
Media represented: films, filmstrips, slides, transparencies, audio recordings, video recordings, free and inexpensive publications, government publications
Producers represented: 621 institutional, U.S. government
Features: [See introduction to 34.]
Subject terms:

energy and environment education	health services
guidance	physical education
health and safety education	

14-02   The Best Records, Books, and Instruments for Dance and Dance Therapy. Dancer's Shop, Children's Music Center, 5373 West Pico Blvd., Los Angeles, CA 90019, 1974. 49p.

Purpose: distributor's catalog; comprehensive
Grade level: all
Arrangement: 12 topical and media groupings
Subjects:

ballet	folk	modern dance
dance therapy/movement for children	jazz dance	rock
	music of many lands	soul

Entries: over 300

price, contents summary
omitted: label, release date, grade level

Indexes: none
Period covered: currently available
Revision and updating: *Note:* no longer available. Replaced by 01-26
Media represented: audio recordings
Producers represented: not known
Features:
Subject terms: dance

14-03   The Best Records for Physical Education, Secondary. Dancer's Shop, Children's Music Center, Inc., 5373 West Pico Blvd., Los Angeles, CA 90019, 1974. 28p.

Purpose: distributor's catalog; comprehensive
Grade level: secondary

14-03 (cont'd)
Arrangement: 13 topical groupings
Subjects: dance   rock music
           gymnastics   skills
           marches   twirling
           physical fitness
Entries: appr. 250

   price; contents note
      omitted: label, release date
Indexes: none
Period covered: currently available
Revision and updating: *Note:* no longer available. Replaced by 01-26.
Media represented: audio recordings
Producers represented: not known
Features: Folk dances and square dances comprise half the listings.
Subject terms: physical education

14-04   **Children's Dances.** Gladys A. Fleming. American Alliance for Health,
            Physical Education and Recreation, 1201 16th Street, NW, Washington,
            DC 20036, 1973. 112p. $5.50. ED 093 821.
Purpose: audiovisual materials listed on pp. 88-92
Grade level: primary, intermediate
Arrangement: by media
Subjects: dance
Entries: appr. 40

   running time, producer or distributor, sale and rental price; release date;
      label and number; evaluation
Indexes: none
Period covered: available at time of publication
Revisions and updating:
Media represented: audio recordings, films
Producers represented: various
Features:
Subject terms: dance

14-05   **Journal of Physical Education and Recreation.** American Alliance for
            Health, Physical Education and Recreation, 1201 16th Street, Wash-
            ington, DC 20036. $25.00/year.
Purpose: "Audiovisuals" column appears very occasionally; chiefly announcements
Grade level: all
Arrangement: random
Subjects: physical education, recreation
Entries: 15-20/year

   running time, producer, purchase and rental price; contents summary
      omitted: grade level
Indexes: indexed in *Media Review Digest* (01-03)
Period covered: current releases
Revision and updating: published 9x/year

14-05 (cont'd)
Media represented: films
Producers represented: various
Features:
Subject terms: physical education

14-06* **Guide to Free-Loan Sports Films (16MM).** Serina Press, Alexandria, VA 22305, 1974. 72p. $5.95.
Purpose: comprehensive
Grade level: all
Arrangement: 46 topical groupings
Subjects:

automobile racing	football	skiing
baseball	golf	sports-general
boating	hunting	snowmobiling
bowling	judo	swimming
fishing	motorcycling	others

Entries: over 500

running time; rental source; contents summary; specified audience
   omitted: release date
Indexes: none
Period covered: available at time of publication
Revision and updating: 2d ed. 1976. $6.95.
Media represented: films
Producers represented: 65 rental sources including federal, state, and foreign governments, industry, organizations
Features:
Subject terms: physical education

14-07* **Catalog of Dance Films.** Susan Braun. Dance Films Association, Inc., 250 West 57th Street, New York, NY 10019, 1974. 1v. (unp.) $6.50pa.
Purpose: comprehensive
Grade level: all
Arrangement: alphabetical title
Subjects:

ballet	mime	social
cine-dance	modern dance	square
dance therapy	religious	theatrical
ethnic (by country)	ritual	others

Entries: appr. 500

running time, producer, distributor, release date; dance company, dancers, choreographer; type of dance; contents summary; December 1973 prices on separate sheet
Indexes: choreographers, composers, dance companies, dance teachers, dancers (by type of dance), film directors and producers, types of dance, others
Period covered: 1930s-1971
Revision and updating: *Film News* (32-18)
Media represented: films
Producers represented: appr. 100, including foreign, television stations, academic

14-07 (cont'd)
Features: "Program suggestions" and "Teacher Education" headings in subject
index provide lead to films for children, films of dances based on legends,
plays, poetry, etc., use of dance in schools, etc. Association also sponsors
Dance Film Festival in June of each year where films of that year and earlier
ones are judged. Award winners are listed in *Film News* (32-18).
Subject terms:

dance	performing arts
ethnic studies	poetry
literature	

14-08* **"The Frontiers of the Possible; A Selective Filmography of Sporting."**
The Lens and the Speaker, v.XIV, Fall, 1976, pp. 3-15. Visual Aids
Service, University of Illinois, 1325 S. Oak Street, Champaign, IL
61820. free.
Purpose: films that illustrate "the will to excel," recommendations
Grade level: all
Arrangement: topical (9 categories)

Subjects:	exploration	Olympics	skiing
	Japanese martial arts	philosophy of sport	surfing
	mountain climbing	racing	miscellaneous

Entries: 34

running time, producer, release date; rental price; grade level; contents synopsis;
awards won, if any; further comments on some of films in the text
Indexes:
Period covered: 1965-74
Revision and updating:
Media represented: films
Producers represented: various
Features:
Subject terms: physical education

14-09* **USTA Tennis Film List 1977.** Julia Rudy. United States Tennis
Association, 51 East 42nd Street, New York, NY 10017, 1977. 47p.
$1.50pa.
Purpose: comprehensive
Grade level: intermediate, secondary
Arrangement: by media and topic
Subjects: entertaining, historic, instructional
Entries: 119

running time, producer/distributor, release date; sale/rental price; contents
summary
        omitted: audience suitability
Indexes: free-loan films
Period covered: 1951-1976
Revision and updating: published annually
Media represented: filmloops, films, video recordings
Producers represented: appr. 45 commercial, industrial, public television

14-09 (cont'd)
Features: Includes 24 free-loan films. USTA regional film libraries (listed) and
USTA Film Library supply separate lists of rental films.
Subject terms: physical education

15–Psychology and Guidance

Media lists included here deal with personal guidance (exclusive of academic counseling) and also with the specific problems of the young and the old, including seven lists of films and other materials specifically on aging and death.

Guides to material dealing with sex roles and specific concerns of women are found in 22–Women's Studies, career guidance media in 03–Career Education. See also 08–Health and Safety Education, 09–Drug Abuse Education, and 10–Sex Education.

Science Books and Films (16-13) is a helpful reference for evaluations of current releases. *High School Psychology Teacher* (Clearinghouse on Pre-college Psychology, American Psychological Association, 1200 17th Street, NW, Washington, DC 20036. 5x/year. free) includes announcements of resources. *Annotated Bibliography of Multi-Ethnic Curriculum Materials* (18-17) recommends media in many formats on interpersonal relationships.

Directory of Spoken-Voice Audio-Cassettes (30-07) annotates sources and titles of many recordings. The National Institute of Mental Health, 5600 Fishers Lane, Rockville, MD 20857, distributes almost 100 publications, single copies of which are free (request *Publications List*).

15-01*   Index to Psychology–Multimedia. 3rd ed. National Information Center
          for Educational Media, University of Southern California, University
          Park, Los Angeles, CA 90007, 1977. 1021p. $47.00; $23.50 microfiche.
          LC 76-1611.
Purpose: comprehensive listing of "Instructional nonbook Media"
Grade level: all
Arrangement: alphabetical title
Subjects: education   psychology
            guidance and counseling   sociology
            health and safety   special education
Entries: appr. 28,000 (including adult & professional)
         type of medium, format data, producer, distributor, release date; grade level;
         contents annotation; out-of-print titles identified
            omitted: price
Indexes: classed subject
Period covered: 1950s-1970s
Revision and updating: *Update of Nonbook Media*
Media represented: audio recordings, filmloops, films, filmstrips, slides, trans-
         parencies, video recordings
Producers represented: several thousand

15-01 (cont'd)
Features: The use of approximately 100 subject headings to access such a large
body of information results in listings many pages in length on one topic.
Subject terms:
career education   psychology
guidance

15-02*   Educators Guide to Free Guidance Materials. 15th ed. Educators
Progress Service, Randolph, WI 53956, 1976. 395p. $10.75pa. LC
62-18761.
Purpose: free materials available for classroom use; comprehensive
Grade level: secondary
Arrangement: by media, subdivided by content
Subjects: career planning   social-personal
responsibility to self and others   use of leisure time
Entries: over 2000
format, ordering information, release date; entries new to this edition are
starred
Indexes: title, subject
Period covered: available at time of publication
Revision and updating: published annually
Media represented: films, filmstrips, slides, audio recordings (tapes), video
recordings, government publications, free and inexpensive publications
Producers represented: appr. 450
Features: Some academic guidance material, but career education is emphasized.
[See also introduction to 34–Free and Inexpensive Publications.]
Subject terms:
career education   health and safety education
guidance   physical education

15-03   Films for Human Development and Home Economics. Pennsylvania
State University, Audio-Visual Services, Willard Building, University
Park, PA 16802, 1973. 63p. free.
Purpose: film library catalog; recommendations
Grade level: all
Arrangement: alphabetical title
Subjects: child development   minority groups
criminology   others
human behavior
Entries: appr. 600
running time, producer, release date, rental price; grade level; synopsis
Indexes: subject, series
Period covered: 1946-1971 (mostly 1960s)
Revision and updating: *Newsletter*
Media represented: films
Producers represented: various, including commercial television

15-03 (cont'd)
Features: [See other university film library catalogs for more recent titles.]
Subject terms:
    guidance   psychology
    home economics

15-04   Aging: A Filmography. Judith Trojan. Educational Film Library Association, 43 West 61st Street, New York, NY 10023, 1974. 16p. $2.00pa.
Purpose: "a comprehensive, critical list"; recommendations
Grade level: all
Arrangement: alphabetical title
Subjects: aging
Entries: over 150
    running time, director, distributor, release date; evaluative annotation; listings only for feature films
        omitted: grade level
Indexes: subject (8 headings only)
Period covered: 1960s-1973
Revision and updating:
Media represented: films
Producers represented: commercial, government, individual filmmakers, public television
Features: Many of the films deal with persons maintaining their creativity into old age, others with the role of grandparents. [Similar lists: 15-15, 15-16, 15-18, 15-21.]
Subject terms: aging

15-05   Annotated Film Bibliography; Child Development and Early Childhood Education. Carol Lou Holt, Child Day Care Association of St. Louis, 915 Olive Street, St. Louis, MO 63101, 1973. 148p. $3.00. ED 093 496.
Purpose: comprehensive
Grade level: primary, intermediate
Arrangement: alphabetical title
Subjects: pre-school and school age, adolescents
Entries: appr. 150 (excluding professional)
    running time, producer or distributor, release date (not in all cases); contents note
        omitted: price, audience suitability
Indexes: subject
Period covered: available at time of publication
Revision and updating:
Media represented: films
Producers represented: appr. 150 commercial, institutional, government, instructional television

15-05 (cont'd)
Features: Professional films for teachers and parents are in the majority and are
   listed in one alphabet along with those for young audiences. The latter can
   be found through the subject index.
Subject terms:
   early childhood education
   psychology

15-06   **"Film Profiles of Youth."** *Booklist.* v.69, September 15, 1972,
   pp. 71-75; v.70, October 1, 1973, pp. 33-36.
Purpose: recommendations
Grade level: secondary
Arrangement: alphabetical title in each article
Subjects: "Young People in Their Many Roles"
Entries: 63 + 41

   running time, release date, sale and purchase price, distributor; critical review
Indexes:
Period covered: 1967-1972
Revision and updating:
Media represented: films
Producers represented: various commercial and academic producers; also young
   filmmakers
Features: [Similar list: "Films for student identity" (*Media and Methods*, v.12,
   March 1976, pp. 38-40, 51-52.]
Subject terms:
   guidance
   psychology

15-07   **"Films on Death and Dying."** Edward A. Mason. *Sightlines.* v.7, no.2,
   pp. 4-7, 1973. Reprint from Educational Film Library Association,
   43 West 61st Street, New York, NY 10023. $0.75pa.
Purpose: filmography of recommended films
Grade level: all
Arrangement: alphabetical title
Subjects: death
Entries: 40 (including 6 not previewed)

   running time, producer, distributor, sale and rental price, release date;
   commentary in text
Indexes:
Period covered: 1952-1973
Revision and updating:
Media represented: films
Producers represented: commercial and public television, various others
Features: The author is an M.D. associated with the Department of Psychiatry,
   Harvard Medical School.
Subject terms: death education

15-08   "**Alive But Alone.**" Adele H. Stern. *Scholastic Teacher, Junior/Senior High Edition.* October 1973, pp. 32-37.
Purpose: mini-course guide and recommended resource list
Grade level: secondary
Arrangement: alphabetical title
Subjects: loneliness and alienation
Entries: 23 (excluding books)
running time, producer, sale and rental price
omitted: release date
Indexes:
Period covered: available at time of publication
Revision and updating:
Media represented: films, filmstrips, slides
Producers represented: various
Features: [Similar list: *Today's Education*, v.66, January/February and March/April 1977 ("Audiovisual Materials" column)
Subject terms:
guidance
psychology

15-09*   **Selected Audiovisuals on Mental Health.** National Institutes of Mental Health, 5600 Fishers Lane, Rockville, MD 20852, 1975. 231p.
ED 112 629.
Purpose: comprehensive; for "persons engaged in educating the public and scientific audiences about mental illness and mental health"
Grade level: secondary
Arrangement: alphabetical by subject (27 categories)
Subjects:

aging	death and suicide	neurosciences
animal studies	education	personality
biochemistry and	group processes	religion
metabolism	learning	sexology
child mental health	mental retardation	social issues
crime and delinquency	minority groups	treatment
cultural studies	motivation	others

Entries: 2300 (including professional)
running time, distributor, release date, sale and rental price; format details for video; contents synopsis
omitted: audience suitability
Indexes: none
Period covered: 1960s-1974
Revision and updating:
Media represented: audio recordings, films, filmstrips, government publications, video recordings
Producers represented: various commercial, academic, government, institutional
Features: *Guide to Mental Health Education Materials*, from the same office (1974. ED 101 258), is a listing of pamphlets, periodicals, and some audio recordings on similar subjects, including drug abuse.

15-09 (cont'd)
Subject terms:
contemporary issues
ethnic studies

psychology
sex education

15-10* **Famous People on Film.** Carol A. Emmens. Scarecrow Press, Metuchen, NJ 08840, 1977. 355p. $13.50. LC 77-3449.
Purpose: comprehensive listing of non-theatrical films on famous personalities
Grade level: all
Arrangement: alphabetical by name
Subjects: biography
Entries: appr. 2100

name, series, producer, distributor, rental source; running time, release date; grade level; contents note; availability on videotape
Indexes: title, subject (occupations)
Period covered: available 1975/1976
Revision and updating:
Media represented: films, video recordings
Producers represented: several hundred
Features: Appr. 100 selected feature films listed on pp. 287-302.
Subject terms:
biography
career education

15-11* **Family Life; Literature and Films: An Annotated Bibliography.** Minnesota Council on Family Relations, 1219 University Avenue SE, Minneapolis, MN 55414, 1972. 375p. $5.50. ED 118 234. **1974 Supplement.** 244p. $6.00. ED 118 235. **1976 Supplement.** $5.00. Price for all three $15.00.
Purpose: recommendations
Grade level: all
Arrangement: topical
Subjects: the family: theoretical, historical, and cross-cultural perspectives
female and male roles: in the family and out
sexuality and sex education
human reproduction and family planning
adolescence and youth
courtship, love, mate selection, engagement

marital interaction and family process
family crises and disorganization
child development and parenthood
middle and later years
self-growth and personal potential
social issues and the family
health
education
counseling

Entries: over 400 in 1972 edition; appr. 300 in 1974 *Supplement* (excluding print)

running time, producer, release date (not in all cases); contents summary, audience suitability
omitted: price
Indexes: none

15-11 (cont'd)
Period covered: 1953-1976
Revision and updating: frequently revised since first ed. 1951
Media represented: audio recordings, films, filmstrips
Producers represented: various, including academic
Features: [Similar list: "Child Abuse: A Bibliography" (Gwendolyn Davis, *School Library Journal*, v.23, November 1976, pp. 29-33).]
Subject terms:

guidance	women's studies
health and safety education	

15-12* **A Selective Guide to Materials for Mental Health and Family Life Education.** 1976 ed. Mental Health Materials Center, 419 Park Ave. South, New York, NY 10016, 1976. 947p. $52.50pa.
Purpose: recommendations of "authoritative, substantial, sound, well-balanced, unbiased" materials; reprints of reviews that appeared in its *Bulletin*
Grade level: secondary
Arrangement: 21 subject categories
Subjects: adults
areas of special concern (alcoholism, crime & delinquency, drug abuse, mental illness, developmental disabilities, mental retardation, physical handicaps & illness, suicide/crisis intervention, intergroup relations) child growth and development
Entries: appr. 200 (excluding books)
running time, producer, release date (av); source, publication date, number of pages (print); price, contents summary and evaluation; appropriate audience subject terms, cross references
Indexes: title
Period covered: 1960s-1974
Revision and updating: previous ed. 1972. *In-Depth Reports* ($12.00/year)
Media represented: films, filmstrips, free & inexpensive publications, slides, government publications
Producers represented: various commercial, government, professional
Features: Primarily a guide for professional and general adult audiences; a 25-page "Memorandum to Discussion Leaders" on how to select and use materials, run effective programs. [See 15-13 for a briefer list from the same source.]
Subject terms:

drug abuse education	psychology
guidance	

15-13* **The MHMC Guide to Recent Mental Health Films.** Mental Health Materials Center, 419 Park Avenue South, New York, NY 10016, 1976. 57p. price not known.
Purpose: evaluations; "a guide to what new films should be considered—or ignored"
Grade level: secondary
Arrangement: topical

15-13 (cont'd)
Subjects: adult and family life
   areas of special concern
   (alcohol use and abuse,
   physical handicaps,
   mental illness,

   mental retardation,
   6 others)
   child growth and development
   (numerous subcategories)

Entries: 230 (including professional)

running time, producer, sale & rental price; rating (excellent, very good, good, fair, no value); critical review & summary with use suggestions
   omitted: release date
Indexes: none
Period covered: not known
Revision and updating:
Media represented: films
Producers represented: various commercial, government, public television, institutional
Features: Includes free-loan films. Chiefly intended for staff and patient training, many selections are suitable for high school use. [See 15-15 for list from the same source.]
Subject terms:
   drug abuse education   psychology
   guidance

15-14* **"Films on Mental Health and Mental Illness Plus."** *EMC Two-76* (*Lifelong Learning*, v.46, September 13, 1976). pp. 3, 6-19, 23-4. University of California, Extension Media Center, Berkeley, CA 94720. free.
Purpose: new additions to EMC collection as a result of analysis and recommendations by Mental Health Materials Center, New York
Grade level: secondary
Arrangement: topical
Subjects: drugs/alcohol/tobacco   others
   psychology/psychiatry/mental health
Entries: 45 (including 11 teachers training films)

running time, release date, producer, rental price; contents synopsis
   omitted: grade level, purchasing information
Indexes: topical title listing serves as index to alphabetical "new acquisitions" listing with annotations
Period covered: 1971-1976
Revision and updating:
Media represented: films, audio recordings
Producers represented: various
Features: "Mental Health Film Classics—Or Just Old Hat?" by Jack Neher of the Mental Health Materials Center in same issue asserts that "mental health film classics still have much to offer and should not be passed by because of age" and mentions 18 films dating to the 1940s still valuable if properly presented. Eleven recent mental health audio recordings are described on pp. 23-24.

15-14 (cont'd)
Subject terms:
    drug abuse education
    psychology

15-15*   About Aging: A Catalog of Films 1977. 3rd ed. Mildred V. Allyn.
    Andrus Gerontology Center, University of Southern California,
    Los Angeles, CA 90007, 1977. 148p. $3.50pa.
Purpose: comprehensive
Grade level: intermediate, secondary
Arrangement: alphabetical title
Subjects: aging: some solutions   death
             aging: the problems   family relationships
             aging: the realities   lifestyles
             aging in other countries   retirement
             biography   others
Entries: appr. 400

    running time, producer/distributor, release date; sale price; rental source,
    annotations supplied by producer or distributor; titles new to this edition
    marked with asterisk (*)
        omitted: grade level
Indexes: subject
Period covered: 1960-1976 (some earlier)
Revision and updating: previous edition 1975
Media represented: films
Producers represented: appr. 130 commercial, academic, government, institutional
Features: Includes separate alphabetical listing of some 40 feature films. [Similar
    list: *Teaching about Aging*, by Francis E. Pratt (Social Science Education
    Consortium, 855 Broadway, Boulder, CO 80302, 1976. 78p. $3.25pa. ED
    135 682) includes brief notes on 11 films and other media.]
Subject terms:
    aging   death education
    biography   world cultures

15-16*   Aging; An Annotated Guide to Government Publications. L. DeLuca,
    and others. University of Connecticut, Library, Storrs, CT 06268,
    1975. 68p. $3.00pa.
Purpose: "the most significant" publications
Grade level: secondary
Arrangement: subject
Subjects: comprehensive studies   government programs   nutrition
             demographics   and conferences   quality of life
             employment of older   health care   social security
                 workers   long-term care   and medicare
                                                              others
Entries: 220

    issuing agency, date, number of pages; order number; contents summary
Period covered: 1960-74

15-16 (cont'd)
Indexes: title, series
Revision and updating:
Media represented: government publications
Producers represented: U.S., state governments, U.N.
Features: [Similar list: *SB 039* from the Superintendent of Documents,
Washington, DC 20402, is a frequently updated listing of currently available
U.S. publications.]
Subject terms: aging

15-17*   Death out of the Closet; A Curriculum Guide to Living with Dying.
Gene Stanford and Deborah Perry. Bantam, 1976. 213p. $1.95pa.
Purpose: recommendations in "Materials and Teaching Strategies" (Ch. IV)
Grade level: all
Arrangement: topical

Subjects:	death and science	personal experience of death
	death rites and rituals	social and ethical issues
	immortality	

Entries: over 100
    format, running time, producer/distributor; sale/rental prices; contents
    summary
       omitted: release date
Indexes: none
Period covered: not known
Revision and updating:
Media represented: audio recordings, films, graphic materials
Producers represented: various
Features: Also lists paintings and musical excerpts and films of literary works on
the theme of death. Study guides to 19 books. [Similar lists: *Helping Children
Cope with Death and Separation* (Joanne Bernstein. ED 125 753) lists
resources for teacher use. "Exploring the Future through Contemporary
Music" (*Media and Methods*, v.12, April 1976. pp. 32-36) and "Images of
the Future in Popular Music" (*Social Education*, v.39, May 1975, pp. 276-
285) both identify songs dealing with death themes.]
Subject terms:
    death education

15-18*   Films and Videotapes on Aging and Death. Pennsylvania State
University, Audio Visual Services, University Park, PA 16802, 1977.
16p. free.
Purpose: film library catalog; recommendations
Grade level: secondary
Arrangement: alphabetical title
Subjects: aging and death
Entries: appr. 70
    running time, producer, release date, rental price; contents summary, grade
    level
Indexes: none
Period covered: 1951-1977 (many quite recent)

15-18 (cont'd)
Revision and updating: *Newsletter*; previous edition 1974
Media represented: films, video recordings
Producers represented: various
Features:
Subject terms:
 aging
 death education

15-19* A Comprehensive Resource Guide to 16mm Mental Health Films.
Mental Health Media Evaluation Project, P. O. Box 1548, Spring-
field, VA 22151, 1977. 112p. $25.00pa. LC 77-81480.
Purpose: comprehensive
Grade level: all
Arrangement: alphabetical title
Subjects: adolescence   family life
    aging and the aged   life situations
    childhood   minority mental health
    community mental health treatment
Entries: appr. 1500
 running time, producer/distributor, production date; grade level; contents
 note
  omitted: price
Indexes: subject
Period covered: 1966-76
Revision and updating:
Media represented: films
Producers represented: appr. 100 academic, commercial, institutional distributors
Features: *An Evaluative Guide to 16mm Mental Heatlh Films* from the same
 source (15-20) represents recommended films culled from this group.
Subject terms:
    guidance   psychology
    ethnic studies   women's studies

15-20* An Evaluative Guide to 16mm Mental Health Films. Mental Health
Media Evaluation Project. P.O. Box 1548, Springfield, VA 22151,
1977. 55p. $15.00pa. LC 77-81481.
Purpose: recommendations for public mental health education, exclusive of
 alcoholism and drug abuse, based on evaluations by Mental Health Associa-
 tion personnel, other professionals and lay personnel
Grade level: all
Arrangement: alphabetical title
Subjects: adolescence   family life
    aging and the aged   life situations
    childhood   minority mental health
    community mental health treatment

15-20 (cont'd)
Entries: over 300

running time, producer/distributor, production date; grade level; contents
note, suggestions for use, evaluator's comments
omitted: price
Indexes: subject
Period covered: 1966-1976
Revision and updating:
Media represented: films
Producers represented: appr. 100 distributors including academic, commercial,
institutional
Features: Includes Mental Health Association rental films. *A Comprehensive
Resource Guide to 16mm Mental Health Films* from the same source (15-19)
represents the larger universe from which the ones here were chosen.
Subject terms:

ethnic studies	psychology
guidance	women's studies

15-21* **KWIC's Film Forum.** Center for the Study of Aging and Human Develop-
ment, Box 3003, Duke University, Durham, NC 27710. free.
Purpose: evaluations by film audiences
Grade level: secondary
Arrangement: alphabetical title in each issue
Subjects: education for the elderly   psychological aspects of aging

Subjects:	education for the elderly	psychological aspects of aging
	living arrangements	social aspects of aging
	physiological aspects of aging	others

Entries: appr. 40/year

running time, producer; release date (generally), sale price, contents summary;
audience suitability (generally); perceived purpose (informational, attitudinal,
social action, etc.), suggested use, rating on scale of 1 to 5, shortcomings
Indexes: none
Period covered: 1963-1974
Revision and updating: published 2-3x/year
Media represented: films, filmstrips, slides, video recordings
Producers represented: various
Features:
Subject terms: aging

16-Science

Consult *Superfilms* (32-22) for award-winning films and *The Guide to Simula-
tions/Games for Education and Training* (41-01) for games both to develop inquiry
approaches and to teach specific concepts. Programs from NOVA, the public television science series, are available from the Public Television Library (43-02) and
from commercial distributors, depending on the program desired. *Directory of*

Spoken-Voice Audio-Cassettes (32-07) lists recordings issued by the American Association for the Advancement of Science, the American Chemical Society and other organizations. *Films on the Future* (17-20) annotates films on the impact of science on society.

Selected U.S. Government Publications (35-01) each month features science and technology publications and may be used to update the sources mentioned below.

Earth Science

Lists of government publications and the agencies from which they may be obtained include:

Superintendent of Documents, Washington, DC 20402
Earthquake Information Bulletin (bimonthly; $3.00/year); SB 032 (Oceanography), SB 160 (Earth Sciences), SB 234 (Weather).

Geological Survey, Reston, VA 22092
Motion Picture Film Services; New Publications of the Geological Survey (monthly); *Popular Publications of the Geological Survey; Teachers' Packet of Geologic Materials* (high school earth science courses); *Selected Packet of Geologic Teaching Aids* (others)

Oceanographer of the Navy, 200 Stoval Street, Alexandria, VA 22332
Oceanographic Films

Federal Aviation Administration, Washington, DC 20591
FAA Film Catalog

NOAA. National Climatic Center, Washington, DC 28801
Climatological Data (monthly edition for each state; $5.10/year)

National Aeronautics and Space Administration, Washington, DC 20546
NASA Educational Publications; Report to Educators

National Ocean Survey, Rockville, MD 20852
Motion Picture Films; frequently updated *Science Packet* contains one each of over 30 publicatons; *Oceanography Packet*

Texas A&M University Sea Grant Program, College Station, TX 77843
Sea Grant '70's (monthly)

Library of Congress, Science and Technology Division, Washington, DC 20540
Unidentified Flying Objects (bibliography)

For lists of maps, charts, and aerial photographs, see 36–Graphic Materials and 39–Maps. Local soil conservation districts may have soil maps for examination or distribution.

Landmarks in History contains a collection of newspaper accounts on microfilm of the Apollo 11 and 12 Moon missions (from Bell & Howell Microphoto Division, Wooster, OH 44691).

Life Science

Index to Illustrations of the Natural World: Where to Find Pictures of the Living Things of North America (Gaylord, 1977. 265p. $29.95) indexes over 6000 illustrations in 178 books published since 1960.

The Superintendent of Documents, Washington, DC 20402 supplies subject bibliographies SB 070 (Mammals and Reptiles) and SB 124 (Zoology), among others.

Physical Science

The Bureau of Mines, 4800 Forbes Avenue, Pittsburgh, PA 15213 issues *Films; Publications and Articles* (annual); and *New Publications* (monthly). The Superintendent of Documents, Washington, DC 20402, supplies subject bibliography SB 053 (Electricity and Electronics).

16-01*   **Educators Guide to Free Science Materials.** 17th ed. Educators Progress Service, Randolph, WI 53956, 1976. 343+74p. $11.25. LC 61-919.
Purpose: free materials available for classroom use; comprehensive
Grade level: all
Arrangement: topical subdivisions within 5 media listings
Subjects: aerospace education   environmental education
                 biology   general science
                 chemistry   nature study
                                                         physics
Entries: over 1800
         ordering information; release date (in many cases); contents note
             omitted: grade level
Period covered: available at time of publication
Revision and updating: published annually
Media represented: films, filmstrips, slides, transparencies, audio recordings, graphic materials, video recordings, free and inexpensive publications, government publications
Producers represented: appr. 370
Features: See introduction to 34—Free and Inexpensive Materials.
Subject terms:
         energy and environment education
         science

16-02*   **"Human Genetics; A Filmography for the Secondary School Student."** *Sightlines*, v.8, no.2, Winter 1974/75, pp. 17-19.
Purpose: recommendations
Grade level: secondary
Arrangement: alphabetical title
Subjects: genetics

16-02 (cont'd)
Entries: 33

running time, producer, release date; contents summary; grade level
(junior high, high school, college)
omitted: price
Indexes:
Period covered: 1965-1972
Revision and updating:
Media represented: films
Producers represented: 18 distributors
Features:
Subject terms: life science

16-03* **Films for Life Sciences.** Audio-Visual Services, Pennsylvania State
University, Willard Building, University Park, PA 16802, 1977. 104p.
free.
Purpose: film library catalog; recommendations
Grade level: intermediate, secondary
Arrangement: alphabetical title
Subjects: agriculture and   botany   physiology
    gardening   ecology-environment   primates
  animal behavior   genetics and heredity   reproduction
  aquatic life   insects   others
  birds   microbiology
Entries: appr. 700 (excluding Cinematographica)

running time, producer, release date; rental price; grade level; contents
summary
Indexes: subject
Period covered: 1950s-1976
Revision and updating: previous edition *Films for Biological Sciences* (1973)
Media represented: films
Producers represented: various commercial, government, academic
Features: "Encyclopaedia Cinematographica Films on Biology" (pp. 63-88) lists
appr. 800 selections, almost all under 5 minutes and silent, intended for
scientific audiences.
Subject terms:
energy and environment education
life science

16-04* **American Biology Teacher.** National Association of Biology Teachers,
11250 Roger Bacon Drive, Reston, VA 22090. $18.00/year.
Purpose: "Review" column; evaluations
Grade level: secondary
Arrangement: random
Subjects: biology
Entries: appr. 25/year

running time, producer/distributor, sales price; release date; signed critical
review

16-04 (cont'd)
Indexes: indexed in *Media Review Digest* (01-03)
Period covered: current releases
Media represented: films, filmstrips, filmloops, transparencies
Producers represented: various
Features: See also 16-15.
Subject terms: life science

16-05*   Sourcebook for Oceans: Our Continuing Frontier. Mary Hellman,
University Extension, University of California, San Diego. Publisher's
Inc., 243 12th Street, Drawer P, Del Mar, CA 92014, 1976. 55p.
$2.50pa. ED 138 505.
Purpose: Filmography on pp. 41-50 compiled by Nadine Covert of Educational
Film Library Association
Grade level: secondary
Arrangement: 16 topical categories
Subjects: American imagery and visions   a new world picture
of the sea   our continuing frontier
can the sea feed the land   pollution
exploration of the sea   ships and the sailor
from work to sport   women and the sea
horrors of the deep   writers at sea
law of the sea   others
mineral resources of the oceans
Entries: appr. 90

running time, producer/distributor, release date; synopsis
omitted: price
Indexes:
Period covered: 1950-1975
Revision and updating:
Media represented: films
Producers represented: appr. 40 distributors
Features: Part of University's Courses by Newspaper program (see also 17-06 and
17-13).
Subject terms;
interdisciplinary studies
oceanography

**16-06   Index to a Set of One Hundred Topographic Maps Illustrating
Specified Physiographic Features.** U.S. Geological Survey, Reston,
VA 22092, 1973. folded map. free.
Purpose: maps for sale by the Survey
Grade level: all
Arrangement: by state
Subjects: glaciation, escarpments, shorelines, volcanic, water, wind, mountain,
plains, plateau, valley features
Entries: 100

scale; contents note; prices listed in introduction

16-06 (cont'd)
Indexes: physiographic features
Period covered: currently available
Revision and updating:
Media represented: maps
Producers represented: U.S. government
Features: May be purchased as the entire set, a smaller set of 25, or individually.
   Also supplied in *Teacher's Packet of Geologic Materials* (see "Earth Science"
   above).
Subject terms: earth science

16-07*   **NASA Film List.** National Aeronautics and Space Administration,
   Washington, DC 20546, 1976. 28p. free.
Purpose: films for non-professional audiences available on free-loan from regional
   NASA film libraries and for sale by the National Audiovisual Center
Grade level: all
Arrangement: topical
Subjects: adventures in research   space in the 70s
            Apollo mission   others
            general films
Entries: appr. 100

   running time, color, release date; contents summary; awards
      omitted: grade level
Indexes: none
Period covered: available at time of publication
Revision and updating: previous edition 1973
Media represented: audio recordings, films, filmstrips, video recordings
Producers represented: U.S. government
Features: "Local video tape transfer is encouraged."
Subject terms: science

16-08*   **Journal of Geological Education.** National Association of Geology
   Teachers c/o Allen Press, Inc., P.O. Box 368, Lawrence, KS 66044.
   $17.50/year.
Purpose: "Film Reviews" column by George T. Ladd appears in most issues;
   evaluations
Grade level: secondary
Arrangement: random
Subjects: geology
Entries: appr. 25/year

   running time, producer, release date; price; grade level; signed review
      assessing content and technical quality
Indexes:
Period covered: current releases
Revision and updating: published 5x/year
Media represented: films
Producers represented: commercial, institutional, government

16-08 (cont'd)
Features:
Subject terms: earth science

16-09*   Science Teacher. National Science Teachers Association, 1742
Connecticut Avenue, NW, Washington, DC 20009. $25.00/year.
Purpose: recommendations by members of the NSTA Science Teaching Materials
Review Committee in "Resources/Reviews" column
Grade level: secondary
Arrangement: random
Subjects: science
Entries: appr. 65/year (excluding books)
Indexes: indexed in *Media Review Digest* (01-03)
Period covered: current releases
Revision and updating: published 9x/year
Media represented: films, filmstrips, simulation games, kits
Producers represented: several
Features:
Subject terms: science

16-10*   Science and Children. National Science Teachers Association, 1742
Connecticut Avenue, NW, Washington, DC 20009. $17.00/year.
Purpose: recommendations by members of the NSTA Teaching Materials Review
Committee in "Resources/Reviews" column; announcements in "Advailables"
Grade level: primary, intermediate
Arrangement: random
Subjects: science
Entries: appr. 35/year (excluding books)

distributor, release date, purchase and rental price; running time, grade
level; signed reviews; title, source ("Ad-vailables")
Indexes: indexed in *Media Review Digest* (01-03)
Period covered: current releases
Revision and updating: published 8x/year
Media represented: films, filmstrips, free and inexpensive publications, graphic
materials
Producers represented: several
Features: Chiefly reviews of books.
Subject terms: science

16-11   AAAS Science Film Catalog. Ann Seltz-Petrash and Kathryn Wolff.
Bowker, 1975. 398p. $17.50. LC 75-11536.
Purpose: comprehensive
Grade level: all
Arrangement: Dewey Decimal in two sections (Junior High—Adult; Primary—
Intermediate)
Subjects: science, including "Impact of the Sciences on Society"

16-11 (cont'd)
Entries: 5600

running time, purchase and rental price, release date; grade level; synopsis "reprinted directly from the distributor's catalogs and promotional material"
Indexes: subject index for each section; title
Period covered: films available September 1974
Revision and updating: 16-13
Media represented: films
Producers represented: over 125 commercial, government, academic, institutional, television
Features:
Subject terms:

energy and environment	history
education	industrial arts
ethnic studies	mathematics
geography	psychology
health and safety	science
education	

16-12* **Films for Mathematics and Physical Sciences.** 5th ed. Pennsylvania State University, Audio-Visual Services, Willard Building, University Park, PA 16802, 1976. 74p. free.
Purpose: film library catalogs; recommendations
Grade level: all
Arrangement: alphabetical title

Subjects:	astronomy	earth science	physics
	biochemistry	materials science	science-scientific
	chemistry	mathematics	method
			space science

Entries: appr. 550

running time, producer, release date; rental price; grade level; contents summary
Indexes: subject
Period covered: 1960s-1975
Revision and updating: previous edition 1973
Media represented: films
Producers represented: various commercial, government, academic
Features: Appendix lists an additional over 100 technical films from the Encyclopaedia Cinematographica collection of scientist-made documentaries.
Subject terms:

earth science	physical science
mathematics	

16-13* **Science Books and Films.** American Association for the Advancement of Science, 1515 Massachusetts Avenue, NW, Washington, DC 20005. $16.00/year.
Purpose: evaluative
Grade level: all

16-13 (cont'd)
Arrangement: Dewey Decimal System
Subjects: mathematics
science

also anthropology
psychology
sociology

Entries: appr. 150/year (excluding print)

running time, distributor, release date, sale & rental price, grade level; signed
critical review; rating (not recommended, acceptable, one or two stars);
Dewey Decimal classification
Indexes: title index in each issue
Period covered: current and recent releases
Revision and updating: published 4x/year
Media represented: films
Producers represented: various, including television
Features: Film reviews were added beginning May 1975. "Because of the rela-
tively high cost of 16mm educational films, the appraisal ratings are more
stringently applied to films than to books."
Subject terms:
mathematics
science

social studies

16-14*   Marine Science Education Materials and Their Usefulness. Richard M.
Schlenker, University of Maine, Orono, ME 01173, 1976. 54p.
ED 128 208.
Purpose: evaluations
Grade level: all
Arrangement: alphabetical title
Subjects: biological
career
law

physical/chemical
pollution

Entries: appr. 100 (excluding curriculum guides, reports, etc.)

source; contents note; grade level
omitted: publication date, price
Indexes: subject, grade level
Period covered: available at time of publication
Revision and updating:
Media represented: free and inexpensive publications
Producers: various academic, government
Features: Also bibliographies, texts, curriculum guides, papers, reports, periodicals,
and 3 films.
Subject terms: oceanography

16-15*   "Resource Materials." Entomological Society of America. *American
Biology Teacher*, v.38, May 1976, p. 307-14, 324.
Purpose: comprehensive
Grade level: secondary
Arrangement: by media
Subjects: entomology

16-15 (cont'd)
Entries: over 100

running time, producer, release date; contents note
omitted: price, grade level
Indexes:
Period covered: 1952-75
Revision and updating:
Media represented: films, free and inexpensive publications, graphic materials
Producers represented: appr. 30
Features: Also lists books, specimens, etc. Mentioned are 65 films, Audubon
Society booklets and illustrations from four sources.
Subject terms: life science

16-16*   Films for Humane Education. Ronald Scott and Joan Stewart. Argus
Archives, Inc., 228 East 49th Street, New York, NY 10017, 1977.
loose-leaf. $2.50. LC 77-075785.
Purpose: recommendations by staff reviewers and after showing to audiences
concerned with humane treatment of animals
Grade level: all
Arrangement: 9 topical groupings
Subjects: exhibitions (zoos, etc.)   research and testing
            food and commercial uses   trapping
            humane education   wildlife
            hunting   miscellaneous
            pets
Entries: 46

running time, producer/distributor, release date; sale/rental price; rental
source; synopsis and critique with discussion suggestions
Indexes: title
Period covered: 1970s
Revision and updating:
Media represented: films
Producers: various
Features: Focus on animal welfare.
Subject terms: life science

17-Social Studies

This chapter is comprised of lists of media for social studies instruction in
general and for all subordinate topics except those embraced by "ethnic studies,"
"history," "international education," and "world cultures." These are covered in
18–Ethnic Studies and 19–World Cultures and International Education.
Films 1977-1978 (32-05) lists over 100 documentary films; others are found
in "Short Films" (32-24) and several other sources mentioned in 07–Film Study

and 32–Films. For the availability of television documentaries on film and video-tape, see 43–Television. Past newsreels are found in *Film Programmer's Guide to 16mm Rentals* (32-03).

Government publications are, of course, especially pertinent to the social studies, and reference is made to 35–Government Publications. Guides cited in 34–Free and Inexpensive Publications list many useful items, and a large proportion of the items listed in 41–Simulation Games are in the social studies.

American History

The Bicentennial year was the occasion for much publishing and also spurred the compilation of a number of resource guides. Emphasis frequently was on American history and culture in general and on the history of individual states, in addition to the Revolution. Examples of media guides are:

"CINE Bicentennial Golden Eagles," *Film News*, v.33, May/June 1976, pp. 8-11; September/October 1976; pp. 18-21 (120 films released 1960s-1976).

Bicentennial Broadside: An Annotated Bibliography and Resource Guide. Michigan Association for Media in Education, 401 South Fourth Street, Ann Arbor, MI 48103, 1975. (over 100 media in many formats including free and inexpensive publications, graphic materials, maps, manipulative materials, plus books recommended for all grades).

The American Film Review Special Bicentennial Issue. ED 120 080. (over 100 films).

"Mixed Media for the Bicentennial." *Previews*, v.4, December 1975, pp. 3-9 (84 recommended filmstrips, films, kits and audio recordings released 1973-1975).

Bicentennial Film Preview Sesson. North Carolina Library Association. ED 118 085. (37 films).

"Short Films Americana." *Media and Methods*, v.13, November 1976, pp. 16-18, 56 (37 films).

"American Culture through Media." *Social Education*, v.40, March 1976, pp. 173-177 (appr. 20 titles).

"A Bibliography of Bicentennial Materials." *Audiovisual Instruction*, v.21, January 1976, pp. 28-31, 73 (25 titles based on Michigan Association list).

also:

Arizona in Filmstrips. Arizona Department of Education, 1976. ED 119 938. (460 films, cassettes and other media).

Colorado Grubstakes '76 and *Supplement No. 1.* Colorado Educational Media Association, 5895 South University Boulevard, Littleton, CO 80121. $3.00. (150 titles, including many photographs and maps).

and materials from government agencies:

National Archives and Records Service, Washington, DC 20408
Documents from America's Past; The Written Word Endures ($12.50)
(reproductions of landmark documents); *Select List of Publications*
(from Presidential libraries).

Superintendent of Documents, Washington, DC 20402
Above Ground Archaeology (S/N 2405-00528. $0.80); *American Revolution
Bicentennial Administration Publications* (SB 144); *Historical Handbooks*
(SB 16). *National Park Service Guide to the Historic Places of the American
Revolution.* [1973. S/N 2405-00517. $1.90] ; posters of historical sites
and parks.

Geological Survey, Reston, VA 22092
*The Geology and Early History of the Boston Area of Massachusetts, a
Bicentennial Approach.* (78p. $1.15. *Bulletin* 1476).

Geological Survey, Box 25286, Federal Center, Denver, CO 80225
Historic Trail Map of the Greater Denver Areas ($1.25).

National Audiovisual Center, Washington, DC 20409
Media for the Bicentennial; US Information Agency Films.

Maps for the study of American history are made accessible by *Index to Maps
of the American Revolution in Books and Periodicals* (Greenwood, 1975. $15.00)
which covers 1000 sources and by atlases published for the Bicentennial, such as
Atlas of the American Revolution (Rand McNally, 1974. $35.00) (54 antique maps),
and *Campaigns of the American Revolution; an Atlas of Manuscript Maps* (Hammond,
1976. $25.00) (British maps reproduced).

The use in high school instruction of books illustrating people, places, and
things in the American past is discussed in "Using Picture Books in the Classroom,"
Media and Methods, v.13, January 1977, pp. 22-25. Scanning the index and state-
by-state listings in *Oral History Collections* (Bowker, 1975. 344p. $32.50) will
help locate tapes on local history. The microfilm collection *Landmarks in History*
(Bell / Howell Microphoto Division, Wooster, OH 44691) includes newspaper
coverage of the events of the 1960s and *The Founding Fathers and the American
Revolution* (same source) presents some 8,000 archival items on microfiche. *The
Birth of America: The Year in Review 1763-1783* (Microfilming Corporation of
America, Glen Rock, NJ 07452) collects some 4,000 issues of period newspapers
on microfilm.

Movies that have helped shape myths about American history are found
through filmographies in *Propaganda on Film* and *The American West on Film*
(both Richard A. Maynard. Hayden Book Company, Rochelle Park, NJ 07662,
1975. $4.95pa. ea.).

Contemporary Issues

The term "contemporary issues" and related terms in the Subject Index will
retrieve materials on a variety of current problems. Publications and films found

through *Alternatives in Print* (01-21) and *Canyon Cinema Catalog* (32-08) provide alternative points of view. See also the introduction to 34—Free and Inexpensive Publications.

Economics

Related references are provided in 04—Consumer Education. The U.S. Department of Labor has published *The Bicentennial History of the American Worker*, by Richard B. Morris (1976. 327p. $5.00 from Superintendent of Documents, Washington, DC 20402. S/N 029-000-00256-8).

Futures

The Congressional Clearinghouse on the Future (3692 House Annex #2, Washington, DC 20515) publishes a free monthly newsletter, *What's Next?*

Geography

The scope of this term includes land use and planning. Sources for maps and aerial photographs are suggested in 36—Graphic Materials and 39—Maps, while 19—World Cultures and International Education deals with worldwide aspects.

Government and Law

Instructional and public television agencies have many programs and series in this area (see 43—Television). A Washington calendar *Inside the Capitol* is available from the Public Citizen Visitors Center, 1200 15th Street, NW, Washington, DC 20005. ($6.00/year; semi-monthly). The catalogs published by the Mental Health Materials Center (15-12 and 15-13) offer guides to materials on crime and delinquency.

Urban Studies

Newsbank is a current awareness reference service on urban affairs, supplying microfiche reproductions of articles from 170 newspapers in 13 subject categories.
Guide to Free-Loan Films on the Urban Condition (Serina Press, Alexandria, VA 22305, 1976. 77p. $7.95) lists over 500 films from many sources.

Values Education

"Values" is used as a subject heading in *Films for the Elementary Classroom* (32-23), *Films on the Future* (17-20), *Superfilms* (32-22), *Social Studies Curriculum Materials Data Book* (17-19), *Index to Psychology* (15-01), among others. Animated and non-narrated films located through *Films for Film Study* (07-01), *From "A" to "Yellowjack"* (07-08), and other guides listed in 07—Film Study can be used. The terms "government and law" and "philosophy and religion" in the Subject Index will suggest further materials.

17-01* **Educators Guide to Free Social Studies Materials.** 16th ed. Educators Progress Service, Randolph, WI 53956, 1976. 616p. $11.75. LC 61-65910.
Purpose: free materials available for classroom use; comprehensive
Grade level: all
Arrangement: topical subdivisions within media listings
Subjects: citizenship   history
           communications and   social problems
           transportation   world affairs
           geography
Entries: over 3900

   format details, ordering information; publication and release dates in many cases; contents summary
Indexes: titles, subject
Period covered: available at time of publication
Revision and updating: published annually
Media represented: free and inexpensive publications, films, filmstrips, slides, audio recordings, video recordings, graphic materials, maps, government publications
Producers represented: over 500
Features: [See introduction to 34—Free and Inexpensive Materials.]
Subject terms:
           drug abuse   social studies
           psychology

17-02 **Films for Sociology.** Pennsylvania State University, Audio-Visual Services, Willard Building, University Park, PA 16802, 1973. 205p. free. ED 134 511.
Purpose: film library catalog; recommendations
Grade level: intermediate, secondary
Arrangement: alphabetical title
Subjects: Africa   human development   South and Central
           anthropology   labor   America
           Asia   minority Americans   urban sociology
           education   psychology   others
           family   sociological jurisprudence
Entries: appr. 1200

   running time, release date, distributor, rental fee; grade level; contents note
Indexes: regional, topical
Period covered: late 1950s-1960s
Revision and updating: *Newsletter;* 2nd ed. 1978
Media represented: films
Producers represented: various commercial, academic, commercial television

17-02 (cont'd)
Features: Note index headings "creativity," "art and society," "social change,"
and many others conducive to conceptual approaches. [See other university
film library catalogs for more recent listings.]
Subject terms:
psychology
social studies

17-03* Films for History and Political Science. 4th ed. Pennsylvania State
University, Audio-Visual Services, Willard Building, University Park,
PA 16802, 1976. 118p. free. ED 134 510.
Purpose: film library catalog; recommendations
Grade level: all
Arrangement: alphabetical title
Subjects: Africa   contemporary issues
            Ancient world   Europe
            Asia   Latin America
            biography   United States
            Black rights   others
Entries: appr. 1200

running time, producer code, release date, rental price; grade level; synopsis
Indexes: subject
Period covered: 1950s-1976
Revision and updating: *Newsletter*; previous edition 1973
Media represented: films
Producers represented: various
Features:
Subject terms:
biography
social studies

17-04 Television News Index and Abstracts. Vanderbilt Television News
Archive, Joint University Libraries, Nashville, TN 37203. limited
distribution.
Purpose: abstracts of evning news programs of the three major networks as
broadcast in Nashville; Vanderbilt University maintains a videotape collec-
tion of these and also of other longer broadcasts of major news events,
presidential speeches, national convention coverage, Watergate hearings,
and "compiled tapes" of the evening news coverage of major events (e.g.
Attica)
Grade level: all
Arrangement: chronological
Entries: several thousand/year

network, day, time, newscaster's name, subject caption for each segment;
outline style summary
Indexes: subject index in each issue; annual subject index
Period covered: taping began 8/5/68
Revision and updating: published 12x/year

17-04 (cont'd)
Media represented: audio recordings, video recordings, television, microform
Producers represented: 3 commercial television networks
Features: Abstracts for 1968-1971 are not published but are available at the
    Archive. Copies of the tapes in the collection may be rented in various
    formats, including audio only. Transcripts of daily news and public affairs
    broadcasts on CBS may be obtained on microform (Microfilming Corpora-
    tion of America, Glen Rock, NJ 07452).
Subject terms:
    mass media
    social studies

17-05   Films for Economics Education. 2nd ed. Pennsylvania State University,
    Audio-Visual Services, Willard Building, University Park, PA 16802,
    1972. 50p. free.
Purpose: film library catalog; recommendations
Grade level: all
Arrangement: alphabetical title
Subjects: agriculture   production and distribution
    American economic history   urban economics
    economic growth and   U.S. economic system
        development   others
    labor-management relations
Entries: appr. 450

    running time, producer code, release date, rental price; grade level; synopsis
Indexes: regional, topical
Period covered: 1949-1971
Revision and updating: *Newsletter*
Media represented: films
Producers represented: various including commercial and public television
Features: [See also *Films for Business and Industrial Organization and Manage-
    ment* (03-16) and other university film library catalogs. Also EMC Two-77
    (see 32-05).]
Subject terms: economics

17-06*   Sourcebook for Crime and Justice in America. Mary Hellman, Univer-
    sity Extension, University of California, San Diego. Publisher's Inc.,
    243 12th Street, Drawer P, Del Mar, CA 92014, 1977. $2.50pa.
Purpose: "Films" p. 36-48; recommendations to "stimulate discussion and
    reflection. Compiled by Esme J. Dick and the staff of the Educational Film
    Library Association.
Grade level: secondary
Arrangement: topical
Subjects: crime: no simple   philosophy of   pretrial detention
        solutions   criminal law   plea bargaining &
    white-collar crime   limits of criminal law   sentencing
    organized crime   civil liberties and   punishment
    urban crime   criminal law   the prison
    sex and crime   police & law   community
    race and crime   enforcement

17-06 (cont'd)
Entries: appr. 100

running time, producer/distributor, release date; contents summary
    omitted: price
Indexes: none
Period covered: 1960s-1975
Revision and updating:
Media represented: films
Producers represented: appr. 60
Features: Includes materials on civil disobedience, on impeachment and unexpected
    items such as Richard Nixon's "Checkers" speech. A project of the University's
    Courses by Newspaper program (see also 16-05 and 17-13).
Subject terms: government and law

17-07   **Learning with Games: An Analysis of Social Studies Educational
    Games and Simulations.** Cheryl Charles and Ronald Stadsklev. Social
    Studies Education Consortium, 855 Broadway, Boulder, CO 80302,
    1973. 175p. $4.95pa. ED 077 826. LC 73-77317.
Purpose: evaluations reprinted from *Social Studies Curriculum Materials Data
    Book* (17-19)
Grade level: all
Arrangement: alphabetical title
Subjects: American history   geography   political science
             consumer economics   history   urban studies
             contemporary problems human relations   war/peace studies
             economics   international relations others
             environmental education
Entries: 70 + 250

user characteristics, time required, producer, price; grade level; contents and
    objectives; evaluation
Indexes: grade level, subject
Period covered: through March 1973
Revision and updating: 17-19
Media represented: simulation games
Producers represented: 80
Features: "Abbreviated Games and Simulations Guide." (p. 159ff.) lists an
    additional 250 games by producer without annotations.
Subject terms:
             education   social studies
             energy and environment

17-08   **Educational Games and Simulations in Economics.** Darrell R. Lewis
    and others. Joint Council on Economics Education, 1212 Avenue of
    the Americas, New York, NY 10036, 1974. $4.00. ED 095 057.
Purpose: recommendations
Grade level: all
Arrangement: alphabetical title

17-08 (cont'd)
Subjects: agriculture   politics
           consumer education   resource allocation
           ecology   urban planning
           history   others
Entries: appr. 150

    producer, price, number of players, time required; grade level; subject,
    evaluative summary
        omitted: publication date
Indexes: none
Period covered: available at time of publication
Revision and updating: 41-01
Media represented: simulation games
Producers represented: appr. 50
Features:
Subject terms: economics

17-09* **"Teaching Futuristics in the Classroom Today."** *Previews*, v.4, February
        1976, p. 5-9.
Purpose: comprehensive
Grade level: secondary
Arrangement: by media
Subjects: futures studies
Entries: 60 (excluding print)

    running time, producer, distributor; contents note
        omitted: release date, price
Indexes:
Period covered: available at time of publication
Revision and updating:
Media represented: audio recordings, films, filmstrips, kits, simulation games,
    slides
Producers represented: various
Features:
Subject terms: futures

17-10* **Social Education.** National Council for the Social Studies. 2030 M
        Street, NW, Washington, DC 20036. $25.00/year.
Purpose: "Instructional Media" appears very rarely; evaluations
Grade level: all
Arrangement: random
Subjects: social studies
Entries: appr. 20/year

    format, price, release date, producer/distributor; grade level; full summary
    and review
Indexes: indexed in *Media Review Digest* (01-03)
Period covered: current releases
Revision and updating: published 7x/year
Media represented: films, filmstrips

17-10 (cont'd)
Producers represented: various
Features: Most of the journal's coverage of media is in articles on specific subjects (see 17-25, also 17-18 "Features"). In "Films for the Social Studies: Pedagogical Tools and Works of Art" (v.40, May 1976, pp. 264, 270-272) Stephen C. Johnson of the Indiana University Audiovisual Center lists the 70 most heavily used ones. Also "The Non-Narrative Film: A Social Studies Resource for K-College" (same issue, pp. 265-269), "American Culture through Media" (v.40, March 1976, pp. 173-177).
Subject terms: social studies

17-11 Alternatives. Nadine Covert and Esmé J. Dick. Educational Film Library Association, 43 West 61st Street, New York, NY 10023, 1974. 12p. $2.00pa.
Purpose: recommendations prepared for a February 1974 workshop
Grade level: secondary
Arrangement: alphabetical title
Subjects: alternative lifestyles   religion
           crafts   work
           politics
Entries: over 100

    running time, distributor, release date; brief synopsis, comment
        omitted: price
Indexes: subject
Period covered: 1969-1973
Revision and updating:
Media represented: films
Producers represented: various commercial and institutional
Features:
Subject terms:
           contemporary issues
           crafts

17-12* Update on Law-Related Education. American Bar Association, 1155 East 60th Street, Chicago, IL 60637. $5.00/year. ED 139 716 (v.1, no.1)
Purpose: "Curriculum Update" in each issue describes audio-visual materials
Grade level: all
Arrangement: by grade level
Subjects: law
Entries: appr. 60/year

    format, running time, producer/distributor, release date; grade level;
    synopsis
        omitted: price
Indexes:
Period covered: current releases
Revision and updating: published 3x/year
Media represented: films, filmstrips

17-12 (cont'd)
Producers represented: various commercial
Features: Supplements 17-18 and 17-24.
Subject terms:
contemporary issues
government and law

17-13* **Moral Choices in Contemporary Society: Sourcebook.** Mary Hellman, University Extension, University of California, San Diego. Publisher's Inc., 243 12th Street, Del Mar, CA 92014, 1977. $2.50pa. ED 138 496.
Purpose: "Films", pp. 36-47, recommended by Nadine Covert and staff of Educational Film Library Association
Grade level: secondary
Arrangement: 16 topical categories
Subjects: aging and the aged   moral education
abortion   nature of morality
crime and punishment   politics—domestic
dilemmas of sex   politics—international
family and morality   pornography and obscenity
law and morality   racism
morality of work and sport   science and morals
morality of business
Entries: appr. 100
running time, producer/distributor, release date; contents summary
omitted: price
Indexes: none
Period covered: 1960s-1970s
Revision and updating:
Media represented: films
Producers represented: appr. 50 distributors
Features: A project of the University's Courses by Newspaper program (see also 16-05 and 17-06).
Subject terms: values education

17-14 **"Films for U.S. History."** Daniel T. Gleason. *History Teacher.* v.5, March 1972, pp. 31-39.
Purpose: "a history teacher's evaluations of films he has found particularly useful"
Grade level: secondary
Arrangement: tabular listing (pp. 38-39) following narrative
Subjects: American history
Entries: 42
running time, producer, distributor, release date; teaching suggestions in main body of article
omitted: price
Indexes:
Period covered: 1956-1968
Revision and updating:
Media represented: films

17-14 (cont'd)
Producers represented: CBS, NBC television networks, others
Features: "Reviews-Media" column appears regularly and contains signed critical
reviews of films, including films produced for television, and other media.
Subject terms:
American history
history

17-15* **Journal of Geography.** National Council for Geographic Education,
115 North Marion Street, Oak Park, IL 60301, $20.00/year.
Purpose: "Media Review" in most issues; announcements and in-depth reviews
Grade level: secondary
Arrangement: random
Subjects: geography
Entries: appr. 20/year

running time, producer, release date (not in all cases); sale price; contents
note (films); critical review (other media)
Indexes: indexed in *Media Review Digest* (01-03)
Period covered: current releases
Revision and updating: published 7x/year
Media represented: films, slides, kits
Producers represented: various
Features:
Subject terms: geography

17-16* **Criminal Justice Audiovisual Materials Directory.** Law Enforcement
Assistance Administration. 2d ed. Superintendent of Documents,
Washington, DC 20402, 1976. 120p. $2.05. S/N 027-000-00436-9.
ED 135 346.
Purpose: comprehensive
Grade level: secondary
Arrangement: topical
Subjects: courts   prevention
police techniques   prisons
and training   public education
Entries: appr. 1000

title, format, running time (films), distributor; rental price; release date
(films); contents summary
omitted: date, price (filmstrips)
Indexes: none
Period covered: 1960s-1970s
Revision and updating:
Media represented: films, filmstrips, slides, video recordings
Producers represented: appr. 130 commercial, academic, government
Features:
Subject terms: government and law

17-17*   Films: Historical Preservation and Related Subjects. National Trust
for Historic Preservation, 740-748 Jackson Place, NW, Washington,
DC 20006, 1976. 87p. price not known.
Purpose: comprehensive; "compiled from libraries throughout the country"
Grade level: intermediate, secondary
Arrangement: 21 topical groupings
Subjects: archaeology   handicrafts   preservation/
architecture   history   restoration
art   history, transportation unique communities
building crafts   horticulture   urban planning
conservation/ecology museums   vanishing trades
Entries: appr. 900

running time, release date (generally), distributor; rental price; contents
note
omitted: grade level, producer, awards won
Indexes: title
Period covered: available at time of publication
Revision and updating:
Media represented: films
Producers represented: various commercial, government, institutional, including
foreign
Features: Includes award winners from the Trust's annual National Film and Video
Competition and films available on loan from the Trust. "The distributor with
the lowest rental charge has been listed." [Similar list: *Films for Arts and
Crafts* (20-02) includes titles on architecture and urban development.]
Subject terms:
American history   urban studies
crafts   visual arts

17-18*   Media; An Annotated Catalogue of Law-Related Audio-Visual Materials.
Susan E. Davison. American Bar Association, 1155 East 60th Street,
Chicago, IL 60637, 1975. 88p. single copies free. ED 107 553.
Purpose: comprehensive
Grade level: all
Arrangement: 7 topical categories
Subjects: The Bill of Rights   the political process
The Constitution   practical law
current issues   teaching of law
origins and basic concepts of law
Entries: over 400

running time, format details, producer, release date, price; contents summary;
grade level
Indexes: title and producer (not in ERIC copy)
Period covered: chiefly 1970s
Revision and updating: previous edition 1973; 17-12
Media represented: audio recordings, films, filmstrips, kits, slides, video recordings
Producers represented: 70, including commercial, academic, bar associations, etc.

17-18 (cont'd)
Features: Films and media for the secondary level make up the bulk of the listings. Supplements *Bibliography of Law-Related Curriculum Materials: Annotated* (1976) and *Gaming* (17-24). The same author highlights about 30 "Curriculum Materials and Resources for Law-Related Education" in *Social Education*, v.41, March 1977, pp. 184-193, in an article chiefly devoted to recommending reference books for teachers, curriculum guides, text, related books for young people, etc.
Subject terms:
    contemporary issues
    government and law

17-19*   **Social Studies Curriculum Materials Data Book.** Social Science Education Consortium, Inc., 855 Broadway, Boulder, CO 80302; 3v. $75.00. **Supplement** $20.00/year. LC 71-164951.
Purpose: "to provide analyses of curriculum materials which will allow administrators, curriculum coordinators, college methods teachers, and elementary and secondary school teachers to select materials which are appropriate to their students, school, and community on the basis of grade levels, discipline, underlying philosophy, goals, strategies, structure, content, innovativeness and merit"; evaluations
Grade level: all
Arrangement: games and simulations, supplementary materials
Subjects: all aspects of social studies, including multi- and inter-disciplinary studies, affective education, women's studies, etc.; humanities
Entries: several hundred

    (games) developer, publisher, publication date; number of players, time required, format data; price; grade level; critical review; subject terms; validation information
Indexes: grade level, subject, author or developer, publisher
Period covered: 1970s, some earlier, bulk 1971-73
Revision and updating: published March 15th and October 15th each year
Media represented: audio recordings, filmstrips, kits, slides, simulation games
Producers: various commercial, academic
Features: Primarily evaluates textbooks and project materials, also teacher resources. [Similar list: 01-15.]
Subject terms:
    guidance   women's studies
    social studies

17-20*   **Films on the Future; A Selective Listing.** Marie Martin. World Future Society, 4916 St. Elmo Avenue, Washington, DC 20014, 1977. 68p. $6.00pa.
Purpose: Films that "can contribute to our study of alternative futures," not all previewed
Grade level: intermediate, secondary
Arrangement: 18 topical groupings

17-20 (cont'd)

Subjects:		
arts	education	ocean/ocean
automation/computers	energy	sciences
biology & medical/	environment/pollu-	science fiction
behavioral sciences	tion/weather	sociology/life
cities/urban	food/population	styles/women
planning	forecasts	space/space
communications/	human values	sciences
transportation	international relations/	technology/business/
ecology	politics	industry

Entries: appr. 250

running time, producer, release date; rental source & order number; synopsis;
awards won
omitted: rental price (in most cases); grade level
Indexes: none
Period covered: 1966-1976
Revision and updating: previous edition 1973
Media represented: films
Producers represented: appr. 60 rental sources
Features: Also lists of 40 "short films" (under 15 min.) and 15 film series. [Similar
list: *Teaching the Future* by Draper L. Kauffman (ETC Publications, Palm
Springs, CA 92262, 1976. $12.95; $7.95pa.) recommends 22 pre-1973 titles.
Subject terms: futures

17-21* **American Issues Forum.** Educational Film Library Association, 43 West
61st Street, New York, NY 10023, 1975. 32p. $1.00pa.
Purpose: recommendations
Grade level: secondary
Arrangement: 9 topical groupings

Subjects:		
America in the world	growing up in America	a more perfect union
the business of America	life, liberty and the	a nation of nations
certain unalienable	pursuit of happiness	working in
rights	land of plenty	America

Entries: appr. 200

running time, distributor, release date; evaluative annotation
omitted: price
Indexes: title
Period covered: available at time of publication
Revision and updating:
Media represented: films
Producers represented: various
Features: Other guides for the Bicentennial are mentioned in the introduction to
this section.
Subject terms:

American history	government and law
economics	international education
ethnic studies	

17-22* **Cities.** Dwight W. Hoover. Bowker, 1976. 231p. $15.50.
Purpose: recommendations selected on the basis of "contemporaneity and availability"
Grade level: all
Arrangement: 23 topical categories
Subjects: the city in perspective   (also cont'd) education, ethnics,
the city in practice   housing, transportation, etc.
also: blacks, crime,
Entries: appr. 200 (excluding print)

running time, format details, producer, sale or rental price; release date; contents summary; grade level
Indexes: title
Period covered: 1964-1974
Revision and updating:
Media represented: audio recordings, filmloops, films, filmstrips, simulation games, slides, transparencies
Producers represented: various commercial and academic
Features: Also lists over 800 books.
Subject terms:
contemporary issues   urban studies
ethnic studies

17-23* **A Selective Bibliography of Audio-Visual Materials Reflecting a Civil Liberties Theme.** Barbara Eichman. American Civil Liberties Union, 22 East 40th Street, New York, NY 10016, 1976. 76p. $1.00pa.
Purpose: comprehensive
Grade level: intermediate, secondary
Arrangement: by media and subject
Subjects: Bill of Rights, Constitution, Supreme Court
Entries: appr. 150

running time, producer or distributor, release date, sale & rental price; grade level; contents summary; information supplied by distributor
Indexes: title, distributor
Period covered: available at time of publication
Revision and updating:
Media represented: audio recordings, films, filmstrips, simulation games
Producers represented: 40 commercial, academic, organizations
Features: Chiefly for secondary level.
Subject terms: government and law

17-24* **Gaming: An Annotated Catalogue of Law-Related Games and Simulations.** Susan E. Davison. American Bar Association, 1155 East 60th Street, Chicago, IL 60637, 1975. 39p. single copies free. ED 114 307.
Purpose: comprehensive
Grade level: secondary
Arrangement: six topical groupings

17-24 (cont'd)
Subjects: basic concepts of law   current issues
           The Bill of Rights   the political process
           The Constitution   teacher resources
Entries: appr. 125

      producer, release date, price; time & number of players required; contents summary; grade level
Indexes: no
Period covered: 1967-1975
Revision and updating: 17-12
Media represented: simulation games
Producers represented: appr. 40
Features: Supplements *Bibliography of Law-Related Curriculum Materials: Annotated* (1976) and *Media* (17-18). The same author highlights about 30 "Curriculum Materials and Resources for Law-Related Education" in *Social Education*, v.41, March 1977, pp. 184-193.
Subject terms:
       contemporary issues
       government and law

17-25*   **"Images of the Future in Popular Music."** *Social Education*, v.39, May 1975, pp. 276-285.
Purposes: "encourage students to examine social problems, to think reflectively about ethical issues, and to probe their personal values"; recommendations to stimulate discussion
Grade level: secondary
Arrangement: 10 topical groupings
Subjects: civil rights   political power
           ecology   rejection of society
           future   self-awareness
           individual freedom and   social change
            personal integrity   war
            old age and death
Entries: 112

      performers and song titles only
Indexes:
Period represented: 1970s
Revision and updating:
Media represented: audio recordings
Producers represented: various
Features: Also resource books for students and teachers. "Exploring the Future through Contemporary Music," by B. Lee Cooper, *Media and Methods*, v.12, April 1976, pp. 32-35, recommends 56 folk and popular songs that may be used to explore the generation gap, technological change, political participation, personal freedom, equal opportunity, civil liberty, old age, and death.
Subject terms: futures

17-26* An Annotated and Classified List of 16mm Films on Urban Studies: New Towns, Urban Problems, City and Regional Planning. (Exchange Bibliography #838). Council of Planning Librarians, P.O. Box 229, Monticello, IL 61856, 1975. 33p. $3.00pa. ED 115 537.

Purpose: comprehensive
Grade level: secondary
Arrangement: 5 topical categories
Subjects: cinematic and artistic impression   new towns and cities
                    of cities   urban planning and
                 ghetto problems, slums and skid   urban renewal
                    rows   urban problems
Entries: over 100

running time, release date; rental source; contents summary; annotations quoted from distributors' catalogs
        omitted: price, audience suitability
Indexes: none
Period covered: 1960-1973
Revision and updating:
Media represented: films
Producers represented: various, including foreign
Features:
Subject terms: urban studies

17-27* A Selected List of Urban, Environmental and Social Problem Gaming/ Simulations. Barbara Steinwachs. Michigan University Extension Gaming Service, 412 Maynard Street, Ann Arbor, MI 48109, 1977. 27p. ED 135 667.

Purpose: comprehensive
Grade level: secondary
Arrangement: by publisher
Subjects: social problems
Entries: appr. 100

producer, price; theme of games; number of players and time required
        omitted: publication date
Indexes: title
Period covered: available at time of writing
Revision and updating: previous editions 1972, 1974, 1976
Media represented: simulation games
Producers represented: University of Michigan and commercial vendors
Features: Primarily designed for professional and community groups; also includes information on games requiring computer facilities.
Subject terms:
            contemporary issues   urban studies
            energy and environment education

17-28* Urban Gaming/Simulation '77; An Ongoing Conference for Educators and Trainers. Larry C. Coppard and Frederick L. Goodman. University of Michigan, Publications Distribution Service, 615 East University Avenue, Ann Arbor, MI 48106, 1977. 376p. $12.00pa.

17-28 (cont'd)
Purpose: evaluations by "persons who have either directed, played, or designed urban gaming/simulations" of "materials . . . of value"
Grade level: secondary
Arrangement: alphabetical title
Subjects: economics   land use
education   others
environmental management
Entries: 66

designer, distributor, price; game intent, resource requirements (time, number of players, computer facilities, materials); subject, instructional uses; detailed play description; extensive signed comments
omitted: production date
Indexes: none
Period covered: "games currently in use"
Revision and updating: annual (planned)
Media represented: simulation games
Producers represented: various academic, commercial, individuals
Features: Primarily designed for higher education and community use.
Subject terms: urban studies

18-Ethnic Studies

Increased interest in this topic in the two-and-one-half years since the first edition is reflected in many recently published comprehensive general titles that cover individual groups adequately. Attention to ethnic diversity among the white population is also a new departure.

For media on countries of origin and their cultures, references cited in 19—World Cultures and International Education are relevant.

Publications of the Council on Interracial Books for Children examine text and trade books for evidences of racism and other biases. No such service exists for non-print media though the social science education consortium has prepared an *Ethnic Materials Analysis Instrument* (ED 128 279).

Selected Audiovisuals on Mental Heatlh (15-09) includes material on minority groups that can be used in high school settings. The *Children's Book and Music Center* places emphasis on multi-cultural education by offering many such recordings in its catalog (01-26). *Multicultural Resources for Children* (Box 2945, Stanford CA 94305, 1977. $4.00) is a bibliography mainly of books but also of posters and study prints, simulation games, bilingual materials, art, music, etc.

The music of ethnic groups is represented in *The Elementary School Library Collection* (01-09) while ethnic dance films may be found in *Catalog of Dance Films* (14-07).

Native Americans

The Reference Encyclopedia of the American Indian (2d ed. Todd Publications, Rye, NY 10580, 1974. 2v. $30.00, provides names and addresses of federal, state, and regional government agencies, the tribes they serve, and their populations. *Federal and State Indian Reservations and Indian Trust Areas* (Superintendent of Documents, Washington, DC 20402, 1974. 604p. $5.90. S/N 0311-00076), a state-by-state listing, gives brief synopses of each reservation's legal status, address and exact location, tribe and its history, economy, government, community facilities, population, etc. Other government publications include *Indian Images: Photographs of North American Indians, 1847-1928* (Superintendent of Documents, 1974. 33p. $1.05. S/N 4701-0107), an exhibition catalog, and from the National Archives, Washington, DC 20408: *Cartographic Records in the National Archives of the United States Relation to American Indians.*

A Guide to Slide and Photograph Collection of Primitive Art (20-06) indicates visuals available from museums. "American Indian Periodical Literature: A Selective Bibliography," by Jim Buchanan (RQ, v.16, Spring 1977, pp. 225-230) lists tribal and religious organizations, schools, and government agencies publishing periodicals. The "Alternative Periodicals" column in *Wilson Library Bulletin* listed Native American periodicals in its February and April 1977 issues.

See also entries 18-10, 18-11, 18-12, 18-21 and 18-22.

Spanish-Speaking

Reference is made to 02–Bilingual Education and to 11–Language Arts (Foreign Language). *Puerto Ricans in the Continental United States: An Uncertain Future* (1976. 157p.) is available free from the U.S. Commission on Civil Rights, Washington, DC 20425. See also entries 18-07, 18-08, and 18-09.

Blacks

Fourteen public television programs and series on Black American culture are available on videotape from the Public Television Library (43-02). *Roots* is distributed on film by a commercial vendor. *Alternatives in Print* (01-21) indexes Black Liberation materials.

The treatment of Blacks in American movies is discussed in these titles, all supplying filmographies:

Black Films and Film-Makers; A Comprehensive Anthology from Stereotype to Superhero. Lindsay Patterson. Dodd, Mead, 1975. $12.50. "Selected Filmography," pp. 269-281, is a listing of some 400 titles. The book's index will locate mention of some of these in the text. Seven films are discussed at length in separate articles.

Blacks in American Movies: A Selected Bibliography. Anne Powers. Scarecrow, 1974. $6.00. "Filmography: Features by and about Blacks 1904-1930," pp. 142-50, lists about 80 films.

The Black Man on Film: Racial Stereotyping. Richard A. Maynard. Hayden Book
Company, Inc. Rochelle Park, NJ 07662. 1974. $4.95. "Filmography"
p. 126-134 of over 60 silents, features stereotypes of the 1930s-1950s, war
propaganda films with Black actors, all-Black features, social drama con-
cerning Blacks, "The Sidney Poitier Stereotype", and Black filmmakers.
See also entries 18-03, 18-05, 18-06, 18-23 and 18-24.

Asian Americans

See 18-14 and 18-16 with over 200 and 49 titles respectively, also 18-02.

White Ethnics

The general guides 18-15 and 18-16 cover every conceivable group. See also
18-25.

18-01   **People: Annotated Multi-Ethnic Bibliography K-12.** Delores D. Gilmore.
Montgomery County Public Schools, Rockville, MD 20850. 1973. 345p.
ED 099 864.
Purpose: comprehensive; supplements earlier bibliographies on Black Americans
Grade level: all
Arrangement: by subject, plus "late entries" section
Subjects: all Americans   Native Americans
             Asian Americans   Puerto Rican Americans
             Jewish Americans   other hyphenated
             Mexican Americans   Americans
Entries: appr. 200 (excluding print)

non-print media marked by asterisk; type of medium, producer, price, grade
level; release date in some cases; contents note only where title is not self-
explanatory
Indexes: title
Period covered: 1960s-1973
Revision and updating:
Media represented: audio recordings, filmstrips, filmloops, kits, graphic materials,
slides, transparencies
Producers represented: various commercial, Pacifica radio
Features: Print media predominate, and there are very few audiovisual titles in
the "Other Hyphenated Americans" chapter. For more recent lists from
similar sources see 18-17 and titles referred to there.
Subject terms:
             ethnic studies

18-02   **Asians and Asian Americans.** San Francisco Unified School District,
San Francisco, CA 94102, 1972. 34p. ED 085 452.

18-02 (cont'd)
Purpose: "a selected bibliography of some good and outstanding audio-visual
educational materials"
Grade level: all
Arrangement: 7 topical groupings
Subjects: Chinese-Americans   Oceania
           East Asia   South Asia
           Hawaii   Southeast Asia
           Japanese-Americans
Entries: over 100

    format, release date; grade level; full critical annotation
        omitted: ordering information
Indexes: no
Period covered: 1960s, some earlier
Revision and updating:
Media represented: films, filmstrips, graphic materials
Producers represented: not known
Features: Films make up two-thirds of the listing, which includes materials on
    ethnic groups in general. As this list was compiled for internal use, it
    must be used in conjunction with a film library catalog. [Similar lists:
    The San Francisco Schools also compiled resource guides for *Black
    America* (ED 085 453) and *North American Indians and Eskimo* (ED
    085 454).]
Subject terms:
    ethnic studies
    world cultures

18-03   Index to Black History and Studies (Multimedia). 2d ed. National
             Information Center for Educational Media, University of Southern
             California, University Park, Los Angeles, CA 90007, 1973. 189p.
             $19.50. LC 73-78921.
Purpose: comprehensive
Grade level: all
Arrangement: alphabetical title
Subjects: Africa–culture   education   professions
           Africa–past   1866-1915   recreation and
           Afro-American culture   employment   sports
           agriculture   famous personalities religions
           arts and crafts   1492-1865   segregation and
           business   housing   integration
           civil rights   literature   social problems
           Civil War period   1915 to present   songs and music
           economic conditions   other countries
Entries: 10,000

    type of medium, format data, producer, distributor, release date; grade
    level; contents annotation; out-of-print titles are so noted
        omitted: price
Indexes: subject, subdivided by media

18-03 (cont'd)
Period covered: mainly 1960s
Revision and updating: 1st ed. 1971
Media represented: filmloops, filmstrips, films, transparencies, audio recordings, video recordings
Producers represented: 500 commercial, institutional, government (including foreign); public television
Features: Other NICEM indexes offer no subject headings starting with "Black" and only "Negro History" under "History—US." The present volume uses only 25 subject terms to access 10,000 titles, which results in unduly long listings under each.
Subject terms:
    Africa   world cultures
    Black studies

18-04* **"Ethnic America."** Linda Artel. *Sightlines*, v.9, Spring 1976, p. 13-20.
Purpose: recommended "quality films"
Grade level: all
Arrangement: 9 ethnic groups
Subjects: cultural traditions   history of ethnic groups
              current efforts
Entries: 33
    running time, producer, director, release date; full summary
        omitted: price, audience suitability
Indexes:
Period covered: 1970-1975 (a few earlier)
Revision and updating:
Media represented: films
Producers represented: 23
Features: [Similar lists: *Focus on Ethnic Literature in the Classroom* (*Indiana English Journal*, v.11, Spring 1977). Indiana Council of Teachers of English, Indiana State University, Terre Haute, IN 47809. 34p. ED 139 037; "American Ethnic Studies and Film" (*Sightlines*, v.11, Fall 1977, p. 18-19.]
Subject terms:
    ethnic studies

18-05   **The Black Experience in Children's Audiovisual Materials.** Office of the Branch Libraries, New York Public Library, 8 East 40th Street, New York, NY 10016, 1973. 32p. $1.00pa. ED 091 067.
Purpose: recommended materials that "have proven to be popular with children'
Grade level: primary, intermediate
Arrangement: by media
Subjects: Blacks
Entries: over 200
    label and number (recordings); running time, producer (films); evaluative summary
        omitted: price, release date, grade level

18-05 (cont'd)
Indexes: none
Period covered: available at time of publication
Revision and updating:
Media represented: audio recordings, films, filmstrips, kits
Producers represented: various
Features: Recordings make up one-half of listings, films one-third. The 61 "Most Used Titles" of the New York Public Library film collection are found in "Films for Kids in the Minority" (*Film Library Quarterly*, v.9, no. 3, 1976, pp. 46-52).
Subject terms:
    Black studies
    world cultures

18-06   **Films for Black Studies: A Selected List.** Pennsylvania State University, Audio-Visual Services, Willard Building, University Park, PA 16802, 1973. 21p. free.
Purpose: "not a complete listing of all the films about black studies which are available from the Penn State collection, but it include many relevant films . . . with an emphasis on the values and contributions of black people"
Grade level: all
Arrangement: alphabetical title
Subjects: Africa   civil rights movement
             Blacks and the arts   welfare and poverty
             Black-White relations   others
             Blacks and cities
Entries: appr. 180

    running time, producer, release date, rental fee; grade level; contents summary
Indexes: subject
Period covered: 1964-1972
Revision and updating: *Newsletter*
Media represented: films
Producers represented: various, including commercial and public television
Features: Chiefly selections for secondary and adult levels.
Subject terms:
    Africa   urban studies
    Black studies

18-07   **Mexican Americans: Resources to Build Cultural Understanding.** Lois B. Jordan. Libraries Unlimited, Littleton, Colo. 80160, 1973. 265p. $8.50. LC 72-94302.
Purpose: recommendations; "Audio-Visual Materials," pp. 121-165
Grade level: secondary
Arrangement: by media
Subjects: Mexican Americans
Entries: 277 (excluding print)

    running time, format, producer, distributor, release date; synopsis of varying length
        omitted: price, addresses of film distributors

18-07 (cont'd)
Indexes: author, title, subject
Period covered: 1949-1971
Revision and updating:
Media represented: films, filmstrips, filmloops, audio recordings, maps, graphic
    materials, slides, transparencies, kits
Producers represented: various
Features: Films and filmstrips total over 200 of the audiovisual entries; there
    are over 700 print titles in Part I.
Subject terms:
      bilingual education   Latin America
      foreign language   Spanish-speaking

18-08   **Spanish Heritage and Influence in the Western Hemisphere.** San
        Francisco Unified School District, San Francisco, CA 94102, 1972.
        49p. ED 085 455.
Purpose: recommendations of "good and outstanding audiovisual educational
    materials"
Grade level: all
Arrangement: by media within 8 topics
Subjects: art, music, food   Spanish language
            early California   Spanish-speaking countries
            Mexican-Americans   and peoples
            pre-Columbian civilization   U.S. expansion
            Spanish influence in the Americas
Entries: appr. 200
      running time, release date; grade level; critical evaluation
      omitted: ordering information
Indexes: none
Period covered: 1950s-1960s
Revision and updating:
Media represented: films, filmstrips, graphic materials
Producers represented: various
Features: The majority of the listings are films, though there are also a good many
    study prints. Includes coverage of Puerto Rico and the Philippines. Compiled
    for internal use, it must be used in conjunction with a film library catalog.
Subject terms:
      Latin America
      Spanish-speaking

18-09   **The Puerto Ricans: An Annotated Bibliography.** Paquita Vivó. Bowker,
        1973. 299p. $15.95. LC 73-8825.
Purpose: Section IV is a comprehensive list of audiovisual media; book attempts
    "complete bibliographic overview"
Grade level: all
Arrangement: alphabetical by title within media groupings
Subjects: Puerto Ricans

18-09 (cont'd)
Entries: appr. 100

running time, producer, availability of teachers' guide; release date in some
cases; brief synopsis
        omitted: distributor, price, grade level
Indexes: author, title, subject
Period covered: 1950s-1972
Revision and updating:
Media represented: films, filmstrips
Producers represented: commercial, academic, government, TV networks
Features: Two-thirds of audiovisual media listed are films, including Spanish
    language films. Sections I-III list books, pamphlets, periodicals, government
    publications (for professional use). [See also chapter on Spanish-speaking
    in 18-14.]
Subject terms:
        Spanish-speaking

18-10   **Bibliography of Nonprint Instructional Materials on the American
        Indian.** Institute of American Indian Studies, Brigham Young
        University, Provo, Utah 84601, 1972. 221p. $2.95pa. ED 070 310.
Purpose: comprehensive
Grade level: all
Arrangement: alphabetical title
Subjects: American Indian
Entries: 1400

type of medium, format details, producer, release date; availability of
teachers' guide; grade level; synopsis; subject terms
        omitted: price
Indexes: subject (36p.)
Period covered: mainly 1960s, some earlier
Revision and updating:
Media represented: films, filmloops, filmstrips, slides, transparencies, graphic
    materials, maps, audio recordings, kits
Producers represented: various, including government
Features: Includes materials on the Eskimo, pre-Columbian peoples, and on art,
    music, industry, and legends of various tribes with detailed subject access.
    [Similar list: *Native American Resources: Annotated Bibliography of Print
    and Non-Print Materials.* Minority Group Study Center, Mankato, MN 56001.
    1975. ED 155 634.]
Subject terms: Latin America, Native Americans

18-11   **Filmography for American Indian Education.** Carroll W. Williams and
        Gloria Bird. Zia Cine Inc., P.O. Box 493, Santa Fe, NM 87501, 1973.
        201p. $5.00. ED 091 101.
Purpose: recommendations
Grade level: all
Arrangement: alphabetical title, plus addenda and BIA films
Subjects: American Indians

18-11 (cont'd)
Entries: appr. 400

running time, distributor, sale and rental price; contents summary
omitted: grade level, release date
Indexes: title
Period covered: available at time of publication
Revision and updating:
Media represented: films
Producers represented: various, including Bureau of Indian Affairs
Features: Frequently lists alternate distributors with varying rental charges.
Subject terms: Native Americans

18-12*   **A Bibliography of Selected Materials of the Navajo and Zuni.** Gallup-
McKinley County Public Schools, Gallup, NM 87301, 1974. 88p.
ED 124 367.
Purpose: comprehensive; "Audiovisual aids" pp. 35-82
Grade level: all
Arrangement: by media
Subjects: Navajo
Zuni
Entries: over 400

running time, producer, release date (not in all cases), sale price; contents
summary, grade level
Indexes: none
Period covered: available at time of publications; 1940s-1973
Revision and updating:
Media represented: audio recordings, filmloops, films, filmstrips, graphic materials,
free and inexpensive publications, kits, maps, transparencies
Producers represented: appr. 100 commercial; also Navajo Tribal Museum, Window
Rock, AZ
Features: Information supplied is taken from publishers catalogs. Also lists books
and Indian-published and other periodicals.
Subject terms:
Native Americans

18-13*   **American Folklore Films and Videotapes; An Index.** Center for Southern
Folklore, 1216 Peabody Avenue, P.O. Box 4081, Memphis, TN 38104,
1976. 338p. illus. $15.00pa.
Purpose: comprehensive
Grade level: all
Arrangement: by media

Subjects:	American folk experience	arts & crafts	folktales
	and tradition	music	folklore and
	ceremonies and	dance	the writer
	celebrations	folk religion	occupational lore

18-13 (cont'd)
Entries: over 1800

> running time, producer, release date; university rental sources (including ordering number); contents summary
> > omitted: price, grade level

Indexes: subject (96p.)
Period covered: through 1975
Revision and updating: annual supplements are planned
Media represented: films, video recordings
Producers represented: various commercial, academic, independent, institutional, instructional television
Features: A handsomely produced and illustrated volume.
Subject terms:

American history	literature
the arts	music
ethnic studies	

18-14* **Ethnic American Minorities; A Guide to Media and Materials.** Harry A. Johnson. Bowker, 1976. 304p. $16.50. LC 76-25038.
Purpose: materials "selected on the basis of availability, authenticity, suitability and relevance . . . in some cases because they were the only ones available"
Grade level: all
Arrangement: 5 subject chapter, subdivided by media
Subjects:

Afro-Americans	Spanish-speaking Americans
Asian-Americans	other ethnic minorities
Native Indian Americans	

Entries: appr. 1100

> running time, producer, release date (not in all cases); grade level; purchase and rental price; contents summary

Indexes: subject, title
Period covered: 1970s, some earlier
Revision and updating:
Media represented: audio recordings, films, filmstrips, graphic materials, slides, transparencies, video recordings
Producers: over 200 commercial, organizations, industrial, academic
Features: Full introductions to each chapter (including bibliographies) by experts. *Selected Films and Filmstrips on Four Ethnic American Minorities* (ED 116 702), compiled by the same author, represents an earlier version recommending primarily filmstrips and excluding "other ethnic minorities."
Subject terms:
> ethnic studies

18-15* **Ethnic Information Sources of the United States.** Paul Wasserman. Gale, 1976. 750p. $45.00. LC 76-4642.
Purpose: "Audiovisual Materials" and "Books and Pamphlets" listed under most headings; descriptive
Grade level: intermediate, secondary
Arrangement: 90 ethnic groups

18-15 (cont'd)
Subjects: ethnic studies
Entries: over 1000 (excluding hard-cover books)

running time, producer/distributor, release date (not in all cases); contents
summary
omitted: distributor's address, number of pages (print), prices,
audience suitability
Indexes: none
Period covered: 1950s-1974
Revision and updating:
Media represented: films, free and inexpensive materials, maps
Producers represented: various institutional, commercial
Features: Excludes Blacks, American Indians and Eskimos. Lists organizations,
newspapers, magazines, radio programs, foundations, research centers, etc.
Includes chapters on Canadians, Portuguese and some other groups not
found in *Building Ethnic Collections* (18-16).
Subject terms: ethnic studies

18-16* **Building Ethnic Collections; An Annotated Guide for School Media
Centers and Public Libraries.** Lois Buttlar & Lubomyr Wynar. Libraries
Unlimited, 1977. 434p. $18.50.
Purpose: "Audiovisual Materials (Multi-Ethnic)" pp. 47-53 and at the end of
each chapter; recommendations on basis of preview or published reviews
Grade level: all
Arrangement: 37 individual ethnic groups
Subjects: (in order of length of listings)

Black-Americans	Appalachian-Americans
American Indians	Chinese-Americans
Mexican Americans	Spanish-speaking Americans
multi-ethnic	British-Americans
Japanese-Americans	German-Americans
Puerto Rican Americans	others
Jewish Americans	

Entries: appr. 471 (excluding print)

running time, producer, release date; grade level; contents summary; format
data
omitted: price (in most cases)
Indexes: title
Period covered: in print 1976 (with some exceptions)
Revision and updating:
Media represented: audio recordings, filmloops, films, filmstrips, graphic materials,
kits, maps, slides, transparencies, video recordings
Producers represented: over 200 commercial, institutional, government, academic
Features: Total 2873 titles in 2286 entries, including fiction, non-fiction,
curriculum publications, filmographies, etc. Strong coverage of white
ethnic groups.
Subject terms: ethnic studies

18-17* Annotated Bibliography of Multi-Ethnic Curriculum Materials. Midwest
Center for Equal Educational Opportunity, University of Missouri, 408
Hitt Street, Columbia, MO 65201. 1974-1977. free. ED 114 378-
114-381, 129 703.
Purpose: recommendations; catalog of materials available on free loan from Center
Grade level: all
Arrangement: by media
Subjects: ethnic studies
Entries: over 100/year (excluding print and professional)

running time or format data, producer, purchase price, release date; grade
level; detailed contents; subject terms (films)
Indexes: planned subject index to series
Period covered: releases of previous 2 years; entire series covers 1967-1976
Revision and updating: original volume 1974; 2 semi-annual supplements
1975—
Media represented: audio recordings, films, filmstrips, graphic materials, free
and inexpensive publications, kits, simulation games
Producers represented: appr. 100
Features: Also books and materials on interpersonal relationships. [Similar
catalogs issued by local or state educational agencies: *Multi-Ethnic Materials,
A Selected Bibliography* (Racine, WI, Unified School District, 1976. 78p.
ED 129 957); *A Bibliography of Materials on the American Indian and
Spanish Speaking* (Michigan Department of Education, 1975. ED 122 985);
With Liberty and Justice for All (Indiana Department of Public Instruction,
1975. ED 120 751); *A Selected Annotated Bibliography of Material Relating
to Racism, Blacks, Chicanos, Native Americans and Multi-Ethnicity* (Michigan
Education Association, Division of Minority Affairs, P.O. Box 873, East
Lansing, MI 48823, 1973-75. ED 117 230-1, 117 290); *A Community of
People; A Multi-Ethnic Bibliography* (Educational Media Department, Portland Public Schools, Portland, OR 97208, 1974. 135p. ED 121 872). See
also 18-01.]
Subject terms:
ethnic studies
women's studies

18-18* Journal of American Folklore. 1703 New Hampshire Avenue, NW,
Washington, DC 20009. $18.00/year.
Purpose: "Record Reviews" and "Film Reviews" are regular columns
Grade level: secondary
Arrangement: topical (films); geographical or ethnic groups (records)
Subjects: folk cultural films, folk music films, folk narrative films
Entries: over 100/year

(films) running time, producer; signed critical review
omitted: release date, price
(records) review essays critiquing a number of records, stating label and
number
omitted: release date, price
Indexes:

18-18 (cont'd)
Period covered: not known
Revision and updating: published 4x/year
Media represented: audio recordings, films
Producers represented: U.S. and foreign
Features: covers various regions and ethnic groups in the United States and
    Europe, Africa, Canada.
Subject terms:

    ethnic studies   world cultures
    music

18-19*   **Materials and Human Resources for Teaching Ethnic Studies: An
Annotated Bibliography.** Social Science Education Consortium,
855 Broadway, Boulder, CO 80302, 1975. 275p. $7.95pa. ED 128 233.
Purpose: descriptive
Grade level: all
Arrangement: by ethnic and religious group, and grade level
Subjects: ethnic groups in U.S. only
Entries: appr. 100 (excluding print)

    producer, contents summary
        omitted: running time, release date (generally), price
Indexes: none
Period covered: 1950s–
Revision and updating:
Media represented: films
Producers represented: various
Features: Primarily an evaluative listing of appr. 1500 curricular materials, books
    for students and teachers. [Similar lists: "Audio-Visual Resources" in *Good
    Reading for the Disadvantaged Reader; Multi-Ethnic Resources*, by George D.
    Spache (Garrard, 1975. $5.75pa.) lists media titles, mediagraphies (some from
    the 1960s) but is primarily a guide to sources. *An Ethnic Dimension in
    American History; A Unit on Immigration, Industrialization, Urbanization
    and Imperialism 1880-1920* (Anti-Defamation League of B'nai B'rith, 315
    Lexington Avenue, New York, NY 10016, n.d. $1.50. ED 130 944) recom-
    mends 25 filmstrips and other media.]
Subject terms: ethnic studies

18-20*   **Appalachian Books and Media for Public and College Libraries.** George E.
Bennett. West Virginia University Library, Morgantown, VW 26505,
1975. 85p. $3.00pa.
Purpose: recommendations; "Media" p. 67-81
Grade level: intermediate, secondary
Arrangement: by media
Subjects: Appalachian regional studies, folklore and music
Entries: appr. 100 (excluding print)

    (films and videotapes) running time, producer, sale price, release date
    (generally, except for audio recordings); contents note
        omitted: grade level

18-20 (cont'd)
Indexes: none
Period covered: in-print materials only
Revision and updating:
Media represented: audio recordings, films, video recordings, graphic materials
Producers represented: various, including television documentaries
Features: "Picture Books" pp. 25-27 identifies 15 books of photographs, drawings and paintings. Phonograph recordings make up almost two-thirds of media listings.
Subject terms:
  energy and environment education   social studies
  music

18-21*   **American Indian Reference Book.** eARTh, P.O. Box 95, Portage, MI 49081, P.O. Box 2275, Alexandria, VA 22301, 1976. 308p. $9.95pa. ED 134 391.
Purpose: pages 243-306 list audiovisual media; comprehensive
Grade level: all
Arrangement: by media
Subjects:
Entries: appr. 475 (excluding print)

  running time, producer, release date (generally);
    omitted: price, grade level, contents
Indexes: none
Period covered: 1950s-1974
Revision and updating:
Media represented: audio recordings, filmloops, films, filmstrips
Producers represented: appr. 100
Features: Compilers are Native Americans. Over 200 films and records each.
  [Similar list: The National Indian Association's funded *Project Media* (1115 Second Avenue South, Minneapolis, MN 55403) aims to establish a comprehensive data base of *Native American Evaluations of Media Materials*. Two volumes published in 1977 ($70.00) contain extensive listings of books. *Index to Bibliographies and Resource Materials* (1975. $4.50pa. 225p. ED 118 341) describes some 500 titles from the 1960s, mainly recordings.]
Subject terms: Native Americans

18-22*   **Cultures in the North:Aleut; Athabascan Indian; Eskimo; Haida Indian; Tlingit Indian; Tsimshian Indian. Multi-Media Resource List.** Center for Northern Educational Research, Alaska University, Fairbanks, AK 99701, 1975. 51p. ED 108 809.
Purpose: comprehensive; chosen from distributor catalogs without previewing
Grade level: all
Arrangement: by tribe
Subjects: Alaskan Natives

18-22 (cont'd)
Entries: appr. 135

running time, producer/distributor; rental source; annotation from catalog description
    omitted: release date (in most cases), grade level, price
Indexes: title
Period covered: available at time of publication
Revision and updating:
Media represented: audio recordings, filmloops, films, filmstrips, manipulative materials, slides, video recordings
Producers represented: various, including museums, National Film Board of Canada
Features: Also books, periodicals, professional materials, materials in production. Inaccurate portrayals are said to be present in almost all available materials, including those listed, and reference books to identify such inaccuracies are suggested.
Subject terms: Native Americans

18-23*   **Interpreting the Black Experience in America to Foreign Students; A Guide to Materials.** Valerie A. Jones & John Stalker. Trevor Arnett Library, Atlanta University, Atlanta, GA 30314, 1976. 76p. ED 125 977.

Purpose: recommendations
Grade level: secondary
Arrangement: by subject

Subjects:	art	history	politics
	civil rights	literature	religion
	drama	music	social & economic
	education	people	sports

Entries: 235 (excluding books)

running time, producer, release date (except recordings); sale & rental price; contents note
Indexes: none
Period covered: 1960s-1975
Revision and updating:
Media represented: audio recordings, films, filmstrips, slides, transparencies
Producers represented: various academic, commercial, television (network & NET)
Features: Over half of listings cover history, politics, civil rights, and social and economic aspects; appr. one-fourth are in the arts.
Subject terms: Black studies

18-24*   **The Black World in Literature for Children; A Bibliography of Print and Non-Print Materials.** Joyce White Mills. Atlanta University School of Library Service, Atlanta, GA 30314, 1975. 42p. $2.00pa.

Purpose: comprehensive
Grade level: primary, intermediate
Arrangement: by age and subject

18-24 (cont'd)

Subjects: arts and recreation history picture materials
biography junior fiction and easy readers
folklore literature sociology

Entries: 63 (excluding print)

format, producer, price; grade level; contents note
Indexes: author-title
Period covered: released 1974-July 1975
Revision and updating: v.II, 1976 ($2.50pa.)
Media represented: filmstrips, audio recordings
Producers represented: various commercial
Features: Bulk of non-print materials for ages 9-13. Critical evaluation of books, only.
Subject terms: Black studies

18-25*   Jewish Films in the United States: A Comprehensive Survey and Descriptive Filmography. Stuart Fox. G. K. Hall, 1976. 360p. $40.00.

Purpose: comprehensive
Grade level: all
Arrangement: chronological and topical groupings
Subjects: documentaries newsreels
feature films TV shows
Israel World War II
Israeli films

Entries: appr. 4,000

running time, producer, release date; language of film; contents note
omitted: availability; audience suitability
Indexes: subject, title
Period covered: pre-1913–1970
Revision and updating:
Media represented: films
Producers represented: various, including foreign
Features: Includes captured German government and SS films. [Briefer lists: *Guide to Feature and Documentary Films for the Hillel Programs.* B'nai B'rith Hillel Foundation, 1640 Rhode Island Avenue, NW, Washington, DC 20036, $1.00 (ED 129 664); *Teaching the Jewish Experience in America: Units and Resources.* Max Nadel. American Association for Jewish Education, 114 Fifth Avenue, New York, NY 10011, 1975. $1.25pa. (ED 125 986).]
Subject terms:
ethnic studies Near East
history

19—World Cultures and International Education

The Subject Index employs the term "history," "international education," and "world cultures" and the narrower ones "Africa," "Asia," "Canada," "Latin America," "Near East," and "Europe."

Ethnic American Minorities (18-14) includes media on countries of origin of Americans from all continents. Recordings from many lands are found in the catalog of the *Children's Book and Music Center* (01-26). *Science Books and Films* (16-13) reviews current films on anthropology. The Great Plains National Instructional Television Library (43-03) sells slide sets on a number of countries. Films of the public television *Tribal Eye* series may be obtained from a commercial distributor. Other programs on foreign cultures are listed in the public television *Video Program Catalogue* and *Supplement* (43-01). *Alternatives in Print* (01-21) is a source for finding Third World publications and media.

The State Department, Washington, DC 20520, publishes *Selected Information Materials* (pamphlets anf free-loan films). *Foreign Affairs* (monthly) announces currently released documents of United States, foreign and international government bodies.

19-01* **United Nations 16mm Film Catalogue 1977-78.** United Nations Office of Public Information, New York, NY 10017, 1977. 43p. illus. free.
Purpose: catalog of UN films only, not including those of specialized agencies
Grade level: all
Arrangement: topical
Subjects: International Zone—series   The UN: its charter and
         Man Builds, Man Destroys—series   organization
                                                  other UN films
Entries: appr. 190

running time, release date; availability in various languages; synopsis; purchase price; distributor if other than UN
    omitted: grade level
Indexes: subject, title
Period covered: 1960s-1977
Revision and updating: previous edition 1975
Media represented: films
Producers represented: United Nations
Features: Also lists films in production. Specialized agencies publish their own lists of films [e.g., WHO (08-08)].
Subject terms:
        energy and environment education   international education
        foreign language

19-02* **Teaching Canada: A Bibliography.** William J. McAndrew and Peter J. Elliott. 2d ed. University of Maine, Orono, ME 04473, 1974. ED 139 702.
Purpose: "Teaching Aids and Audio-Visual Materials" p. 76-86; descriptive
Grade level: all
Arrangement: by media

19-02 (cont'd)
Subjects: Canada
Entries: appr. 150

> running time (films), producer/distributor, sale/rental price; contents
> note (films)
>> omitted: grade level, release date; format details and contents
>> (filmstrips, filmloops); price (slides, kits)

Period covered: available at time of publication
Revision and updating: 1st ed. 1971
Media represented: audio recordings, filmloops, films, filmstrips, kits, graphic
materials, simulation games, slides
Producers represented: various
Features: Includes free-loan films, sources for slides, artifacts, maps, prints.
Subject terms: Canada

19-03*   Films of a Changing World: A Critical International Guide. Volume II.
Jean Marie Ackermann. Society for International Development, 1346
Connecticut Avenue, NW, Washington, DC 20036, 1976. 73p. $4.00pa.

Purpose: reviews that appeared in *International Development Review 1972-1976;*
evaluations
Grade level: secondary
Arrangement: chronological
Subjects: development, social change
Entries: appr. 150

> running time, producer/distributor, release date; sale/rental price; signed
> critical review
>> omitted: grade level

Indexes: title, subject, geographical
Period covered: 1969-1975 (some earlier)
Revision and updating: *Volume I* published 1972; *International Development
Review* (quarterly; $20.00/year)
Media represented: films
Producers represented: commercial, academic, institutional, government, U.N.,
U.S., and foreign
Features: Emphasis is on films that break down cultural stereotypes. [Similar
list: 19-24.]
Subject terms:
> international education
> world cultures

19-04*   China: A Resource and Curriculum Guide. Arlene Posner and Arne J.
de Keijzer. 2nd ed. University of Chicago Press, 1976. 317p. $15.00;
$3.95pa. LC 75-9061.

Purpose: "Audiovisual Materials," pp. 73-148 (evaluations); "Materials from the
People's Republic of China," pp. 263-275 (comprehensive)
Grade level: secondary
Arrangement: by media, with some subject subdivision
Subjects:

19-04 (cont'd)
Entries: over 150 (excluding print)
  (a-v materials) format data, running time, release date, distributor; price;
  grade level; contents summary and critique; official materials; contents
  summaries only, source for photographs only
    omitted: release dates and prices (official materials)
Indexes: title
Period covered: materials available in early 1975
Revision and updating: previous edition 1973
Media represented: audio recordings, films, filmstrips, graphic materials, kits,
  video recordings, free and inexpensive publications
Producers represented: various
Features: 115 films, including 29 produced in the People's Republic; 31 film-
  strips and multi-media kits, others.
Subject terms: Asia

19-05* **Educational Media Resources on Egypt.** University of Michigan Audio-
  Visual Education Center, Ann Arbor, MI 48109, 1977. 57p. price not
  known.
Purpose: comprehensive
Grade level: all
Arrangement: alphabetical title

Subjects:	agriculture	Egyptian art	modern Egypt
	Arab world	Egyptian contributions	Nile river
	archaeology	to civilization	political and
	architecture	geography	social problems
	cities	history	pyramids
	Egypt in literature	Middle East	Suez canal
			others

Entries: 424
  running time (films), number of frames (filmstrips), producer, release date
  (in most cases); grade level; contents summary
    omitted: price
Indexes: subject (indicates medium and grade level)
Period covered: 1960s-1976 (some earlier)
Media represented: audio recordings, filmloops, films, filmstrips, kits, slides,
  video recordings
Producers represented: appr. 100
Features:
Subject terms:
  Near East
  philosophy and religion

19-06* **Films for Anthropological Teaching.** Karl G. Heider. 6th ed. American
  Anthropological Association, 1703 New Hampshire Avenue, NW,
  Washington, DC 20009, 1977. 187p. $5.00pa.
Purpose: comprehensive; not all previewed
Grade level: secondary

19-06 (cont'd)
Arrangement: alphabetical title

Subjects:		
archaeology	folklore	ritual
art and music	language	social conflict
change, moderniza-	life cycle	& resolution
tion, etc.	paralinguistics,	social organization
economics	kinesics, etc.	& kinship
ethology	play and sports	technology
fieldwork		

Entries: 780

running time, producer/distributor, release date (in most cases); sale/rental
price, rental source; description from distributors' catalogs; references to
reviews in *American Anthropologist* (19-21)
Indexes: geographical, topical, title, name
Period covered: 1930s-1976
Revision and updating: previous edition 1972
Media represented: films
Producers represented: various
Features: *Ethnographic Film* by the same author (University of Texas Press,
Austin, TX 78712, 1976. 166p. $9.95) contains a filmography of some
60 recommended films (pp. 135-152); see *Films for Arts and Crafts* (20-02)
for films documenting dances of various cultures.
Subject terms:
ethnic studies
world cultures

19-07* **"An Asian Studies Filmography."** *The Lens and the Speaker*, v.XV,
Fall 1977, pp. 21-38. Visual Aids Services, University of Illinois, 1325
South Oak Street, Champaign, IL 61820. free.
Purpose: descriptive
Grade level: all
Arrangement: topical

Subjects:	
agriculture and economics	painting and calligraphy
China	performing arts
crafts	religion and philosophy
India	Southeast Asia
Japan	others

Entries: over 300

running time, release date; order number & rental price; grade level; contents
synopsis
Indexes: none
Period covered: 1950s-1976
Revision and updating:
Media represented: films
Producers represented: not known
Features: [Similar list: 19-18.]

19-07 (cont'd)
Subject terms:
Asia   philosophy and religion
performing arts   visual arts

19-08*   Guide to Free-Loan Films about Foreign Lands. Serina Press, 70
Kennedy Street, Alexandria, VA 22305, 1975. 283p. $12.95pa.
Purpose: comprehensive
Grade level: all
Arrangement: geographical
Subjects: agriculture   feature films   painting
architecture   festivals   sports
art   history   theater
dances   industry   war
education   music   others
energy
Entries: appr. 3000

running time, rental source; contents summary; audience restirctions
omitted: release date
Indexes: subject
Period covered: available at time of publication
Revision and updating:
Media represented: films
Producers represented: consulates and embassies, airlines, free-loan film
distributors, others
Features:
Subject terms: world cultures

19-09*   A Filmography of the Third World; An Annotated List of 16mm Films.
Helen W. Cyr. Scarecrow Press, Inc., Metuchen, NJ 08840, 1976. 319p.
$11.00. LC 76-22584.
Purpose: comprehensive
Grade level: all
Arrangement: geographical
Subjects: "non-Western nations and ethnic minorities of North America and
Europe"
Entries: appr. 2200

running time, producer, distributor, release date; contents summary;
director, etc. for theatrical films
omitted: grade level, price
Indexes: director, cinematographers, scenarists and composers; title
Period covered: 1960s-1975, some older ones that are classics or where recent
coverage is inadequate
Revision and updating:
Media represented: films
Producers represented: over 200 distributors in U.S. and Canada

19-09 (cont'd)
Features: Short, feature-length, and fictional films included. "The Third World in Europe" (pp. 253-255), 15 "titles that reflect either a European view of Third World peoples or Third World experiences in Europe," is an unusual and valuable listing.
Subject terms:
     ethnic studies   world cultures
     international education

19-10*   **Africa from Real to Reel; An African Filmography.** Steven Ohrn and Rebecca Riley. African Studies Association, 218 Shiffman Center, Brandeis University, Waltham, MA 02154, 1976. 154p. illus. $15.00pa.
Purpose: comprehensive
Grade level: secondary
Arrangement: alphabetical title
Subjects: films about Africa and Africans
Entries: appr. 1300
    running time, producer, release date (not in all cases); geographical area or ethnic group pictured; rental sources; contents notes or summaries
    omitted: audience suitability, price
Indexes: geographical
Period covered: 1929-75
Revision and updating:
Media represented: films
Producers represented: various U.S. and Canadian commercial, academic, government, including television
Features: [Similar lists: *Films on Africa: An Educators Guide to 16mm Films Available in the Midwest.* (African Studies Program, University of Wisconsin, 1220 Linden Drive, Madison, WI 53706, 1974. 74p. $1.00. ED 127 246) indexes 270 recommended, 50 not recommended and some 400 other films released 1960s-1974, including free-loan films available from embassies, UN missions, etc. *Africa on Film: Myth and Reality*, by Richard A. Maynard, (Hayden Book Company, 1974. $4.95pa.) contains a filmography of 27 recommended films 1930-1968 that do not perpetuate myths.]
Subject terms: Africa

19-11*   **Teacher's Resource Handbook for Latin American Studies; Annotated Bibliography of Curriculum Materials, Preschool through Grade Twelve.** John N. Hawkins. Curriculum Inquiry Center, University of California, 405 Hilgard Avenue, Los Angeles, CA 90024, 1975. 230p. $2.50pa. ED 133 239.
Purpose: comprehensive; an "attempt was made to be as inclusive as possible"
Grade level: all
Arrangement: by grade level, subject, medium
Subjects: Caribbean   Mexico
          Central America   South America
          Latin America

19-11 (cont'd)
Entries: appr. 1100 (excluding books)
running time, producer, release date; sale and rental price (not in all cases);
grade level; contents descriptions by producers
Indexes: none
Period covered: 1960s-1975
Revision and updating:
Media represented: audio recordings, films, filmstrips, graphic materials, kits,
manipulative materials, maps, transparencies, slides
Producers represented: various commercial, government, academic
Features: Entries total 1346, including books.
Subject terms: Latin America

19-12* **Teacher's Resource Handbook for Asian Studies: An Annotated**
Bibliography of Curriculum Materials, Preschool through Grade
Twelve. John N. Hawkins. Curriculum Inquiry Center, Graduate
School of Education, University of California, 405 Hilgard Avenue,
Los Angeles, CA 90024, 1976. 194p. $3.00pa. ED 133 241.
Purpose: comprehensive; an "attempt was made to be as inclusive as possible"
Grade level: all
Arrangement: by grade level, subject, medium
Subjects: Asia   South Asia
East Asia   Southeast Asia
Pacific Islands
Entries: 1081 (excluding books)
Indexes: none
Period covered: 1950s-1973
Revision and updating:
Media represented: audio recordings, films, filmstrips, graphic materials, kits,
manipulative materials, maps, slides, transparencies
Producers represented: various commercial, government, academic
Features: Also 452 books. [Similar list: *Guide to Slides on Asia* (Asia Society,
112 East 64th Street, New York, NY 10021. $0.30) lists about 40 sources,
indicating number of slides, subject coverage and use restrictions.]
Subject terms: Asia

19-13* **Teacher's Resource Handbook for Near-Eastern Studies; An Annotated**
Bibliography of Curriculum Materials, Preschool through Grade Twelve.
John N. Hawkins and Jon Maksik. Curriculum Inquiry Center, Graduate
School of Education, University of California, 405 Hilgard Avenue, Los
Angeles, CA 90024, 1976. 111p. $2.50pa. ED 133 242.
Purpose: comprehensive; some evaluations
Grade level: all
Arrangement: by grade level, subject, medium
Subjects: Arab-Israeli conflict   North Africa & the Sudan
Arab Middle East   Religion
non-Arab Middle East

19-13 (cont'd)
Entries: 700 (excluding books)

running time, producer, release date; sale and rental price (not in all cases); grade level; contents descriptions supplied by producers

Indexes: none
Period covered: available at time of publication
Revision and updating:
Media represented: audio recordings, films, filmstrips, maps, slides, transparencies
Producers represented: various commercial, government, academic
Features: Also books. [Similar list: 19-05.]
Subject terms:

Africa   philosophy and religion
Near East

19-14*   **Film Resources on Japan.** University of Michigan Audio-Visual Center, Ann Arbor, MI 48109, 1975. 55p. ED 110 002.
Purpose: comprehensive
Grade level: all
Subjects: 1) films   3) sponsored films
            2) films produced before 1960   4) filmstrips
Entries: appr. 550

running time, producer, release date (#1 and 2 only); grade level (#1 and 4 only); contents note (#1 only)

Indexes: subject (#1 only)
Period covered: available at time of publication
Revision and updating:
Media represented: films, filmstrips
Producers represented: appr. 75
Features:
Subject terms: Asia

19-15*   **The War Film.** Ivan Butler. A. S. Barnes & Co., Cranbury, NJ 08512, 1974. 191p. $10.00.
Purpose: "Chronological List of War Films" pp. 153-186; comprehensive
Grade level: intermediate, secondary
Arrangement: subject
Subjects: atomic threat   Spanish Civil War
            Civil War   World War I
            Korean War   World War II
            Napoleonic wars
Entries: over 400

director, cast, release date only; discussion of films in body of book

Indexes: subject index refers to discussion in text
Period covered: 1910-1971
Revision and updating:
Media represented: films
Producers represented: various, including foreign studies

19-15 (cont'd)
Features: [Similar list: *The War Film*. Norman Kagan. Pyramid, 1971, discusses
some 60 feature films "of great popular and critical success," 1915-70.]
Subject terms:
history   mass media
international education

19-16*   Teacher's Resource Handbook for Russian and East European Studies:
         An Annotated Bibliography of Curriculum Materials Preschool through
         Grade Twelve. John N. Hawkins and Jon Maksik. Curriculum Inquiry
         Center, Graduate School of Education, University of California, 405
         Hilgard Avenue, Los Angeles, CA 90024, 1976. 54p. $2.50pa. ED
         133 240.
Purpose: comprehensive; an "attempt was made to be as inclusive as possible"
Grade level: all
Arrangement: by grade level, subject, medium
Subjects: Eastern bloc countries, Soviet Union
Entries: 383 (excluding books)
         running time, producer, release date (not in all cases); sale and rental price
         (not in all cases); grade level; contents descriptions supplied by producers
Indexes: none
Period covered: available at time of publication
Revision and updating:
Media represented: audio recordings, films, filmstrips, graphic materials, kits,
         maps, slides, transparencies
Producers represented: various commercial, government, academic
Features: Also 250 books.
Subject terms:
         Asia
         Europe

19-17*   Teacher's Resource Handbooks for African Studies; An Annotated
         Bibliography of Curriculum Materials Preschool through Grade Twelve.
         John N. Hawkins and Jon Maksik. African Studies Center, University
         of California, Los Angeles, CA 90024, 1976. 68p. $1.50pa. ED 137 213.
Purpose: comprehensive; "Materials Assessment Sheet" and "Cross-Cultural
         Evaluation Sheet" provided
Grade level: all
Arrangement: by grade level
Subjects: Africa (General)   Southern Africa
            Eastern/Central Africa   Western Africa
Entries: appr. 370 (excluding books)
         running time, producer/distributor, release date (not in all cases); sale/
         rental price; contents note
Indexes: none
Period covered: available at time of publication
Revision and updating:

19-17 (cont'd)
Media represented: audio recordings, films, filmstrips, graphic materials, kits,
    maps, slides, transparencies
Producers represented: various commercial, government, academic
Features: Total of 662 entries includes books. Bulk of a-v entries are for films.
Subject terms: Africa

19-18* **Asia through Film.** Center for Japanese Studies, 108 Lane Hall,
    University of Michigan, Ann Arbor, MI 48109, 1976. 64p. $3.50pa.
Purpose: "an annotated guide to films on Asia in the University of Michigan
    Audiovisual Education Center"; evaluative
Grade level: all
Arrangement: by subject
Subjects: China   South Asia
           Japan   Southeast Asia
Entries: appr. 250 (excluding adult)

    running time, producer & distributor, release date; rental price; grade
    level; detailed contents summary; evaluation of content and technique
Indexes: subject and grade level indexes for each section
Period covered: 1950s-1974 (relatively few after 1970)
Revision and updating:
Media represented: films
Producers represented: appr. 40 distributors
Features: Includes out-of-print films. [Similar lists: *Guide to Films on Asia* (Asia
    Society, 112 East 64th Street, New York, NY 10021, 1976? $0.30) presents
    evaluations of about 40 films by experts. Evaluations of 34 "Films on South-
    east Asia," many on arts and crafts, appeared in *American Anthropologist*,
    v.78, September 1976, pp. 716-726. See also 19-07.]
Subject terms: Asia

19-19* **Multimedia Materials for Studies on World Peace.** Harry A. Johnson
    and Wayne F. Virag. Virginia State College, Petersburg, VA 23803,
    1975. 146p. $5.95pa.
Purpose: "An Annotated Bibliography of Resources" pp. 25-146; comprehensive
Grade level: secondary
Arrangement: 6 topical groupings
Subjects: conflict/resolution   environment
           decision-making   human rights/social justice
           development   population
Entries: over 200 (excluding print)

    running time, format details, distributor, sale and rental prices; contents
    summary
        omitted: release date
Indexes: none
Period covered: available at time of preparation
Revision and updating:
Media represented: audio recordings, films, filmstrips, free and inexpensive
    publications, graphic materials, kits, simulation games, transparencies

19-19 (cont'd)
Producers represented: various
Features: Includes free-loan films. [Similar list: *Global Perspectives: A Bibliography* (Social Studies Development Center, Indiana University, Bloomington, IN 47401, 1975. 45p. ED 114 350) notes some 60 media in various formats that emphasize "the inter-relatedness of world problems"; *Media Supported Teaching for Peace*, American Association of School Librarians, 1201 16th Street, NW, Washington, DC 20036. 1975. $2.50.
Subject terms:
    international education
    energy and environment education

19-20* **"Archaeological Films: The Past as Present."** Thomas Wight Beale and Paul F. Healy. *American Anthropologist*, v.77, December 1975, pp. 889-922; v.78, March 1976, pp. 116-142, June 1976, pp. 359-386.
Purpose: evaluations
Grade level: secondary
Arrangement: by geographical area and topic
Subjects: introductory films and archaeological technique (December 1975), Old world (March 1976), New world (June 1976)
Entries: 144

    running time, producer, sale and rental prices; rental sources; signed critical review with full summary
        omitted: release date (in many cases)
Indexes: title index in December 1975 and December 1976 issues
Period covered: available at time of writing
Revision and updating:
Media represented: films
Producers represented: various, including television and many foreign sources (including BBC)
Features: Includes free-loan films. [Similar list: "Archaeology; The Ancient Past on Film" (*EMC One-77*. Extension Media Center, University of California, Berkeley, CA 94720) on pp. 2-8 recommends appr. 100 available from the Center, some reviewed here; see also 19-06.]
Subject terms:
    history   world cultures
    Native Americans

19-21* **American Anthropologist.** American Anthropological Association, 1703 New Hampshire Avenue, NW, Washington, DC 20009. $30.00/year.
Purpose: "Audiovisual Reviews" column
Grade level: secondary
Arrangement: random
Subjects: anthropology
Entries: over 100/year

    running time, producer, sale/rental price; signed review
        omitted: audience suitability
Indexes: indexed in *Media Review Digest* (01-03); annual index in December issue

19-21 (cont'd)
Period covered: current releases
Revision and updating: published 4x/year
Media represented: films
Producers represented: various commercial, academic, U.S. and foreign
Features: While many reviews are of documentaries of scholarly interest, many
others point to films suitable for school use. Column occasionally devoted
to filmography on one subject, e.g., 19-20, 22-06.
Subject terms: world cultures

19-22* **"Audio-Visual Aids for English History since 1750: A Critical Review."**
Clara I. Gandy. *History Teacher*, v.10, November 1976, pp. 21-58.
Purpose: evaluations in narrative style
Grade level: secondary
Arrangement: topical
Subjects: geography and economics   literature and the arts
government and politics   social issues
Entries: over 100

running time (films), producer; critique
omitted: format data (filmstrips), release date, price
Indexes:
Period covered: available at time of writing
Revision and updating: supplements 11-09
Media represented: audio recordings, films, filmstrips, maps, slides, transparencies
Producers represented: several, including British sources
Features: Includes primary source materials.
Subject terms: history

19-23* **History Teacher.** Society for History Education. California State
University, Long Beach, CA 90840. $12.00/year.
Purpose: "Reviews" column in each issue; evaluations
Grade level: secondary
Arrangement: random
Entries: appr. 45/year

running time, producer/distributor, sale/rental price; signed critical review
omitted: release date
Indexes: indexed in *Media Review Digest* (01-03)
Period covered: recent releases
Revision and updating: published 4x/year
Media represented: audio recordings, films, filmstrips, kits, slides, simulation
games
Producers represented: various
Features: Occasional mediagraphies on one subject (see 19-22, 17-14, 11-09).
Subject terms: history

19-24* **Political Change: A Film Guide.** James Morrison & Richard Blue.
Audio Visual Library Service, University of Minnesota, 3300 University
Avenue, SE, Minneapolis, MN 55414, 1975. 87p. $3.95pa. LC 75-14268.

19-24 (cont'd)
Purpose: Selections from several hundred films on basis of technical quality,
    subject relevance, intellectual substance and thought-provoking quality,
    objectivity, and dramatic and aesthetic interest
Grade level: secondary
Arrangement: alphabetical title in two sections (highly recommended, less
    appropriate)
Subjects: political change in developing and developed countries
Entries: appr. 150

running time, producer/distributor, release date; language; sale price;
subject (i.e., country); rental price range (section I), full critical review,
including use suggestions (section II), contents summary
Indexes: geographical
Period covered: 1960s-1973
Revision and updating:
Media represented: films
Producers represented: various U.S. and foreign
Features: Includes feature-length and free-loan films. Approximately 35 are
    about the United States. *Revolutionary Films/Chicago '76* (Chicago Art
    Institute, 1976. 53p. illus. $2.50pa.) describes some 70 American and
    foreign films about revolution shown at the Institute during the Bicen-
    tennial.
Subject terms:

contemporary issues	international education
government and law	

20—Visual Arts

Industrial aspects of graphic arts and photography are covered in
21—Vocational Education under Industrial Arts, while filmmaking is also
considered in 07—Film Study.

Slide Buyers' Guide (42-02) is a comprehensive index to suppliers of slides.
A number of public television shows on art may be ordered on videotape through
Video Program Catalogue 1976/77 (43-02).

For art of specific culture groups, consult the Subject Index terms "ethnic
studies," "world cultures," and their narrower terms.

"Films on Southeast Asia" in *American Anthropologist* (September 1976,
pp. 716-726, v.78) includes 16 films on weaving. About 25 films on American art
and art museums and over 100 on architecture are listed in *Films: Historic Preservation and Related Subjects* (17-17).

Pictorial books and listings of them are noted in 36—Graphic Materials. *Art
Index* (qu) indexes reproductions appearing in museum bulletins and other art
periodicals.

The National Gallery of Art, Extension Service, Washington, DC 20565,
issues a catalog, *Slide Lectures and Films*, and similar catalogs are available from
other museums.

20-01   **Catalogue of Reproductions of Paintings 1860-1973.** UNESCO, Paris, 1974. 343p. $13.20pa.
Purpose: selective index to available reproductions
Grade level: all
Arrangements: alphabetical by artist
Subjects: painting
Entries: 1534

    publisher, price, process used; size and location of original
Indexes: artists, publishers, printers
Period covered: available at time of publication
Revision and updating: previous ed. 1969
Media represented: graphic materials (art reproductions)
Producers represented: appr. 100; worldwide, including commercial producers and museums, but excluding publishers specializing in the educational market
Features: Illustrations are in black-and-white. No reproductions from books, portfolios, or postcards. [The companion volume, *Catalogue of Reproductions of Paintings prior to 1860* (UNESCO, 1972), is o.p.]
Subject terms: visual arts

20-02*   **Films for Arts and Crafts.** Pennsylvania State University, Audio-Visual Services, University Park, PA 16802, 1977. 94p. free.
Purpose: film library catalog; recommendations
Grade level: all
Arrangement: alphabetical title

Subjects: ancient cultures   crafts/decorative arts   musicians
          architecture/urban   dance   photography
            development   esthetics   theater
          art   motion pictures   others
          artists   music
Entries: appr. 600

    running time, producer, release date, rental price; contents summary, grade level
Indexes: subject, series
Period covered: 1951-75
Revision and updating: previous edition 1974; *Newsletter*
Media represented: films
Producers represented: various
Features: "Encyclopaedia Cinematographic Films on Dance" (pp. 84-88) lists approximately 90 scientist-produced films documenting dances of various cultures; "Reference Collection" (pp. 89-93) lists appr. 100 out-of-print and limited-interest films. Both collections are available for rent.
Subject terms:
      the arts
      film study

20-03   **Worldwide Art Catalogue Bulletin.** Worldwide Books, Inc., 37-39
           Antwerp Street, Boston, MA 02135. $22.50/year.
Purpose: reviews of catalogs of art exhibits; evaluative
Grade level: all
Arrangement: alphabetical by country
Subjects: architecture   photography
           design   textiles
           graphic arts   others
Entries: appr. 650/year

    subject of exhibit, exhibit dates and locations; price, ordering information;
    full synopsis and critical review
Indexes: title, artists, chronological, media, topical; annual index is a compilation
    of indexes appearing in each issue
Period covered: current
Revision and updating: published 4x/year
Media represented: graphic materials (exhibition catalogs)
Producers represented: museums, galleries
Features: Number of illustrations and of color plates is noted in annotations.
    Issues dated 1976 were actually published in 1977.
Subject terms: visual arts

20-04   **School Arts.** Davis Publications, Inc., Worcester, MA 01608. $9.00/year.
Purpose: "Resource Materials" listed in each issue; recommendations
Grade level: all
Arrangement: random by publisher or producer
Subjects: art
Entries: 15/year (excluding books and professional)

    format, producer, price; synopsis (not in all cases)
        omitted: grade level, release date
Indexes: indexed in *Media Review Digest* (01-03)
Period covered: current releases
Revision and updating: published 10x/year
Media represented: films, filmstrips, graphic materials
Producers represented: various
Features: Mainly books for teachers.
Subject terms: visual arts

20-05   **Index to Art Reproductions in Books.** Scarecrow Press, Metuchen,
           NJ 08840, 1974. 372p. $12.50. LC 74-1286.
Purpose: "to aid in the location of reproductions in some excellent art books
    published during the last two decades"; comprehensive
Grade level: all
Arrangement: alphabetical by artist
Subjects: architecture   photography
           graphic art   sculpture
           painting   stage design
Entries: appr. 7000

    title of art work, page reference, size of reproduction, color or black/white

20-05 (cont'd)
Indexes: title
Period covered: 1960-1971
Revision and updating:
Media represented: graphic materials
Producers represented: appr. 63 books
Features:
Subject terms: visual arts

20-06* **A Guide to Slide and Photograph Collections of Primitive Art in the Midwestern United States.** June M. Axelrod. Art Libraries Society of North America, P.O. Box 3692, Glendale, CA 91201, 1976. 20p. $3.50pa.
Purpose: collections of 15 museums and academic institutions in Ohio, Indiana, Illinois, Michigan, Minnesota, Iowa, Missouri, South Dakota
Grade level: all
Arrangement: by institution
Subjects: primitive art
Entries: description of collection and total number of slides and photographs held
Indexes: name-subject
Period covered: available fall 1975
Revision and updating:
Media represented: graphic materials, slides
Producers represented: various
Features: [Similar list: *A Guide to Slide and Photograph Collections of Primitive Art from Boston to Washington, D.C.* (1975), by the same author, summarizes the collections of 13 institutions in the Northeast. See also 01-05.]
Subject terms:

ethnic studies	world cultures
visual arts	

20-07* **Contemporary Crafts Market Place.** 1977-78. ed. Bowker, 1977. 341p. $15.95pa.
Purpose: "Audiovisual Materials," pp. 133-150; comprehensive
Grade level: all
Arrangement: by subject
Subjects:

clay	paper
fiber	wood
glass	general
leather	others
metal	

Entries: appr. 450

        format, title, producer, grade level
            omitted: release date, price; running time or other format details
Indexes: none
Period covered: available at time of publication
Revision and updating: published biennially

20-07 (cont'd)
Media represented: filmloops, films, filmstrips, slides, video recordings
Producers represented: appr. 125, including museums, academic, commercial, institutional
Features: "Includes some art, design, foreign and historical film materials."
Subject terms: crafts

21-Vocational Education

The lists detailed in this chapter deal primarily with career training. Media *about* careers will be found via 03—Career Education.

Guides to free and inexpensive materials explicitly designed for schools (34-02, 34-03, 34-04, 34-07) are helpful for all aspects of vocational education.

Agricultural Education

Local Cooperative Extension Service offices generally provide a link to state agriculture departments, schools of agriculture and their publications. *Films for Life Sciences* (16-03) recommends 33 titles on agriculture and gardening.

Mediagraphies specifically for agricultural education are entered as 21-01, 21-02, 21-14, 21-16, and 21-21.

Business Education

Mediagraphies for business education including distributive education are entered as 21-04, 21-05, 21-18, and 21-19.

Home Economics

Reference is made to 04—Consumer Education and 08—Health and Safety Education for additional sources. Videotapes on child and infant care and child development are found under "Patient Education" in the *Health Sciences Video Directory* (08-10). Posters on food and nutrition are available from the Food and Drug Administration, 5600 Fishers Lane, Rockville, MD 20852. There is information also from the Department of Agriculture and from local extension service offices (see above). The Center for Science in the Public Interest, 1757 S Street, NW, Washington, DC 20009, publishes nutrition posters, a magazine, school food guides, and information on food supply.

Mediagraphies for home economics and nutrition are entered as 21-06, 21-07, 21-08, 21-09, 21-17, 21-22, 21-23, and 21-25.

Industrial Arts

Lists dealing with safety aspects are detailed in 08–Health and Safety Education. *Metric Education; An Annotated Bibliography for Vocational, Technical and Adult Education* (12-08) and other references in 12–Mathematics and Metric Education are pertinent. The National Audiovisual Center (01-10) supplies many technical and instructional films, including films on safety. Government publications on science and technology are featured in *Selected U.S. Government Publications* (35-01). Note a number of films on building crafts and skills in *Films: Historic Preservation and Related Subjects* (17-17). *Guide to Free-Loan Training Films* (Serina Press, Alexandria, VA 22305, 1975. $7.95) lists some 900 films.

Mediagraphies specifically for industrial arts are entered as 21-12, 21-13, 21-15, and 21-27.

Health Services

Expanding employment opportunities in allied health fields have brought about expanded instructional programs, and one mediagraphy is included (21-20). Subject terms "nutrition" and "home economics" and 08–Health and Safety Education also apply.

21-01*   **New Instructional Materials for Agricultural Education 1977.** American Vocational Association, 1510 H Street, NW, Washington, DC 20005, 1977. 35p. free.
Purpose: comprehensive
Grade level: secondary
Arrangement: random within 10 categories
Subjects: agricultural economics   field crops
            agricultural engineering   horticulture
            agricultural occupations   soils
            animal science   others
            diseases and pests
Entries: 200
       title, format, producer, price, release date; contents summary
Indexes: none
Period covered: 1976 publications, a few 1975
Revision and upating: published annually
Media represented: filmstrips, free and inexpensive publications, slides, transparencies
Producers represented: state agencies, academic institutions
Features: Includes curriculum units, printed materials; excludes commercially distributed items.
Subject terms: agricultural education

21-02   **Agricultural Education in a Technical Society: An Annotated Bibliography of Resources.** Mary R. Brown and Eugenie L. Moss. American Library Association, 50 North Huron Street, Chicago, IL 60611, 1973. 228p. $10.00. LC 72-7501.

21-02 (cont'd)
Purpose: comprehensive list of print media; "government documents; periodicals and other serials," pp. 170-180
Grade level: secondary
Arrangement: by media
Subjects: agricultural education
Entries: 94

> frequency, date publication began, ordering information; price; intended audience; evaluative annotation, indicating whether scholarly or popular

Indexes: none
Period covered: available at time of publication
Revision and updating: *Government Periodicals and Subscription Services*
Media represented: government publications
Producers represented: U.S. government
Features: Books and other guides to media lists make up most of this very well done, very comprehensive guide. Several of the government periodicals are free.
Subject terms: agricultural education

21-03 **Films for Business and Industrial Skills.** 5th ed. Pennsylvania State University, Audio-Visual Services, Willard Building, University Park, PA 16802, 1974. 58p. free.
Purpose: film library catalog; recommendations
Grade level: secondary
Arrangement: alphabetical title
Subjects: strong listings under:

atomic energy	machining	office practice
computers and computer	mechanical drawing	occupational
technology	motion picture	guidance
electronics	production	welding
		others

Entries: appr. 600

> running time; release date, distributor, rental fee; contents summary; grade level

Indexes: subject
Period covered: 1940-1972
Revision and updating: *Newsletter*
Media represented: films
Producers represented: various commercial and government
Features: Mainly training films, but some are suitable for introducing various occupations.
Subject terms:

business education	industrial arts
career education	

21-04* **Journal of Business Education.** 4000 Albemarle Street, NW, Washington, DC 20016. $12.00/year.

21-04 (cont'd)
Purpose: descriptive announcements in most issues
Grade level: secondary
Arrangement: random
Subjects: includes some not directly related to business education
Entries: appr. 50/year

title, source, ordering information
Indexes: indexed in *Media Review Digest* (01-03)
Period covered: current releases
Revision and updating: published 8x/year
Media represented: films, free and inexpensive publications, government publications, kits
Producers represented: various
Features:
Subject terms: business education

21-05 * **Simulations and Games; A Guidebook for Distributive Education.**
Jimmy G. Koeninger. Distributive Education Laboratory, Ohio State
University, 1885 Neil Avenue, Columbus, OH 43210, n.d. 83p.
ED 112220
Purpose: recommendations to generate student interest
Grade level: secondary
Arrangement: alphabetical title
Subjects: economics & business management & supervision
human relations
Entries: 57

author, publisher, copyright date, price; number of players & time required;
description of game, including instructional purposes served
Indexes: subject
Period covered: 1964-71 (most 1968-69)
Revision and updating:
Media represented: simulation games
Producers represented: appr. 20
Features: "Games not abstracted" pp. 67-9 (appr. 20)
Subject terms: business education

21-06* **Forecast for Home Economics.** Scholastic Magazines, 50 West 44th
Street, New York, NY 10036. $8.00/year (free with bulk subscriptions to CO-ED).
Purpose: "Visual News 'N' Views" by Vera M. Falconer in most issues recommends "good new materials"
Grade level: secondary
Arrangement: topical
Subjects: careers guidance
clothing and textiles health and personal hygiene
consumer education marriage, family and children
foods and nutrition women and men

21-06 (cont'd)
Entries: appr. 150/year

> format data, running time, producer; evaluative summary with teaching
> suggestions
> > omitted: release date, price

Indexes: indexed in *Media Review Digest* (01-03)
Period covered: current releases
Revision and updating: published 9x/year
Media represented: films, filmstrips, kits, slides
Producers represented: various
Features:
Subject terms:

consumer education	home economics
guidance	women's studies

21-07* **Secondary Teaching Materials and Teacher References.** Society for
Nutrition Education, 2140 Shattuck Avenue, Berkeley, CA 94704,
1977. 25p. $3.00pa.
Purpose: recommendations of "useful materials"
Grade level: secondary
Arrangement: 2 media groupings (pamphlets, audiovisuals)
Subjects:

adolescents	nutritive values
basic nutrition facts	processed foods
calorie control	snacks
dental health	world food supply
food groups, habits, selection, etc.	others

Entries: 141 (excluding books and teacher materials)

> running time, format data, publisher or producer/distributor, release or
> publication date, sale price; subject descriptors

Indexes: author/source
Period covered: 1970-1977
Revision and updating: previous edition 1974; *Journal of Nutrition Education*
(21-25)
Media represented: films, filmstrips, graphic materials, free and inexpensive publi-
cations, manipulative materials, slides, video recordings, government publi-
cations
Producers represented: various
Features: Includes Spanish language materials, also books, curriculum guides,
journal articles.
Subject terms: nutrition

21-08* **Elementary Teaching Materials and Teacher References.** Society for
Nutrition Education, 2140 Shattuck Avenue, Berkeley, CA 94704,
1975. 19p. $3.50pa.
Purpose: "selected . . . materials useful as teaching tools"; recommendations
Grade level: primary, intermediate
Arrangement: by media
Subjects: nutrition

21-08 (cont'd)
Entries: appr. 100 (excluding books)

publisher or producer, date (not in all cases), price; format data; grade level; subject descriptors

Indexes: none
Period covered: 1960s-1974
Revision and updating: previous edition 1973; *Journal of Nutrition Education* (21-25)
Media represented: audio recordings, films, filmstrips, free and inexpensive publications, graphic materials, kits, manipulative materials, slides, government publications
Producers represented: various institutional, commercial, government
Features:
Subject terms: nutrition

21-09* **Journal of Home Economics.** American Home Economics Association, 2010 Massachusetts Avenue, NW, Washington, DC 20036. $13.00/year.
Purpose: "New Publications and Visuals" in most issues; descriptive
Grade level: secondary
Arrangement: random

Subjects:	clothing	foods
	consumer education	nutrition
	energy	population
	family	sex roles

Entries: appr. 30/year

running time, source, price
Indexes: indexed in *Media Review Digest* (01-03)
Period covered: current releases
Revision and updating: published 5x/year
Media represented: films, free and inexpensive publications, government publications
Producers represented: various
Features: Mostly professional materials.

Subject terms:	
consumer education	home economics
guidance	

21-10* **Index to Vocational and Technical Education (Multimedia).** 3rd ed. National Information Center for Educational Media, University of Southern California, University Park, Los Angeles, CA 90007, 1977. 936p. $47.00; $23.50 microfiche. LC 76-1616.
Purpose: comprehensive
Grade level: all
Arrangement: alphabetical title

21-10 (cont'd)

Subjects:	agriculture	engineering	plastics
	automation	guidance and	plumbing
	automobile	counseling	printing
	aviation	home economics	refrigeration
	business & economics	mathematics	science
	construction	machine shop	woodwork
	electronics	photography	others

Entries: appr. 32,000 (including adult & professional)

> type of medium, format data, producer, distributor, release date; grade
> level; contents annotation; out-of-print titles identified
> > omitted: price

Indexes: classed subject
Period covered: 1940s-1976
Revision and updating: *Update of Nonbook Media*
Media represented: audio recordings, filmloops, films, filmstrips, slides, transparencies, video recordings
Producers represented: appr. 300
Features:
Subject terms:

agricultural education	home economics
career education	industrial arts

21-11*   Industrial Arts—Metals Technology; A Curriculum Guide for Intermediate and Secondary Level Programs. Missouri Department of
Education, Jefferson City, MO 65101, 1974. 174p. ED 099 474.

Purpose: descriptive; "Industrial arts free and inexpensive learning materials"
p. 10-2 to 10-11; also listings at end of each chapter
Grade level: intermediate, secondary
Arrangement: 9 topical groupings

Subjects:	art metal work	metal work forging practices
	bench metal work	metal work foundry practices
	heat-treatment of metals	sheet metal practices
	machining metals	welding
	metal work	

Entries: over 200

> ordering source; publication date, contents note, instructional suggestions
> (free and inexpensive materials only)
> > omitted: running time (in most cases) price, release date

Indexes: none
Period covered: available at time of writing
Revision and updating:
Media represented: filmloops, films, filmstrips, free and inexpensive publications,
graphic materials
Producers represented: various government and institutional
Features: [Similar list: Companion guide *Industrial Arts—Woods and Wood Technology* (099 473) lists some 50 films and other media.]
Subject terms: industrial arts

21-12*   **Industrial Education.** Macmillan Professional Magazines, Inc., One
Fawcett Place, Greenwich, CT 06830. $12.00/year.
Purpose: "Books and AV" and "Aids from Industry" columns announce materials
"that may be helpful"
Grade level: secondary
Arrangement: random
Subjects: industrial arts
Entries: several hundred/year
ordering information; contents note
Indexes: indexed in *Media Review Digest* (01-03)
Period covered: current publications and releases
Revision and updating: published 9x/year
Media represented: films, filmstrips, free and inexpensive publications, graphic
materials, slides, transparencies, filmloops
Producers represented: various commercial, industry sources
Features: Annual directory of over 150 sources of "Free Teaching Aids and
Resources" in a spring issue. Very few audiovisual media in "Books and
AV" column. [See also 21-27.]
Subject terms: industrial arts

21-13*   **School Shop.** Prakken Publications, P.O. Box 623, 416 Longshore
Drive, Ann Arbor, MI 48107. $10.00/year.
Purpose: "Instructional Resources" column announces materials
Grade level: secondary
Arrangement: random
Subjects: shop
Entries: appr. 60/year (excluding books)

running time, producer, sale and rental price (not uniform); contents note;
ordering information for pamphlets
omitted: release date
Indexes: indexed in *Media Review Digest* (01-03)
Period covered: current releases
Revision and updating: published 10x/year
Media represented: films, filmstrips, free and inexpensive publications, govern-
ment publications, slides, transparencies
Producers represented: various
Features: "New Audiovisuals for Industrial Educators" (v.36, January 1977,
pp. 26-28) describes 25 titles reviewed in the previous year.
Subject terms: industrial arts

21-14*   **List of Available Publications.** Department of Agriculture, Office
of Communications, Washington, DC 20250, 1976. 185p. free.
(also available from Superintendent of Documents, Washington, DC
20402. $2.00. S/N 001-003-00030-5).
Purpose: comprehensive
Grade level: all
Arrangement: topical; separate listing of visual aids

21-14 (cont'd)
Subjects: agricultural economics   home economics
            agricultural engineering   plant science
            animal science   recreation
            conservation   soil science
            forestry   others
Entries: appr. 3600

   title, order number, series, publication date; publications for sale only so
   indicated; series descriptions state audience suitability
Indexes: subject, title
Period covered: publications available July 1976
Revision and updating: *Selected U.S. Government Publications* (35-01)
Media represented: government publications, graphic materials, maps
Producers represented: U.S. government
Features:
Subject terms:
            agricultural education   home economics
            energy and environment education   life science

**21-15*   A Bibliography of Free Loan Materials for Trade and Industrial
            Education.** Roger H. Lambert & others. 3rd ed. Wisconsin Vocational
            Studies Center, University of Wisconsin, Madison, WI 53706, 1976.
            45p. ED 132 276.
Purpose: catalog of free-loan materials available within state; descriptive
Grade level: secondary
Arrangement: 32 topical groupings
Subjects: automotive   electronics
            construction   others
Entries: appr. 1000 (including books)

   title, publication date, pagination, price (if any).
Indexes: "disadvantaged materials"
Period covered: 1970s
Revision and updating: annual
Media represented: free and inexpensive publications, government publications
Producers represented: academic, institutional, departments of education
Features: Also books. [Similar list: *Resource Information for Industrial Arts.*
            (Research and Curriculum Unit for Vo-Technical Education, Mississippi
            State University, Mississippi State, MS 39762, 1976. 42p. ED 127 435)
            lists over 100 sources of free and inexpensive publications and free-loan
            films.]
Subject terms: industrial arts

21-16*   A Bibliography of Free Loan Materials for Agriculture Education.
            Roger H. Lambert. 3rd ed. Wisconsin Vocational Studies Center,
            University of Wisconsin, Madison, WI 53706, 1976. 40p. ED 132 279.
Purpose: catalog of materials available within state; descriptive
Grade level: secondary
Arrangement: 30 topical groupings

21-16 (cont'd)
Subjects: include forestry, landscaping, wildlife management in addition to
    agriculture
Entries: appr. 900 (including books)
    title, publication date, pagination, price (if any)
Indexes: "disadvantaged materials"
Period covered: 1970s
Revision and updating: annual
Media represented: free and inexpensive publications, government publications
Producers represented: academic, institutional, departments of education
Features: Also books.
Subject terms: agricultural education

21-17*   **Catalog Food and Nutrition Information and Educational Materials
    Center.** National Agricultural Library, 10301 Baltimore Boulevard,
    Beltsville, MD 20705, 1973. 286p. free. **Supplements 1-4,** 1974-1976.
Purpose: catalog of print and non-print media available on loan to selected
    professional target audiences (not schools)
Grade level: secondary
Arrangement: 15 topics
Subjects:

consumer education	menu planning
equipment	nutrition science and education
food preparation and production	recipes
food standards and legislation	sanitation & safety
food technology	others
history (of food and nutrition)	

Entries: over 800 (excluding print)
    running time, format details, producer, release date (not in all cases); subject
    terms; contents summary
        omitted: price
Indexes: subject, author, title, media; cumulative index covering *Catalog* and
    Supplements 1 and 2
Period covered: 1960s-1975
Revision and updating: Supplements issued 2x/year
Media represented: audio recordings, filmloops, filmstrips, films, graphic materials,
    kits, manipulative materials, slides, transparencies, video recordings
Producers represented: various commercial, institutional
Features: While use of this library is restricted to USDA employees, state school
    food service personnel, school food service training programs, professional
    and research institutions and selected libraries, many selections would be
    useful in secondary classes, and schools can use this catalog as a selection
    tool. [Similar list: appr. 450 AV items of *Catalog* and *Supplement 1* (1973
    accessions only) are also separately issued as *Audiovisual Guide to the
    Catalog of the Food and Nutrition Information and Educational Materials
    Center* from the same address.
Subject terms:
        home economics
        nutrition

21-18* **A Bibliography of Free Loan Materials for Distributive Education.** Roger H. Lambert. 3rd ed. Wisconsin Vocational Studies Center, University of Wisconsin, Madison, WI 53706, 1976. 25p. ED 132 277.
Purpose: catalog of materials available within state; descriptive
Grade level: secondary
Arrangement: 21 topical groupings
Subjects: advertising   food distribution   insurance
           apparel and accessories hardware & building   personal services
           automotive   materials   petroleum
           finance and credit   hotel & lodging   recreation & tourism
           floristry   industrial marketing   others
Entries: appr. 500 (including books)
       title, publication date, pagination, price (if any)
Indexes: "disadvantaged materials"
Period covered: 1970s
Revision and updating: annual
Media represented: free and inexpensive publications, government publications
Producers represented: academic, institutional, departments of education
Features: Also books. [Similar list: *Instructional Materials for Distributive Education.* Cornell Institute for Research and Development in Occupational Education, Stone Hall, Cornell University, Ithaca, NY 14853, 1975. 110p. ED 123 402 (evaluations of curriculum materials).]
Subject terms: business education

21-19* **A Bibliography of Free Loan Materials for Business Education.** Roger H. Lambert. 3rd ed. Wisconsin Vocational Studies Center, University of Wisconsin, Madison, WI 53706, 1976. 28p. ED 132 274.
Purpose: catalog of materials available within state; descriptive
Grade level: secondary
Arrangement: appr. 40 topical groupings
Subjects: business English   consumer education
           business law   office education
           business math
Entries: appr. 500 (including books)
       title, publication date, pagination, price (if any)
Indexes: "disadvantaged materials"
Period covered: 1970s
Revision and updating: annual
Media represented: free and inexpensive publications, government publications
Producers represented: academic, institutional, departments of education
Features: Also books.
Subject terms:
       business education
       consumer education

21-20* **A Bibliography of Free Loan Materials for Health Occupations Education.** Roger H. Lambert & others. 3rd ed. Wisconsin Vocational Studies Center, University of Wisconsin, Madison, WI 53706, 1976. 25p. ED 132 275.

21-20 (cont'd)
Purpose: catalog of materials available on free loan within state; descriptive
Grade level: secondary
Arrangement: 38 subject categories
Subjects:　dental assisting　　　home health aide　　　occupational therapy
　　　　　　dental hygiene　　　　medical laboratory　　physical therapy
　　　　　　dental laboratory　　　　technology　　　　　psychiatric aide
　　　　　　　technology　　　　　medical recorder　　　rehabilitation
　　　　　　environmental health　　mental health　　　　others
　　　　　　food service supervisor　nursing
Entries: appr. 475 (including books)

　　　　title, publication date, pagination, price (if any)
Indexes: "disadvantaged materials"
Period covered: 1970s
Revision and updating: annual
Media represented: free and inexpensive publications
Producers represented: academic, institutional, departments of education
Features:
Subject terms: health services

21-21*　　Selected References and Aids for Teaching Agricultural Mechanics to
　　　　　Students of Agricultural Education. Virginia Polytechnic Institute
　　　　　and State University, College of Education, Department of Agricultural
　　　　　Education, Blacksburg, VA 24061, 1975. 57p. ED 109 486.
Purpose: comprehensive
Grade level: secondary
Arrangement: 9 topical groupings
Subjects:　agricultural power　　　　　　　metal work
　　　　　　construction　　　　　　　　　safety
　　　　　　electricity　　　　　　　　　　shop
　　　　　　general　　　　　　　　　　　soil and water conservation
　　　　　　machinery　　　　　　　　　　water management
Entries: appr. 300

　　　　format data, source, release date, price; contents note
Indexes:
Period covered: available 1973
Revision and updating:
Media represented: films, filmstrips, free and inexpensive publications, graphic
　　　　materials, slides, transparencies
Producers represented: various commercial and industrial
Features: Also books.
Subject terms:
　　　　　　agricultural education
　　　　　　industrial arts

21-22*　　Audiovisuals for Nutrition Education. Society for Nutrition Education,
　　　　　2140 Shattuck Avenue, Berkeley, CA 94704, 1975. 28p. $2.50pa.

21-22 (cont'd)
Purpose: "selected evaluative reviews from the *Journal of Nutrition Education*"
Grade level: all
Arrangement: by media
Subjects: nutrition
Entries: appr. 150 (excluding adult)

> format data, producer, release date (not in all cases), price; critical review
> with instructional suggestions; grade level

Indexes: author/publisher/producer, subject, title
Period covered: 1969-1975
Revision and updating: *Journal of Nutrition Education* (21-25)
Media represented: audio recordings, films, filmstrips, free and inexpensive
publications, graphic materials, kits, manipulative materials, slides, transparencies, video recordings
Producers represented: appr. 130 institutional, academic, commercial
Features: Additional titles mentioned in text.
Subject terms: nutrition

21-23*   **Cooking for Entertaining.** Nancy Tudor and Dean Tudor. Bowker, 1976.
256p. $19.95. LC 76-9841.
Purpose: "Nonprint Materials" at end of each section; comprehensive
Grade level: intermediate, secondary
Arrangement: topical

Subjects:	design and service	specific courses
	history	specific food
	international cuisine	specific kinds of meals
	menu and entertaining	techniques
	special appliances	wine and food

Entries: appr. 150 (excluding print)

> format data, running time, producer, release date; sale price; contents
> summary
>   omitted: grade level

Indexes: subject, title
Period covered: 1960-1975
Revision and updating:
Media represented: audio recordings, filmloops, films, filmstrips, slides
Producers represented: various
Features: Includes free-loan films.
Subject terms:
   ethnic studies
   home economics

21-24*   **Child Care Resource Materials.** Jeanne Webb. Nebraska State Department of Economic Development, Lincoln, NE 68509, 1976. 103p.
ED 134 345.
Purpose: descriptive
Grade level: secondary
Arrangement: 19 topical groupings

21-24 (cont'd)

Subjects: activities
caring for children
day care
nursery school

parent-child relationships
playgroups
others

Entries: appr. 140

running time, producer; contents summary
omitted: release date, price
Indexes: none
Period covered: not known
Revision and updating:
Media represented: films, filmstrips, kits
Producers represented: 12, including state agencies, U.N., commercial
Features: Also books. Films predominate.
Subject terms:
health services
home economics

21-25* **Journal of Nutrition Education.** Society for Nutrition Education,
2140 Shattuck Avenue, Berkeley, CA 94704. $10.00/year.
Purpose: "Audiovisuals" and "Pamphlets" columns; recommendations
Grade level: all
Arrangement: by grade level and topic

Subjects: basic nutrition facts
consumer education
dairy foods
dental health

food supply
infant feeding
mass media
meat

pregnancy and
nutrition
vegetarian diets
others

Entries: appr. 125/year (excluding professional)

running time, format data, producer, release date, sale/rental price;
synopsis including teaching suggestions
Indexes:
Period covered: current releases
Revision and updating: published 4x/year
Media represented: audio recordings, films, filmstrips, free and inexpensive
publications, graphic materials, manipulative materials, slides
Producers represented: various
Features: Action for Children's Television publications which point out the
nutrition messages received by children through commercials are noted,
among others.
Subject terms:
nutrition
mass media

21-26* **Instructional Materials for Occupational Education.** Cornell Institute
for Research and Development in Occupational Education, Stone Hall,
Cornell University, Ithaca, NY 14853, 1975. 545p. ED 122 068.
Purpose: evaluations by classroom teachers on basis of accuracy, bias, appropriateness, verbal and visual fluency, usefulness and versatility

21-26 (cont'd)
Grade level: secondary
Arrangement: by subject
Subjects: automobile mechanics   cosmetology
             building trades   data processing
             business education   distributive education
             child care   practical nursing
Entries: appr. 70 (excluding print)

   format data, producer, release date (not in all cases), price; contents note;
   rating (excellent, useful, or unacceptable)
Indexes: none
Period covered: to 1974
Revision and updating:
Media represented: filmloops, filmstrips, manipulative materials, slides,
   transparencies
Producers represented: various
Features: No table of contents. Bulk of contents deals with print.
Subject terms: vocational education

21-27*   **"Films on Energy and Industrial Materials."** Edward B. Evans.
            Industrial Education, v.65, May/June 1976, p. 33-34.
Purpose: recommendations
Grade level: secondary
Arrangement: 5 subject categories
Subjects: energy and environment   resources
             extraction and refining   spinoffs and emerging
             man-made materials, structures,   technologies
               and processes
Entries: 50

   running time, distributor, contents note
      omitted: release date, price
Indexes:
Period covered: available at time of publication
Revision and updating:
Media represented: films
Producers represented: 11 producers and distributors, including government
   and industry
Features: Chiefly free-loan films.
Subject terms:
         energy and environment education
         industrial arts

22–Women's Studies

The first edition annotated three lists in 15–Psychology and Guidance, all of them journal articles. Women's changing social and political roles and Title IX requirements have focused educators' concerns on sexism; separate treatment seems justified in this edition.

Material on sex roles may also be found through related terms "guidance," "sex education," "contemporary issues," and in 15-11, 15-19 and 15-20. The Public Television Library (43-02) supplies a number of programs on sex bias, and four Women's Studies programs are listed in *Index to College Television Courseware* (43-10).

"The Masculine Image: A Film-Centered Approach" by Bonnie Wagner (*Media and Methods*, v.13, September 1976, pp. 50-52) recommends 24 feature films that can help boys explore concepts of masculinity. "Women and work" (*RQ*, v.16, Winter 1976, pp. 168-174) lists recent government publications on women in the working world as does *SB 111* from Superintendent of Documents, Washington, DC 20402.

The Extension Media Center, University of California, Berkeley, CA 94720, sells audiotapes on the history of women in the United States. Women's rights pamphlets from the period 1814-1912 are available on microfiche (Bell & Howell Microphoto Division, Wooster, OH 44691).

22-01*   Womanhood Media Supplement: Additional Current Resources about Women. Helen R. Wheeler. Scarecrow, 1975. 482p. $15.00.
Purpose: "Non-Book Resources" pp. 97-295; comprehensive
Grade level: secondary
Arrangement: by topic (pamphlets); alphabetical (others)
Subjects: women's liberation and related subjects
Entries: appr. 1300 (excluding books, periodicals)

publisher, date, number of pages, contents note (pamphlets); running time, producer, release date (not in all cases), format data, slae and rental price, contents note (non-print)

Indexes: none
Period covered: 1960s-1974
Revision and updating: *Womanhood Media* (1972) accessed some 250 entries, excluding books and periodicals, some of which are repeated here
Media represented: audio recordings, filmloops, films, filmstrips, free and inexpensive publications, graphic materials
Producers represented: various, including foreign
Features: Primarily a basic book collection, directory of sources, periodicals, special issues of periodicals, plays, radio programs, etc. "Women's Liberation: A Non-Print Media Compilation," Alice Schaeffer, (*Previews*. v.2, February 1974, pp. 5-9) and *Images of Women: A Bibliography of Feminist Resources for Pennsylvania Schools* (1973. ED 090 470) also offer multimedia resource listings.
Subject terms: women's studies

22-02* **Women's Films in Print.** Bonnie Dawson. Booklegger Press, 555 29th Street, San Francisco, CA 94131, 1975. 165p. $4.00pa.
Purpose: comprehensive list of 16mm films made by women
Grade level: all
Arrangement: by filmmaker's name
Subjects: all
Entries: 800

running time, release date, sale and rental price; contents note omitted: audience suitability
Indexes: title, subject
Period covered: 1922-1975
Revision and updating:
Media represented: films
Producers represented: 370 U.S. women filmmakers
Features: Includes some Weston Woods films. [Similar list: "Women on Film" by Carol Emmens (*Booklist*, v.72, January 1, 1976, pp. 630-634) recommends 20 recent films (plus filmstrips) to supplement *Women's Films in Print, Women in Focus* (22-08).
Subject terms: women's studies

22-03* **Positive Images; Non-Sexist Films for Young People.** Linda Artel and Susan Wengraf. Booklegger Press, 555 29th Street, San Francisco, CA 94131, 1976. 167p. $5.50pa.
Purpose: recommendations, based on feminist content and technical quality; all previewed unless otherwise indicated
Grade level: all
Arrangement: alphabetical title; video, filmstrips and slide shows, and photographs in separate chapters
Subjects: adolescence   marriage
         biography   masculinity
         Black women   older women
         consciousness raising films   sports
         history   work
                                  others
Entries: over 400

running time, producer, release date, sale and rental price; grade level; critical review
Indexes: subject
Period covered: 1960s-1976
Revision and updating:
Media represented: films, filmstrips, slides, video recordings, graphic materials
Producers represented: appr. 100 distributors
Features: Approximately 45 children's films separately listed in subject index. [Similar list: "Non-Sexist Films for Children." *Sightlines*. v.8, Fall 1974, pp. 7-8, 17-18.]
Subject terms:
         biography   women's studies
         guidance

22-04* **Women's Films; A Critical Guide.** Indiana University Audio-Visual
Center, Bloomington, IN 47401, 1975. 121p. $5.95pa.
Purpose: films recommended for purchase by Indiana University Film Library
and for women's studies programs
Grade level: secondary
Arrangement: by subject
Subjects: abortion   personal statements   third world women
           compilation   portraits   welfare
           documentaries   problem pregnancies   women make movies
           day care   rape   working mothers
           ironic commentaries   self-defense   others
           jobs
Entries: appr. 180

running time; producer, release date; rental/sale price; critical review
omitted: audience suitability
Indexes: title
Period covered: 1960s-1974, some earlier
Revision and updating:
Media represented: films
Producers represented: 65 commercial, academic, government, institutional
Features: [Similar list: *Women: A Select Bibliography* (1975. ED 112 320)
contains one chapter listing over 100 films and videotapes available from
the University of Michigan Audio-Visual Education Center.]
Subject terms:
        sex education
        women's studies

22-05* **Films about Women.** Pennsylvania State University, Audio-Visual
Services, Willard Building, University Park, PA 16802, 1975. 10p.
free.
Purpose: film library catalog; recommendations
Grade level: secondary
Arrangement: alphabetical title
Subjects: changing roles   profiles/biographies
           marriage/pair bonds   other
Entries: appr. 80 (+20 on dittoed supplementary sheet)

running time, producer, release date; rental price; grade level; contents
summary
Indexes: subject
Period covered: 1970s, some 1960s
Revision and updating: *Newsletter*
Media represented: films
Producers represented: various
Features: Traditional and non-traditional viewpoints are represented.
Subject terms:
        biography   women's studies
        sex education

22-06*   **"Women in Film: An Introduction."** Louise Lamphere. *American Anthropologist*, v.79, March 1977, pp. 192-216.
Purpose: evaluations of both "ethnographic" and "political" films
Grade level: secondary
Arrangement: random
Subjects: women in the United States and in developing countries
Entries: 47
          running time, producer, sale/rental price; signed critical review
              omitted: release date (in some cases)
Indexes: title index in December issue
Period covered: 1954-1974
Revision and updating:
Media represented: films, video recordings
Producers represented: various academic, commercial, independent
Features: Introduction supplies overview, pointing out gaps and needs; also
          references to reviews of additional films in the magazine 1971-1975.
          [Similar list: "International Women on Film," by Carol Emmens
          (*Sightlines*, v.9, no.1, Fall 1975, pp. 13-15) recommends 20 titles on
          women in developing and developed countries.]
Subject terms:
          women's studies
          world cultures

22-07*   **A Partial List of Educational, Instructional and Documentary Films
          Treating Women's Roles, Problems, and Communication Strategies.**
          Richard Edwards and Bruce E. Gronbeck. 1975. 42p. ED 113 763.
Purpose: comprehensive; "potentially beneficial films" culled from catalogs of
          26 film libraries; not all previewed by compilers
Grade level: secondary
Arrangement: subject
Subjects (in order of length of listing)

working women	dating and marriage	family life
birth control, abortion	search for self-fulfillment	history of women's
sex role stereotyping and	coping with a male	movement
re-education	oriented society	rape
socialization of the	motherhood	directions for
young	sex education	women's
		movement
Entries: appr. 185		others

          running time, format, producer, grade level; summary and critique; rental
          libraries where available
Indexes: none
Period covered: mid-60s-1974 (some much earlier)
Revision and updating:
Media represented: films, video recordings
Producers represented: various

22-07 (cont'd)
Features:
Subject terms:
    women's studies
    sex education

22-08*   Women in Focus. Jeanne Betancourt. CEBCO Pflaum, Fairfield, NJ
    07006, 1974. 186p. illus. $10.00. LC 74-78728.
Purpose: "Films that present real women;" recommendations
Grade level: secondary
Arrangement: alphabetical title
Subjects: women
Entries: 90

    running time, producer/distributor, release date; sale/rental price; contents
    synopsis and critical review; suggested audience; related feminist reading
Indexes: filmmakers, themes
Period covered: 1958-1973
Revision and updating:
Media represented: films
Producers represented: appr. 80 independent filmmakers, mainly women
Features: Biographical information about filmmakers, also filmography, quote
    and photo; programming suggestions; bibliography
Subject terms: women's studies

**22-09*   Films by and/or about Women: Directory of Filmmakers, Films,
    and Distributors.** Women's History Research Center, Inc., 2325 Oak
    Street, Berkeley, CA 94708, 1972. 72p. $3.00pa. ED 127 217.
Purpose: comprehensive
Grade level: secondary
Arrangement: 15 topical groupings
Subjects: avant garde   female portraits
             classics   Third World
             experimental   others
Entries: appr. 1300

    running time, filmmaker, distributor, release date (not in all cases); sale/
    rental price; contents note
Indexes: female filmmakers
Period covered: 1960s-1971
Revision and updating:
Media represented: films
Producers represented: various independent filmmakers, commercial, academic,
    British Film Institute, National Film Board of Canada
Features: Also several hundred "films without complete information," "film-
    makers without complete information," "last minute additions." [Similar
    list: 22-02.]
Subject terms:
        film study
        women's studies

Section III
Lists by Media

30–Audio Recordings

References here list spoken recordings only, or both spoken and musical recordings in all formats (disc, tape, cassette, etc.). Lists comprised entirely of musical recordings are considered in 13–Music. The term "radio" in the Media Index will locate listings of recorded broadcasts.

Media Review Digest (01-03) indexes periodical reviews of recordings in a separate section. Reviews appear regularly in special columns in *Booklist* (01-12), generally on the fifteenth of the month, and in *Previews* (01-11). For journals reviewing musical recordings, see 13–Music.

Recordings of books are discussed in the introduction to 11–Language Arts. The Division for the Blind and Physically Handicapped, Library of Congress, Washington, DC 20542, provides free recordings (also large type and Braille books) through cooperating public libraries to persons legally entitled to this service. Catalogs issued by this agency include *Magazines in Special Media* (1977) *Cassette Books 1974-1976* (1977), *Talking Books Adult* (1976), *For Younger Readers* (1976), and *I Went to the Animal Fair* (1975), all supplemented by the bimonthly *Talking Topics.* They contain a few references to commercial recordings available also to the general public.

The purchase price of some cassette recordings includes permission to duplicate for educational purposes, as in the case of the National Center for Audiotapes (30-06) and some commercial vendors.

Public radio and television stations "that lend, rent and/or sell programs" are listed in *Audiovisual Marketplace 1977* (Bowker, 1977). An American Television and Radio Archive is to be created at the Library of Congress in connection with the revised copyright law effective January 1, 1978. Some tapes of National Public Radio programs are released through the National Center for Audio Tapes (30-06). A local affiliate provides a catalog of 140 of its programs (*The Great Atlantic Radio Conspiracy.* 2743 Maryland Avenue, Baltimore, MD 21218).

30-01* **Schwann–1 Record and Tape Guide.** W. Schwann, Inc., 137 Newbury Street, Boston, MA 02116. $1.00 per issue (combined subscription to *Schwann–1* and *–2*, $18.00/year).
Purpose: "A selective reference guide to recorded music for the dealer in his store and the consumer in his home"; based on information supplied by manufacturers; descriptive
Grade level: all
Arrangement: new listings; mono and electronic stereo records; composers; electronic music; classical collections; musicals, movies, TV shows; current popular; jazz; other (may vary from issue to issue)
Subjects: all
Entries: appr. 45,000

  label and number; availability on cartridge, cassette; symbols indicate stereo recordings and records being discontinued
  omitted: release date, price

30-01 (cont'd)
Indexes: title, ballets, operas
Period covered: recordings currently offered for sale
Revision and updating: each monthly issue replaces previous one; also semi-annual
    supplement *Schwann—2* (30-2)
Media represented: audio recordings
Producers represented: 1000 labels
Features: May be used to determine current prices and availability of recommended
    recordings, excluding open reel. "New Listings" section includes spoken
    recordings.
Subject terms:
    music
    performing arts

**30-02*   Schwann—2 Record and Tape Guide: Semi-Annual Supplement to the
    Monthly Schwann—1.** $0.95 per issue (combined subscription to
    Schwann—1, and *—2*, $18.00/year).
Purpose: based on information supplied by manufacturers; descriptive
Grade level: all
Arrangement: composers; classical collections; spoken and miscellaneous; musical
    shows, operettas, film; international pop & folk; non-current popular; jazz
    (may vary from issue to issue)
Subjects: spoken recordings category includes:
    bird songs and nature sounds   plays
    documentaries and history   poetry
    humor   prose
    instruction   speech
    language instruction
Entries: over 10,000, including 1500 non-musical

    label and number; availability on cartridge and cassette; symbols indicating
    stereo recordings and records that are being discontinued
        omitted: release date, price
Indexes: none
Period covered: recordings currently offered for sale; domestic popular recordings
    over 2 years old
Revision and updating: published February and August of each year; each issue
    replaces previous one; also "New Listings" in monthly *Schwann—1* (30-01)
Media represented: audio recordings
Producers represented: over 1000 labels
Features: Excludes recordings sold only by direct mail (i.e., most specifically
    published for the educational market)
Subject terms:
    foreign language   performing arts
    music   poetry

30-03*   Harrison Tape Guide. 141 East 25th Street, New York, NY 10010.
    $5.50/year.

30-03 (cont'd)
Purpose: "a comprehensive listing of pre-recorded tapes in all configurations"
Grade level: all
Arrangement: popular, shows, religious, electronic, spoken, language lessons,
    poetry, children's, classical, opera (may vary from issue to issue); "What's
    New"
Subjects: all
Entries: 25,000 to 30,000
    label and number, price
Indexes: none
Period covered: recordings currently offered for sale
Revision and updating: published 6x/year; each issue replaces previous one
Media represented: audio recordings (reel-to-reel, cassette, cartridge)
Producers represented: over 100
Features: Single issues are sold in stores selling tapes; *Schwann Record and Tape
    Guides* (30-01 and 30-02) do not list reel-to-reel recordings. The Harrison
    guide is most valuable for listings of new releases. Little overlap with *Index
    to Educational Audiotapes* (30-04)
Subject terms:
    music
    performing arts

30-04*   Index to Educational Audiotapes. 4th ed. National Information Center
    for Educational Media, University of Southern California, University
    Park, Los Angeles, CA 90007, 1977. 750p. $47.00; $23.50 microfiche.
Purpose: comprehensive listing of "commercially produced educational audiotapes"
Grade level: all
Arrangement: alphabetical title
Subjects: all; listings in order of length:
    literature and drama   history
    psychology   music
    social science and   science
        sociology   others
Entries: over 28,000 (including adult)
    full format details, producer/distributor, grade level (not in all cases); out-
    of-print titles so indicated
    omitted: price, release date (generally)
Indexes: classed subject
Period covered: 1960s-1977 (some earlier)
Revision and updating: 3rd ed. 1973; *Update of Nonbook Media*
Media represented: audio recordings (reel-to-reel, cassette, cartridge), radio
Producers represented: appr. 400, including British and Canadian academic,
    radio and TV stations, commercial
Features: Lists recordings available from National Center for Audiotapes (30-06);
    supplements 30-07. Subject index has no entry for speeches or other
    documentaries.
Subject terms: all subjects

30-05* **Index to Educational Records.** 4th ed. National Information Center for Educational Media, University of Southern California, University Park, Los Angeles, CA 90007, 1977. 746p. $47.00; $23.50 microfiche.
Purpose: comprehensive listing of "commercially produced educational records"
Grade level: all
Arrangement: alphabetical title
Subjects: all
Entries: over 25,000 (including adult)

full format details, including record size and rpm's; producer, distributor, grade level (in some cases); contents note; out-of-print titles so indicated
omitted: price, release date
Indexes: classed subject
Period covered: not known
Revision and updating: 3rd ed. 1974; *Update of Nonbook Media*
Media represented: audio recordings (disc)
Producers represented: appr. 400 commercial, academic, foreign
Features: Music listings largest single group, followed by literature, drama, foreign language. *Schwann Record and Tape Guides* (30-01 and 30-02) have more entries, are more up-to-date, and, of course, are far less expensive, but they lack subject access.
Subject terms: all subjects

30-06 **National Center for Audio Tapes 1974-76 Catalog.** National Center for Audio Tapes, University of Colorado, Stadium Building, Boulder, CO 80302, 1973. 93 + 151 + 85p. $4.50pa.
Purpose: catalog of non-profit distributing center
Grade level: all
Arrangement: numeric
Subjects: all
Entries: 14,000

running time, producer; grade level; synopsis; price schedule
omitted: release date
Indexes: classed subject; title
Period covered: available at time of publication
Revision and updating:
Media represented: audio recordings (cassette, reel)
Producer represented: appr. 200 commercial, academic, institutional, radio stations, government
Features: Purchase price includes permission to duplicate tapes. Social sciences account for one-third of the listings. Includes foreign language tapes, including many non-Western languages, Canadian Broadcasting Corporation programs, recordings of children's literature, full-length speeches and lecture series, music festivals, conferences on current issues, State Department reports, taped courses in science, the arts, philosophy, religion, music appreciation, driver training, and many others. [Similar list: The University of Michigan also operates a tape recording service, though on a smaller scale (Audio-Visual Education Center, Ann Arbor, MI 48103). Both are priced at a fraction of the cost of commercial "audio-text" services.]

30-06 (cont'd)
Subject terms: all subjects

30-07* **Directory of Spoken-Voice Audio-Cassettes.** Gerald McKee. Cassette
Information Services, Box 17727, Los Angeles, CA 90057, 1976.
176p. $10.00pa. LC 73-19090.
Purpose: comprehensive
Grade level: secondary
Arrangement: alphabetical by issuing organization
Subjects: all
Entries: appr. 800 series

title of cassette series; price; synopsis, running time (in many cases)
omitted: release date
Indexes: subject-title
Period covered: available at time of publication
Revision and updating: previous editions 1972, 1974; *CIS Newsletter* (quarterly,
$6.00/year)
Media represented: audio recordings (cassette), radio
Producers represented: over 400 commercial, academic, institutional
Features: Separate listing of "Children's Cassette Producers," pp. 163-165;
entry for "old-time radio" in subject index. This directory supplements
Schwann Record and Tape Guides (30-01 and 30-02), *Harrison Tape Guide*
(30-03) and *NICEM Indexes* (30-04 and 30-05).

30-08* **Schwann Children's Record and Tape Catalog.** W. Schwann, Inc.,
137 Newbury Street, Boston, MA 02116, 1976. 18p. $1.25pa.
($0.75 at record stores)
Purpose: comprehensive; children's selections excluding popular music
Grade level: all
Arrangement: alphabetical title
Subjects: adventure stories folk songs
Christmas songs music
educational and historical others
Entries: over 1700

label and number; symbol indicating availability in stereo, cartridge,
cassette; separate price list
Indexes: none
Period covered: recordings available as of November each year
Revision and updating: published annually in December
Media represented: audio recordings
Producers represented: appr. 60
Features: Recordings mainly of interest to primary and intermediate grades.
Subject terms:
literature social studies
music

30-09   **Chicorel Index to the Spoken Arts on Discs, Tapes and Cassettes.**
Chicorel Publishing Co., 275 Central Park West, New York, NY 10024,
1973-1974. 3v. $60.00ea. LC 71-106198.
Purpose: comprehensive
Grade level: intermediate, secondary
Arrangement: dictionary (author, title, editor, performer, director, etc.)
Subjects: plays, poetry, readings from novels, short stories, essays, etc., com-
mentaries, conversations, discussions, readings of historical documents,
political speeches
Entries: appr. 1300

label and number, length of recording (in some cases), price, release date;
subject terms; contents listing; note of printed text supplied
Indexes: subject, author, titles of individual plays, stories, etc., interfiled in
dictionary arrangement
Period covered: retrospective
Revision and updating: 3rd volume (7B) updates first two (7, 7A)
Media represented: audio recordings, radio
Producers represented: various commercial and institutional, including foreign
Features: Subject index has entries under "American documents," "international
documents," "Black writers," "radio plays," "motion pictures" (sound
tracks), etc. [Similar lists: *Selected Sound Recordings of American, British
and European Literature in English* (11-15), and *Available Recordings of
American Poetry and Poets* (11-16).]
Subject terms:
<table>
<tr><td>literature</td><td>social studies</td></tr>
<tr><td>performing arts</td><td>world literature</td></tr>
<tr><td>poetry</td><td></td></tr>
</table>

30-10*   **Educators Guide to Free Audio and Video Materials.** 24th ed. Educa-
tors Progress Service, Randolph, WI 53956, 1977. 234p. $10.50pa.
LC 55-2784.
Purpose: free recordings for classroom use; comprehensive
Grade level: all
Arrangement: 16 topics
Subjects:
<table>
<tr><td>accident prevention and safety</td><td>fine arts</td><td>language arts</td></tr>
<tr><td>business and economics</td><td>guidance</td><td>religion and philosophy</td></tr>
<tr><td>communication and transportation</td><td>health and physical education</td><td>science</td></tr>
<tr><td>engineering</td><td>holidays and recreation</td><td>social problems</td></tr>
<tr><td>environmental education</td><td>home economics</td><td>social studies</td></tr>
<tr><td></td><td>industrial education</td><td></td></tr>
</table>
Entries: 1500

new entries starred; ordering information; contents note
omitted: release date, grade level
Indexes: subject, title
Period covered: available at time of publication
Revision and updating: published annually
Media represented: audio recordings, video recordings

30-10 (cont'd)
Producers represented: appr. 80
Features: See introduction to 34—Free and Inexpensive Publications.
Subject terms: all subjects

30-11 **"Children's Recordings."** Barbara S. Miller. *Booklist.* v.69, March 1, 1973, pp. 621, 623-635.
Purpose: "a selection of quality recordings . . . which merit a permanent place"
Grade level: primary, intermediate
Arrangement: 7 subject groupings
Subjects: activity and rhythm   music
documentaries   poetry
folk and fairy tales   prose
Entries: 200

label and number, price, release date; age level; contents note
Indexes: none
Period covered: 1967-1971
Revision and updating:
Media represented: audio recordings (discs)
Producers represented: various
Features: Three-quarters of listings are in literature and language arts. All
recordings listed are monaural.
Subject terms:
early childhood education   music
language arts

30-12* **Sources of Broadcast Audio Programming.** Marvin R. Bensman and Dennis Walter. Memphis State University, Memphis, TN 1975. 332p. ED 109 724.
Purpose: union catalog; comprehensive
Grade level: all
Arrangement: alphabetical title
Subjects: radio
Entries: several thousand

name of program, original date of production; name of collector
Indexes: none
Period covered: 1930s-1957
Revision and updating:
Media represented: audio recordings, radio
Producers represented: 104 private collectors
Features: "Commercial Phonograph Records of Broadcasts" (pp. 6-8) lists 33
for sale recordings. Suggestions on how to obtain copies of recordings
held by collectors, lists of organizations and institutions that preserve,
sell and exchange recordings. [Similar list: *Directory of Spoken-Voice
Audio-Cassettes* (30-07) also lists sources of old-time radio recordings.]
Subject terms: mass media

30-13*   **Radio Soundtracks; A Reference Guide.** Michael R. Pitts. Scarecrow Press, Inc., Metuchen, NJ 08840, 1976. 161p. $6.50.
Purpose: comprehensive guide to recordings of radio broadcasts
Grade level: all
Arrangement: topical
Subjects: tape recordings, long-playing records (programs, performers, albums)
Entries: 1094

> (tape recordings) name of program, network, date of broadcast; length; contents note; (long-playing records) name of program or album; label & number
> omitted: sources for tape recordings

Indexes: name and title
Period covered: 1920s-1950s
Revision and updating:
Media represented: audio recordings, radio
Producers represented: various
Features: Listing of over 600 tape recordings of interest mainly to collectors.
Subject terms: mass media

31-Filmloops

The term filmloops includes cartridged films that are of various size and fit various projectors.

The Elementary School Library Collection (01-09) recommends a minimal collection for elementary grades. Filmloops are not reviewed with great frequency. Such reviews as do appear are indexed along with "Films and Videotapes" in *Media Review Digest* (01-03). *Films and Other Media for Projection* (01-20) offers comprehensive coverage for recent years.

31-01*   **Index to 8mm Motion Cartridges.** 5th ed. National Information Center for Educational Media, University of Southern California, Universtiy Park, Los Angeles, CA 90007, 1977. 589p. $47.00; $23.50 microfiche.
Purpose: comprehensive listing of "commercially produced educational 8mm motion cartridges"
Grade level: all
Arrangement: alphabetical title
Subjects: all; listings in order of length:

science	social science & sociology
industrial and technical education	fine arts
physical education and recreation	others
health and safety	

Entries: appr. 26,000 (including adult)

> complete format data, including whether silent, optical or magnetic sound, super-8, etc.; gradel level; producer; contents note; release date; out-of-print titles so indicated
> omitted: price

31-01 (cont'd)
Indexes: classed subject
Period covered: 1960s-1975, some earlier
Revision and updating: 4th ed. 1975
Media represented: filmloops
Producers represented: appr. 450 commercial, academic, government
Features: Listings in science comprise over one-third of total.
Subject terms: all subjects

31-02   The College Film Library Collection: 8mm Films and 35mm Films.
v.2, Grace-Ann Kone. Bro-Dart Publishing Company, Williamsport,
PA 17701, 1971. 234p. $9.95 (both volumes $14.95). LC 77-164769.
Purpose: recommended for college and advanced high school courses
Grade level: secondary
Arrangement: topical, generally following Dewey Decimal system
Subjects: all
Entries: 8000
    format data, running time, availability in various formats; producer, price;
    synopsis
        omitted: release date
Indexes: subject
Period covered: not known
Revision and updating:
Media represented: filmloops, films, filmstrips
Producers represented: appr. 150
Features: The 8mm filmloops take up all but about 30 pages. Noted here despite
    its early publication date because of strong listings in the areas of sports
    skills and arts and crafts.
Subject terms: all subjects
        the arts
        physical education

32-Films

Films of all sizes, lengths, and genres are considered in this chapter (except
for cartridged films, which are covered in 31—Filmloops. All headings in Sections I
and II contain film lists and multi-media lists that include films. Also relevant are
07—Film Study and that subject term.

The introduction to 43—Television discusses how to find television programs
on film. Appropriate lists are referred to in that chapter.

Reviews of instructional and entertainment films appear in numerous
periodicals, including separate columns in each issue of *Booklist* (01-12) and
Previews (01-11).

Media Review Digest (01-03) indexes these reviews and provides information
on awards and ratings accorded entertainment, documentary, and educational

films. *Readers Guide to Periodical Literature* and *Art Index* also index film reviews, as does *Film Literature Index* (quarterly).
Learning (01-17) and *Media and Methods* (01-19) annually pick the year's best films for schools. Committees of the American Library Association similarly choose "notable children's films" and superior "films for young adults." Lists of 16 films released in 1975 appeared in *Booklist* (01-12) for June 1, 1977, of young people's films released 1975/1976 in the May 1, 1977, issue. Periodicals reporting on film festivals and film awards include *Film News* (32-18), *Sightlines* (32-13), and *Film Review Digest* (32-26). *Worldwide Encyclopedia of Film Awards* (Eduardo Darino, P.O. Box 5173, New York, NY 10017. price not known) attempts an international listing of awards from Acapulco to Zagreb.

32-01*   Index to 16mm Educational Films. 6th ed. National Information Center for Educational Media, University of Southern California, University Park, Los Angeles, CA 90007, 1977. 4v. $109.50; $67.50 microfiche. LC 76-1626.
Purpose: comprehensive listing of "commercially produced educational films"
Grade level: all
Arrangement: alphabetical title
Subjects: all
Entries: appr. 100,000 (including adult)

full format details, producer, distributor; grade level; contents summary; release date; out-of-print titles so indicated
omitted: price
Indexes: classed subject
Period covered: 1920s-1970s
Revision and updating: 5th ed. 1975; *Update of Nonbook Media*
Media represented: films
Producers represented: several thousand
Features: [Similar list: *Films and Other Media for Projection* (01-20) offers comprehensive coverage of recent years only.]
Subject terms: all subjects

32-02*   Feature Films on 8mm and 16mm; A Directory of Feature Films Available for Rental, Sale, and Lease in the United States and Canada. 5th ed. James L. Limbacher. Bowker, 1977. 422p. $19.95. LC 79-163905.
Purpose: comprehensive index to catalogs of American and some Canadian distributors
Grade level: all
Arrangement: alphabetical title
Subjects: feature films
Entries: 17,000

format, running time, credits, producer, distributor code; original release date
omitted: price; contents
Indexes: directors
Period covered: 1920s-current

32-02 (cont'd)
Revision and updating: previous editions 1971, 1974; supplemented 4x/year in
    Sightlines (32-13)
Media represented: films, video recordings
Producers represented: commercial, institutional, foreign governments
Features: Lacking any subject access (even to documentaries) or notations as to
    contents of films, this index is used to determine whether a given feature
    length film is available for educational showing and through what distributors
    it is available.
Subject terms: film study

32-03*   Film Programmer's Guide to 16mm Rentals. Kathleen Weaver. 2nd
    ed. Reel Research, P.O. Box 6037, Albany, CA 94706, 1975. 207p.
    $8.75pa.
Purpose: "This *Guide* is particularly geared to reflect the expanding interest in
    the history of cinema in underground and experimental films and in social
    and political documentaries" plus "standard repertory of Hollywood features
    and foreign classics"
Grade level: intermediate, secondary
Arrangement: alphabetical title; separate listings of documentaries and newsreels
Subjects: films
Entries: 10,000

    running time, director, distributors and their rental prices; one-line summary
    for documentaries only
Indexes: directors, early cinema (1890-1915)
Period covered: releases through summer 1975
Revision and updating: previous edition 1972
Media represented: films
Producers represented: 60 U.S. distributors
Features: Includes foreign films, appr. 1000 documentaries, 30-40 newsreels.
    No educational films.
Subject terms: all subjects
    film study
    social studies

32-04*   Educators Guide to Free Films. 37th ed. Educators Progress Service,
    Randolph, WI 53956, 1977. 731p. $12.75. LC 45-412.
Purpose: free films for classroom use; comprehensive
Grade level: all
Arrangement: 22 topics
Subjects:

accident prevention and safety	driver education	home economics
aerospace education	entertainment	industrial education
agriculture	environmental education	music
arts and crafts	geography	religion
business education	guidance	schools & educational opportunities
communication and transportation	health and physical education	science
consumer education	history	social programs
		sports and recreation

32-04 (cont'd)
Entries: appr. 5000

new entries starred; format and ordering information; release date in some cases '
omitted: grade level
Indexes: title, subject
Period covered: available at time of publication
Revision and updating: published annually
Media represented: films
Producers represented: appr. 475
Features: See introduction to 34—Free and Inexpensive Publications.
Subject terms: all subjects

32-05*   **Films 1977-1978.** University of California Extension Media Center, Berkeley, CA 94720, 1977. (*Lifelong Learning*, June 13, 1977). 360p. free.
Purpose: film rental and sale catalog; recommendations
Grade level: all
Arrangement: alphabetical title
Subjects: all; specialize in

anthropology/archaeology/
  ethnology
arts and humanities
business/industry
death and dying
documentaries
drug and alcohol abuse
  education
ecology
energy
ethnic studies

film study
foreign countries/geography
futures studies
health and medical sciences
life styles/alternatives
psychology/psychiatry/mental
  health
the sciences
social studies/issues
women

Entries: over 3500

running time, rental or sale price; copyright (or release or production) date; summary of content, point of view and stylistic treatment with critical comment
omitted: grade level
Indexes: classed subject
Period covered: available from EMC during the years stated
Revision and updating: published biennially; an older film generally withdrawn for each new addition; *EMC One* and *EMC Two* (each year) list new acquisitions and feature filmographies (see 06-11, 08-12)
Media represented: films
Producers represented: several hundred commercial, academic, government
Features: Index Category Outline and Reference Guide to Index Categories permit superior subject access; documentaries and feature films (including excerpts) are separately indexed. The EMC catalog is singled out here as one of the finer examples of university film library catalogs. Others are those issued by Pennsylvania State University (07-01, 11-03, 16-03, 16-12,

32-05 (cont'd)
Features (cont'd): 17-03, 20-02, 32-23).
Subject terms:

the arts	foreign language	philosophy and
biography	futures	religion
career education	health and safety	physical education
consumer education	education	psychology
energy and environment	literature	science
education	mass media	social studies
film study	mathematics	nutrition
		women's studies

32-06 **The College Film Library Collection; 16mm Films. v.1. Emily S. Jones.**
Bro-Dart Publishing Company, Williamsport, PA 17701, 1971. 154p.
$7.95 (both volumes $14.95). LC 77-164768.
Purpose: recommended films for college and advanced high school courses
Grade level: secondary
Arrangement: topical, generally following Dewey Decimal system
Subjects: all
Entries: appr. 1800

running time, producer, distributor, release date; price; critical evaluation;
asterisk marks films "especially high in quality as a motion picture"
Indexes: subject
Period covered: 1960-1970, available for purchase at time of publication
Revision and updating:
Media represented: films
Producers represented: several hundred commercial, institutional, government,
academic, independent, NET
Features: "110 feature films which have become milestones in the history of
motion pictures" (pp. 127-133); "Film as Art," illustrated by 53 films
(pp. 86-89). Strong section on the arts, including art, theater, dance,
motion pictures, and music.
Subject terms:
the arts
film study

32-07* **Landers Film Reviews; The Information Guide to 16mm Films and
Multi-Media Materials.** Landers Associates, P.O. Box 69760, Los
Angeles, CA 90069. $35.00/year.
Purpose: evaluations and announcements
Grade level: all
Arrangement: alphabetical title (films); by producer (other media)
Subjects: all
Entries: appr. 1250/year

(films) running time, producer, release date; sale and rental price; grade
level; contents summary and critical review; subject terms; references to
related titles; (media other than films) format, price; contents note
Indexes: subject and title in each issue, cumulated annually

32-07 (cont'd)
Period covered: current releases
Revision and updating: published 5x/year
Media represented: filmloops, films, filmstrips
Producers represented: several hundred
Features: Distributors are charged a fee for reviews. Two third of entries are
    for films
Subject terms: all subjects

32-08* **Canyon Cinema Catalog No. 4.** Canyon Cinema Cooperative, Room
220, Industrial Center Building, Sausalito, CA 94965, 1976. 270p.
illus. $2.00pa.
Purpose: film rental catalog; comprehensive
Grade level: secondary
Arrangement: 8mm and 16mm films, each by filmmaker
Subjects: independently produced films
Entries: over 1000

running time, release date, rental fee; synopsis, excerpts from reviews
Indexes: subject and genre
Period covered: available at time of publication
Revision and updating: *Canyon Cinemanews* (bimonthly, $3.00/year); previous
    edition 1972
Media represented: films
Producers represented: several hundred independent filmmakers in the U.S.
    and abroad
Features: Film-Makers' Cooperative, 175 Lexington Ave., New York, NY 10016,
    is another distributor for avant-garde filmmakers.
Subject terms:
        contemporary issues
        film study

32-09 **Films—Too Good for Words: A Directory of Nonnarrated 16mm Films.**
Salvatore J. Parlato. Bowker, 1972. 209p. $13.95. LC 72-12831.
Purpose: a few silent movies, "Candid Camera" segments, and films with music
    track only are included in this listing of educational films recommended for
    their visual qualities
Grade level: all
Arrangement: 13 topical areas
Subjects: action   fun   science
            the arts   literature   war and peace
            city and suburbs   nature   values
            expression   other places,   miscellaneous
            fantasy   other customs
Entries: appr. 1000

format, producer, distributor, copyright date; comments on music, awards
won
        omitted: grade level
Indexes: title, subject

32-09 (cont'd)
Period covered: through 1971
Revision and updating:
Media represented: films
Producers represented: appr. 100
Features: Full of a wealth of suggestions for enriching almost any subject area.
[Similar lists: See also 08-12 and 32-22 by the same author, both noting
nonverbal films; also 32-16, 32-25 and "The Non-Narrative Film: A Social
Studies Resource for K-College" (*Social Education*, v.40, May 1976,
pp. 265-269).]
Subject terms:
film study   values education
humanities

32-10*   **David Sohn's Film Notes on Selected Short Films.** David A. Sohn.
Cebco Pflaum, Fairfield, NJ 07006, 1975. 113p. illus. $3.75pa.
LC 75-19529.
Purpose: recommendations of films of "enduring quality"
Grade level: all
Arrangement: alphabetical title
Subjects: all
Entries: appr. 100

running time, producer; grade level; subject descriptors; summary and
critical review
omitted: release date, price
Indexes: subject, filmmakers, themes
Period covered: not known
Revision and updating:
Media represented: films
Producers represented: 17 distributors
Features: Sohn is also the author of *Good Looking: Film Studies, Short Films
and Filmmaking* (North American Publishing Company, 401 N. Broad
Street, Philadelphia, PA 19108, 1976. 238p. $8.95; $5.95pa.), a collection
of previously published articles.
Subject terms: all subjects

32-11   **The Documentary Tradition from Nanook to Woodstock.** Lewis
Jacobs. Hopkinson and Blake, 329 Fifth Ave., New York, NY 10016,
1971. 530p. illus. $6.50pa. LC 72-168866.
Purpose: survey of the development of documentary film through anthology of
contemporary commentaries; recommendations
Grade level: intermediate, secondary
Arrangement: five chronological chapters, each concluding with "A Selection
of Documentaries of the Period"
Subjects: documentary film
Entries: 450

producer, release date; use book's index to find discussion in text
Indexes: name and title

32-11 (cont'd)
Period covered: 1920s-1970
Revision and updating: use *Media Review Digest* (01-03) and journals mentioned
    in introduction
Media represented: films
Producers represented: U.S. and foreign, television stations
Features: Almost half the documentaries listed are from the 1960s, the next
    largest number from the 1940s. Films selected "best illuminate the artistic
    and social concerns of their times and . . . had the most influence in
    advancing the genre." Omits "those documentaries commonly classified
    as industrials, educationals, art and architecture, training films, and other
    types of sponsored films." [See also 07-01, 07-08, 32-05, and 32-24.]
Subject terms:
        film study
        social studies

32-12*   **EFLA Evaluations.** Educational Film Library Association, 43 West
        61st Street, New York, NY 10023. $50.00 and up/year.
Purpose: receipt of *Evaluations* is a membership service of EFLA provided to
    members paying $50.00 or more
Grade level: all
Arrangement: alphabetical by title in each batch
Subjects: all
Entries: appr. 400/year

    running time, producer/distributor, sale/rental price, release date; synopsis
    and critical comments on treatment, technical quality, suggested uses;
    subject terms, rating, audience level
Indexes: cumulated title index with each issue; annual subject index
Period covered: current and recent releases
Revision and updating: 10x/year
Media represented: films
Producers represented: commercial, institutional, independent filmmakers
Features: Reviews of films previously announced in *Sightlines* (32-13). EFLA
    also sponsors the annual American Film Festival (members receive the
    Guide) and publishes filmographies (see 15-04, 17-11, 17-21).
Subject terms: all subjects

32-13*   **Sightlines.** Educational Film Library Association, 43 West 61st
        Street, New York, NY 10023. $15.00/year.
Purpose: "Filmlist" in each issue lists educational films prior to review in
    Evaluations (32-12)
Grade level: all
Arrangement: alphabetical title
Subjects: all
Entries: appr. 500/year

    running time, producer, distributor, purchase price; contents note
Indexes: subject
Period covered: current releases

32-13 (cont'd)
Revision and updating: published 4x/year
Media represented: films, video recordings
Producers represented: various
Features: American Film Festival winners listed in Summer issue. Children's
Film Supplement beginning Fall 1977. Also carries frequent filmographies
(see 22-06, "Features," 16-02, 18-04).
Subject terms: all subjects

32-14   New York Times Film Reviews: A One-Volume Selection 1913-1970.
George Amberg. Quadrangle, 1972. 495p. illus. $12.50. LC 75-176229.
Purpose: reviews originally printed in the *New York Times* and selected from the
multi-volume *New York Times Film Reviews*
Grade level: all
Arrangement: chronological
Subjects: entertainment film
Entries: appr. 400

producer, director, cast; release date; critical review
Indexes: title
Period covered: 1913-1970
Revision and updating: *New York Times Index* "Motion Pictures–Reviews"
Media represented: films
Producers represented: U.S. and foreign
Features: [Similar list: The *New York Times Directory of the Film* (Arno, 1971)
lists Academy Award winners, New York Film Critics Circle Award winners,
"Ten Best" films of the year and reprints reviews of award winning films
only.]
Subject terms: film study

32-15*   Catalog of Educational Captioned Films for the Deaf. Bureau of
Education for the Handicapped, Office of Education, Washington,
DC 20202. 1976. 118p. free.
Purpose: catalog of films available to "groups with at least one hearing imapired
individual"
Grade level: all
Arrangement: alphabetical title
Subjects: all
Entries: appr. 850

running time, producer, release date; contents summary; subject descriptors;
grade level; synchronization of sound track with captions
Indexes: subject
Period covered: 1940s-1973
Revision and updating:
Media represented: films
Producers represented: appr. 200
Features: Supplementary list of appr. 80 films in "reserve collection." "Main-
streaming" of handicapped pupils may make some schools eligible for this
service. [Similar lists: see 32-09 and other lists referred to there.]
Subject terms: all subjects

32-16*   **More Films Kids Like; A Catalog of Short Films for Children.** Maureen Gaffney. American Library Association, Chicago, IL 60611, 1977. 159p. illus. $5.50pa. LC 77-12174.

Purpose: recommendations chosen on the basis of tests with children out of 400 pre-selected non-sexist, non-violent, non-racist, non-condescending, generally non-didactic films that "reflect the needs and interests of children" and demonstrate "imaginative use of the film medium and high production quality"

Grade level: primary, intermediate

Arrangement: alphabetical title

Subjects: action and adventure   city life   values to discuss
           animals   folk tales   visual experiences
           body movement   humor and   (non-narrated)
           children (by ethnic   nonsense   others
             group)

Entries: appr. 200

format, including whether animated, narrated, live; running time, producer/ distributor, release date; suggestions for use and suitability with various audiences

Indexes: subject indexes to this and previous edition

Period covered: 1971-76 (some earlier)

Revision and updating: supplements *Films Kids Like* (1973)

Media represented: films

Producers represented: over 40 distributors

Features: "Film Activities Kids Like," pp. 113-123.

Subject terms:
        the arts   literature
        film study   values education

32-17   **Nonfiction Film: A Critical History.** Richard M. Barsam. Dutton, 1973. 332p. illus. $6.95pa. LC 72-82161.

Purpose: history of documentary film; recommendations

Grade level: intermediate, secondary

Arrangement: Appendix A (pp. 297-311): alphabetical listing of major films; Appendix B (pp. 313-316): Chronological listing of award-winning American documentaries

Subjects: documentary film

Entries: 175

running time, credits, distributor, release date; use book's index to find discussion in text

Indexes: title

Period covered: 1920s-1970

Revision and updating: use *Media Review Digest* (01-03) and journals mentioned in introduction

Media represented: films

Producers represented: U.S. and foreign

32-17 (cont'd)
Features: Valuable for lists of awards by Motion Picture Academy of Arts and
    Sciences and National Board of Review of Motion Pictures. Focus is on
    work of noted filmmakers. [See also 07-01, 07-08, 32-05, 32-24.]
Subject terms:
    film study
    social studies

32-18* **Film News**. 250 West 57th Street, New York, NY 10019. $6.00/year.
Purpose: "Classroom and Community Films" in each issue reviews and previews
    prize-winning films and others
Grade level: all
Arrangement: by media (features, miscellaneous, religious)
Subjects: instructional and documentary films
Entries: 150-200/year

    format, distributor, release date; signed critical reviews; awards won; short
    unsigned announcements of filmstrip releases
        omitted: price, grade level
Indexes: separate title indexes for films and filmstrips in each issue; indexed in
    Media Review Digest (01-03)
Period covered: current releases
Revision and updating: published 5x/year
Media represented: films, filmstrips
Producers represented: various (including foreign, if distributed in the U.S.)
Features: Coverage of film festivals such as CINE Golden Eagle awards, American
    Film Festival, Birmingham International Educational Film Festival, etc.,
    though with considerable delay. For example, see 07-11 and 14-07 "Features."
Subject terms: all subjects

32-19 **Parents' Magazine and Better Homemaking**. 52 Vanderbilt Ave.,
    New York, NY 10017. $7.95/year.
Purpose: "Family Movie Guide" carries appraisals of current films, rated for
    adults, teenagers, and children
Grade level: all
Arrangement: alphabetical title
Subjects: entertainment film
Entries: 130-160/year

    critical annotation; ratings for ages 8-12, 13-17, 18+ (listing only, with
    reference to date of review for titles reviewed in previous issues)
Indexes: listing serves as index to original reviews; indexed in *Media Review
    Digest* (01-03)
Period covered: currently being shown
Revision and updating: revised and published monthly
Media represented: films
Producers represented: commercial
Features: May be used to guide students' viewing of current movies.
Subject terms:
    film study
    mass media

32-20   **Films in Children's Programs.** 3rd ed. Wisconsin Library Association, 201 West Mifflin Street, Madison, WI 53703, 1972. 39p. $2.00. ED 077 237.
Purpose: films recommended for aesthetic quality and technical excellence
Grade level: intermediate
Arrangement: alphabetical title
Subjects: children's films
Entries: 92

format, producer, release date (generally), purchase price; critical annotations include suggestions for related children's books, folk tales, poetry
Indexes: no
Period covered: 1960s
Revision and updating: 1st ed. 1969; 2nd ed. 1970; 4th ed. 1975 (not an ED document)
Media represented: films
Producers represented: appr. 35, including foreign, academic, government
Features:
Subject terms: language arts

32-21*   **American Film Institute Catalog of Motion Pictures; Feature Films 1961-1970.** New York, Bowker, 1976. 2v. $90.00. LC 79-128587.
Purpose: comprehensive listing of films shown in U.S.
Grade level: all
Arrangement: alphabetical title
Subjects: all
Entries: appr. 1800

alternate title, running time, credits, full synopsis; subject terms
Indexes: subject, literary and dramatic sources, country of origin, names
Period covered: 1961-1970 releases
Revision and updating: part of projected 22-volume set covering 1893 to present
Media represented: films
Producers represented: U.S. and foreign
Features: No indication of critical reception or box office success. Subject index permits retrieval of films about occupations, historical periods and events, themes and relationships, persons, places, institutions, etc. Literary index locates films made from plays, operas, ballets, short stories, novels, etc.
Subject index: all subjects
literature
world literature

32-22*   **Superfilms; An International Guide to Award-Winning Educational Films.** Salvatore J. Parlato, Jr. Scarecrow Press, Inc., Metuchen, NJ 08840, 1976. 365p. $13.50.
Purpose: recommendations; winners at 255 festivals
Grade level: all
Arrangement: alphabetical title

32-22 (cont'd)
Subjects: all; longer listings under

art	history	sports and recreation
biography	literature	TV programming
biology	minorities	urban living
children's stories	music	values
film techniques	nonverbal	women's studies

Entries: appr. 1500

running time, producer, release date; awards won; grade level; evaluative annotation
omitted: price
Indexes: subject (appr. 100 categories), company-title
Period covered: 1950s-1974, a few earlier
Revision and updating: use *Media Review Digest* (01-03) and journals mentioned in introduction to this chapter
Media represented: films
Producers represented: over 100
Features: Note pithy observations on film selection in 3-page introduction.
Subject terms: all subjects

32-23*   Films for the Elementary Classroom. 3rd ed. Audio-Visual Services Pennsylvania State University, University Park, PA 16802, 1975. 102p. free.
Purpose: "rated suitable for grade levels up to and including junior high"
Grade level: primary, intermediate
Arrangement: alphabetical title
Subjects:

arts and crafts	Indians of the	understanding our-
birds	Americas	selves and others
biography	insects and spiders	US geography
creative stimuli	literature	US history
ecology	mammals	values
enrichment	mathematics	world geography
health and safety	stories	world history

Entries: over 1200

running time, release date, rental price, producer, grade level, contents summary
Indexes: subject
Period covered: 1950s to 1974; some earlier
Revision and updating: *Newsletter*
Media represented: films
Producers represented: various commercial, academic, television, government
Features:
Subjects: all subjects

32-24*   "Short Film: The Pick of the Flicks." Anne Lynagh. *Media and Methods*, v.12, December 1975, p. 22-26, 61-73.
Purpose: recommendations
Grade level: secondary

32-24 (cont'd)
Arrangement: 10 categories
Subjects: America
comedy/satire
documentaries
growing up/careers
media/film
the poetic
Entries: appr. 1000

portraits
series
stories–fictional &
otherwise
values/special experiences

running time, producer, rental price; brief contents summary
omitted: release date
Indexes: none
Period covered: available at time of publication
Revision and updating: December 1976 issue (pp. 16-17, 19-20) has 80 titles
recommended by staff of Educational Film Library Association
Media represented: films
Producers represented: various
Features:
Subject terms:
biography
film study
guidance

literature
social studies
values education

32-25*   The Short Film: An Evaluative Selection of 500 Recommended
Films. George Rehrauer. Macmillan Information, 1975. 199p.
$12.50.
Purpose: recommendations based on author's experience, students' evaluations,
published reviews
Grade level: all
Arrangement: alphabetical
Subjects: allegory
animation
entertainment
film as art
Entries: 500

film techniques
films without words
story
others

running time, distributor, release date; grade level; contents annotation,
subject terms, references to reviews
omitted: price
Indexes: subject
Period covered: 1950s-1972
Revision and updating:
Media represented: films
Producers represented: appr. 65 commercial, academic, government
Features:
Subject terms: all subjects
film study
guidance

psychology
social studies

32-26*   **Film Review Digest.** Kraus-Thomson Organization Limited, Millwood, NY 10546. $45.00/year.
Purpose: excerpts from film reviews in 27 periodicals, including 5 British and one Canadian
Grade level: all
Arrangement: alphabetical title
Subjects: entertainment film
Entries: appr. 400/year
> director, producer, studio, actors, opening date, rating (at first mention) or reference to previous entry; review excerpts up to 1/4 page
Indexes: title, name-title, reviewer
Period covered: current and recent releases
Revision and updating: published 4x/year
Media represented: films
Producers represented: domestic and foreign
Features: Academy awards listed in Spring issue. Hardbound cumulation published in August may be purchased separately (1975/1976 issue. 394p. illus. $35.00). [Similar list: *Filmfacts* (Division of Cinema, University of Southern California, P.O. Box 69610, West Station, Los Angeles, CA 90069. $40.00/year) supplies very full synopses, critiques, credits, and excerpts from reviews in 16 newspapers and periodicals semi-monthly, but with over a year's delay after the release of a film.]
Subject terms: film study

32-27*   **Let's See It Again; Free Films for Elementary Schools.** J. A. Kislia. CEBCO Pflaum, Fairfield, NJ 07006, 1975. 126p. $2.95pa.
Purpose: free-loan 16mm films recommended by author after screening 400 films in an elementary school
Grade level: primary, intermediate
Arrangement: alphabetical title
Subjects: all
Entries: appr. 180
> running time, source, release date; critical review and synopsis; rating, grade level, subject
Indexes: subject
Period covered: 1950s-1972
Revision and updating:
Media represented: films
Producers represented: appr. 30 academic, government (including foreign), institutional
Features:
Subject terms: all subjects

32-28*   **Today's Education.** National Education Association, 1201 16th Street, NW, Washington, DC 20036. $8.00/year.
Purpose: "Audiovisual Materials" column by William J. Cuttill of Indiana University Audiovisual Center recommends films, each issue on a separate topic

32-28 (cont'd)
Grade level: all
Arrangement: topical
Subjects: all
Entries: appr. 45/year

    running time, producer; contents note; grade level
        omitted: release date, price
Indexes: indexed in *Media Review Digest* (01-03)
Revision and updating: published 4x/year
Media represented: films
Producers represented: various
Features: [See also 34-06.]
Subject terms: all subjects

33-Filmstrips

    Both sound and silent filmstrips are included in this designation, and sound may be provided by a variety of recorded media.
    The bulk of *The Elementary School Library Collection* (01-09) audio-visual media listings consists of filmstrips. Regular columns reviewing filmstrips appear in each issue of *Booklist* (01-12) and *Previews* (01-11). These and other reviews are indexed in *Media Review Digest* (01-03).
    Annual columns featuring the "best" filmstrips of the year appear in the December issue of *Learning* (01-17) in addition to the two listed in this chapter (33-04 and 33-05).

33-01*   **Index to 35mm Educational Filmstrips.** 6th ed. National Information Center for Educational Media, University of Southern California, University Park, Los Angeles, CA 90007, 1977. 3v. $86.50; $45.50 microfiche. LC 76-1642.
Purpose: comprehensive listing of "commercially produced educational filmstrips"
Grade level: all
Arrangement: alphabetical title
Subjects: all
Entries: appr. 70,000 (including adult)

    full format details including information on whether filmstrip is with or without caption, or accompanied by record, script, tape; contents summary; grade level; release date; distributor; out-of-print titles so indicated
        omitted: price
Indexes: classed subject index (v.1)
Period covered: 1950s-1970s
Revision and updating: published biennially; *Update of Nonbook Media*
Media represented: filmstrips
Producers represented: several thousand

33-01 (cont'd)
Features: For comprehensive coverage of recent years, *Films and Other Media for Projection* (01-20) may be used.
Subjects: all subjects

33-02* **Educational Sound Filmstrip Directory.** 10th ed. DuKane Corporation, 2900 DuKane Drive, St. Charles, IL 60174, 1976. 13p. free.
Purpose: index to producers' catalogs; comprehensive
Grade level: all
Arrangement: 29 topics
Subjects: all
Entries: over 100

> name and address of producer only
Indexes: none
Period covered: available at time of publication
Revision and updating: appr. annual
Media represented: filmstrips
Producers represented: appr. 230
Features: DuKane is a manufacturer of viewing equipment.
Subject terms: all subjects

33-03* **Educators Guide to Free Filmstrips.** 29th ed. Educators Progress Service, Randolph, WI 53956, 1977. 174p. $10.00. LC 50-11650.
Purpose: free visuals for classroom use; comprehensive
Grade level: all
Arrangement: 17 topics

Subjects:	accident prevention and safety	driver education	home economics
	aerospace education	environmental education	industrial education
	agriculture	geography	music
	arts and crafts	guidance	religion
	business education	health and physical education	science
	communications and transportation	history	social problems
			sports and recreation

Entries: appr. 550

> full ordering information; release date in a few cases; entries new to this edition are starred; availability of teacher's guide, script, etc.
> omitted: grade level
Indexes: title, subject
Period covered: available at time of publication
Revision and updating: published annually
Media represented: filmstrips, slides, transparencies
Producers represented: appr. 100 institutional, government, etc.
Features: [See introduction to 34—Free and Inexpensive Publications.]
Subject terms: all subjects

33-04* **"Filmstrips and Slides Roundup; Best of the Year."** Diana Spirt. *Previews*, v.5, April 1977, pp. 2-6.

33-04 (cont'd)
Purpose: recommendations selected from 510 entries from over 60 producers
    and distributors
Grade level: all
Arrangement: topical
Subjects:

anthropology	health	outdoor education
art	history	pets
communications	home economics	photography
death and dying	language arts	science
early childhood	literature & drama	social studies
environment &	marriage	sociology
ecology	mathematics	women's studies
guidance	music	

Entries: over 70

format details, producer, prices; grade level; titles of component parts;
reference to earlier *Previews* critical review
Indexes:
Period covered: 1975-76 releases
Revision and updating: annual feature
Media represented: filmstrips, slides
Producers represented: over 40
Features: Social studies and related topics are largest single group.
Subject terms: all subjects

33-05* **"First Class Filmstrips."** Adele Patterson. *Media and Methods*, v.13,
    April 1977, p. 40-41, 56-63.
Purpose: "materials that can be purchased with confidence . . . the best we have
    seen"; recommendations by 17 teachers and librarians
Grade level: secondary
Arrangement: 3 topical groupings
Subjects: humanities
    literature and language arts skills (categories vary from year to year)
    social studies
Entries: 29

producer, price; signed critical review
    omitted: format data, running time
Indexes:
Period covered: March 1976 and later releases
Revision and updating: previous listings in April 1976 and March 1975
Media represented: filmstrips
Producers represented: various
Features: Finds "lessening quality" in filmstrip medium.
Subject terms:

humanities	social studies
language arts	

34-Free and Inexpensive Publications

This chapter includes lists of pamphlets issued by organizations such as trade and professional associations, citizens' groups, and others. Lists of government publications only are found in the following chapter. Free and inexpensive non-print media are referenced in appropriate chapters.

Because much of this material is fugitive, retrospective lists are inappropriate, and any list must be frequently revised to be of use. Since users should replace them as frequently as they are revised, inexpensive guides are a good choice.

Free and inexpensive materials generally are not evaluated for objectivity or suitability for particular classroom situations. This is true of those listed in the *Educators Guides*, published by Educators Progress Service, as well as of others. Many come from sources of high authority. Others have obvious bias, and opposing views must be presented if such material is used in school. The guides here suggested can lead to publications with many different points of view.

There is some duplication among the various guides addressed to the school market. Even so, many important and highly respected sources are not found in any of them. *Alternatives in Print* (01-21) and *Sources* (01-22) must be consulted to locate output of the Center for Science in the Public Interest, Scientists Institute for Public Information, Women's Action Alliance, and American Civil Liberties Union, among others.

Preferred procedures for requesting materials generally are suggested in the guides addressed to teachers. *Educators Guides* to subject areas (e.g., 15-02, 16-01 and 17-01) overlap with those to specific media (e.g., 30-10 and 32-04).

34-01   **Vertical File Index.** H. W. Wilson Co., New York, NY $14.00/year.
Purpose: "subject and title index to selected pamphlets. Inclusion does not constitute a recommendation"
Grade level: all
Arrangement: alphabetical by subject
Subjects: all
Entries: over 2000/year

author, title, publisher, date of publication; price; number of pages; some contents notes
Indexes: title
Period covered: currently published
Revision and updating: published 11x/year
Media represented: free and inexpensive publications, government publications
Producers represented: various private, government, institutional, commercial, U.S. and foreign
Features: Although few free items are listed and many of the items listed are definitely not inexpensive, this index does give access to publications that may not turn up in other bibliographies, and it is very generally found in public libraries.
Subject terms: all subjects

34-02* **Free and Inexpensive Learning Materials.** 18th ed. George Peabody College for Teachers, Nashville, TN 37203, 1976. 250p. $3.50pa.
Purpose: recommendations based on factual contents, timeliness, utility
Grade level: all
Arrangement: appr. 100 subject headings
Subjects: all
Entries: over 3000

ordering information; price; contents note; grade level (in some cases)
Indexes: subject
Period covered: available at time of publication
Revision and updating: revised biennially; 1000 new listings since previous edition
Media represented: free and inexpensive publications, graphic materials, maps, government publications
Producers represented: various
Features: Priced items are generally under $2.00.
Subject terms: all subjects

34-03* **Educators Grade Guide to Free Teaching Aids.** 22nd ed. Educators Progress Service, Randolph, WI 53956, 1976. looseleaf. $24.50. LC 56-2444.
Purpose: free materials available for classroom use; comprehensive
Grade level: primary, intermediate
Arrangement: 14 curricular areas and section on visual and audiovisual aids
Subjects: accident prevention and safety; aerospace education; business education (incl. consumer education); clubs, hobbies, holidays; communication and transportation; environmental education; fine arts; guidance; home economics; health and physical education; industrial education; language arts and arithemetic; science; social studies
Entries: appr. 2000

format, source; contents note
Indexes: source
Period covered: available at time of publication
Revision and updating: published annually
Media represented: free and inexpensive publications, government publications, graphic materials, maps
Producers represented: appr. 600
Features: See the introduction to 34—Free and Inexpensive Publications. This, other Educators Progress publications, and *Selected Free Materials for Classroom Teachers* (34-07) are the only major guides addressed to schools that list only free materials.
Subject terms: all subjects

34-04* **Educators Index of Free Materials.** 86th ed. Educators Progress Service, Randolph, WI 53956, 1977. 264p. $29.00. LC 44-32700.
Purpose: free materials for classroom use; comprehensive
Grade level: secondary

34-04 (cont'd)
Arrangement: eight subject groupings, one for audiovisual aids
Subjects: audiovisual aids
clubs, hobbies, scouting
and special days
fine arts
health, physical education
language arts
science and mathematics
social studies
special areas (consumer education, driver education, guidance,
others)
vocational education
Entries: appr. 3000
Indexes: source index
Period covered: available at time of publication
Revision and updating: published annually
Media represented: free and inexpensive publications, maps, graphic materials,
government publications
Producers represented: appr. 800 commercial, trade and professional associates,
government (including foreign), academic
Features: See introduction to 34—Free and Inexpensive Publications. This, other
Educators Progress publications, and *Selected Free Materials for Classroom
Teachers* (34-07) are the only major guides addressed to schools that list
only free materials.
Subject terms: all subjects

34-05 **Magazines for Libraries.** 2nd ed. Bill Katz. Bowker, 1972. 822p.
$25.00. LC 72-6607. **Supplement.** 1974. 328p. $17.50.
Purpose: "Free Magazines" (main volume, pp. 328-357; *Supplement*, pp. 131-135)
make up one chapter of this widely used guide to selecting periodicals,
found in many public libraries
Grade level: all
Arrangement: alphabetical title
Subjects: all
Entries: over 100

full ordering information; signed review; grade level
Indexes: title
Period covered: available at time of publication
Revision and updating: 1st ed. 1969; *Supplement* notes ceased publications;
supplemented also by Katz's regular column in *Library Journal* (semi-
monthly)
Media represented: free and inexpensive publications, government publications
Producers represented: business and government, including foreign
Features: [Similar list: *Free Magazines for Teachers and Libraries.* 2nd ed.
Ken Haycock. Ontario Library Association, 2397A Bloor Street W,
Toronto M6S 1P6, Canada. $5.50.]
Subject terms: all subjects

34-06* **Today's Education.** National Education Association, 1201 16th
Street, NW, Washington, DC 20036. $8.00/year.
Purpose: "Free or Inexpensive" is a regular feature
Grade level: all

34-06 (cont'd)
Arrangement: by subject
Subjects: all
Entries: appr. 80/year
    ordering information
        omitted: grade level
Indexes:
Period covered: current and recent publications
Revision and updating: published 4x/year
Media represented: free and inexpensive publications, government publications
Producers represented: various, including NEA
Features: Includes professional materials, catalogs, etc. For film column, see
    32-28.
Subject terms: all subjects

34-07*   Selected Free Materials for Classroom Teachers. Ruth H. Aubrey.
    5th ed. Fearon Publishers, Inc., Belmont, CA 94002, 1975. 130p.
    $2.75pa.
Purpose: "carefully screened," recommended on basis of importance, effective
    presentation, usefulness, freedom from undesirable advertising and bias
Grade level: intermediate, secondary
Arrangement: by publisher within appr. 50 curricular categories
Subjects: business   industrial education
             career education   social science
             health education   others
             home economics
Entries: over 2000
    source, titles available, ordering information; grade level; full contents
    summary
Indexes: combined subject-publisher
Period covered: available at time of publication
Revision and updating: previous edition 1971; 124 new sources listed
Media represented: filmstrips, free and inexpensive publications, government
    publications, graphic materials, transparencies, films, maps
Producers represented: 562
Features: This and Educators Progress Service publications are the only major
    guides to free materials exclusively. [Similar list: *The Catalog of Free Things*
    by Jeffrey Feinman and Mark Weiss (William Morrow, 1976. 258p. $6.95pa.)
    lists some 700 free pamphlets from organizations and government agencies,
    but they are not preselected for classroom use.]
Subject terms: all subjects

34-08*   Index to Free Periodicals. Pierian Press, Ann Arbor, MI 48104.
    $15.00/year.
Purpose: author-title-subject index to free periodicals
Grade level: all
Arrangement: alphabetical title
Subjects: all

34-08 (cont'd)
Entries: over 1000 articles

    volume, date, pages
       omitted: publisher's address
Indexes:
Period covered: current publications
Revision and updating: published 2x/year
Media represented: free and inexpensive publications
Producers represented: over 50 periodicals
Features: [Similar list: "A School Librarian Recommends Free Magazines"
(*American Libraries*, v.8, February 1977, p. 89) names five in addition
to 25 free magazines recommended in preceding article, "A New Look at
Free Magazines" (pp. 85-88) by C. Edward Wall, Editor-in-Chief of the
Index.]
Subject terms: all subjects

35—Government Publications

    The federal government publishes maps, posters, and charts and produces
films, filmstrips, and other audiovisual aids. References dealing specifically with
such media are found in 01—Comprehensive Lists, 36—Graphic Materials and
39—Maps. The subject chapters in Section II also refer to appropriate agencies
and their (print and non-print) output. Only those lists that deal primarily with
printed matter and are limited enough to be of potential use to the educator
are considered here.

    Prices of government publications have increased substantially in recent
years. Even so, many remain in the inexpensive category and many remain free,
officially or unofficially. Material priced for sale by the Superintendent of
Documents may be distributed free by issuing agencies (*Government Publications*,
by Philip Leidy. 4th ed. Columbia University Press, 1976, on pp. 369-374 lists
agencies from which materials may be obtained free or purchased directly).
Members of Congress, while mandating that the Government Printing Office be
self-sustaining, obtain publications for free distribution to constituents. Ralph
Nader in January 1975 estimated that only 15 percent of government documents
are sold, the rest being distributed free (see ED 125 956). Publications of the
General Accounting Office, Washington, DC 20548, the investigative arm of
Congress, are free to "local governments, college . . . students, non-profit
organizations."

    Although the federal government is the largest publisher in the United
States and possibly in the world, its output is rarely reviewed. Some of it is
fugitive and of interest for a limited time only. For these reasons, keeping up
with current publications is as important here as it is in purchasing other free
and inexpensive publications. Ordering government publications by mail can be
a slow process. Retail bookstores are operated in the following cities: Atlanta,
Birmingham, Boston, Chicago, Cleveland, Columbus, Dallas, Denver, Detroit,

Houston, Jacksonville, Kansas City, Los Angeles, Milwaukee, New York, Philadelphia, Pueblo, (Colorado), San Francisco, Seattle, and Washington, They sell publications of general interest and maintain complete catalogs.

Consumers Guide to Federal Publications and *Government Periodicals and Subscription Services* (Government Printing Office, Washington, DC 20402) provide additional information, including how to obtain subject bibliographies on over 270 topics. Selected ones (SB numbers) are referred to in appropriate chapters.

State publications vary considerably from state to state as do policies on free distribution. Consult the legislative manual of your state or the telephone directory of your state capital to learn the names and addresses of state agencies.

Public Affairs Information Service Bulletin (weekly), found in many libraries, selectively lists publications of federal, state, local, and international bodies.

35-01* **Selected U.S. Government Publications.** Superintendent of Documents, Washington, DC 20402 or Pueblo, CO 81009. free.
Purpose: available government publications likely to be of popular interest; comprehensive
Grade level: all
Arrangement: topical, random
Subjects: (not each in every issue)

business and industry	the military
education	national news
energy and environment	on foreign shores
highways and skyways	science & technology
the land	to your health
the law	others

Entries: appr. 2000/year

full ordering information; brief description
omitted: grade level indication
Indexes: none
Period covered: current output and retrospective; in-print materials
Revision and updating: published 12x/year
Media represented: government publications, graphic materials, maps
Producers represented: U.S. government
Features: Anyone who wants to take advantage of the large publishing output of the U.S. government must follow this free 16-page publication. Order forms are included with each issue.
Subject terms: all subjects

35-02 **A Guide to Popular Government Publications for Libraries and Home Reference.** Linda C. Pohle. Libraries Unlimited, Inc., Littleton, CO 80160, 1972. 224p. $9.50. LC 70-189256.
Purpose: recommended free and inexpensive government publications of popular interest
Grade level: all
Arrangement: alphabetical by topic

35-02 (cont'd)
Subjects: (listings of 3 or more pages)

Armed Forces	international relations	travel
child and infant care	medicine and health	trees
drugs	national parks	U.S. history
fine arts	occupations	vocational education
fish and wildlife	taxes	World War II

Entries: 1394

full ordering information, including price; evaluative annotations
  omitted: grade level suitability
Indexes: subject (15p.), title
Period covered: 1960s-1971
Revision and updating:
Media represented: government publications, maps, graphic materials
Producers represented: U.S. government
Features: Of the various guides to government publications, this easy-to-use
  listing is likely to be the most useful to schools. The introduction gives
  valuable pointers on how to obtain documents. Although many of the
  specific titles may no longer be in print, information as to the type of
  materials issuing from various agencies is of continuing value. Prices of
  government publications have been subject to significant increases, so
  prices given here should be disregarded.
Subject terms: all subjects

35-03*   Government Reference Books 74/75. 4th vol. Alan Schorr. Libraries
Unlimited, Inc., Littleton, CO 80160, 1976. 263p. $11.50. LC 76-
146307.
Purpose: comprehensive
Grade level: all
Arrangement: topical
Subjects:

agriculture	engineering	medicine
arts and architecture	environmental science	music
astronomy	general reference	physics
biology	geography	political science
chemistry	history and area studies	recreation and
data processing	languages	travel
earth science	law	sociology
economics and business	literature	statistics
education	mathematics	urbanology

Entries: over 1300

ordering information, publication date, price; contents summary and
  annotation
Indexes: combined author-title-subject
Period covered: 1974-1975 imprints
Revision and upating: published biennially
Media represented: government publications
Producers represented: U.S. government

35-03 (cont'd)
Features: Since government publications go out of print quickly, a list of only
the past two years' output is quite adequate for the small library, whether
public or school, and for the individual purchaser.
Subject terms: all subjects

35-04   State Government Reference Publications: An Annotated Bibliography.
David W. Parish. Libraries Unlimited, Inc., Littleton, CO 80160, 1974.
237p. $11.50. LC 74-81322.
Purpose: selected publications of each state
Grade level: all
Arrangement: alphabetical by state and territory
Subjects: all
Entries: 808

issuing agency, dates of publication, price (if any); full descriptions of
contents, special features
Indexes: combined author-title, subject
Period covered: available at time of publication
Revision and updating:
Media represented: government publications, free and inexpensive publications
Producers represented: state and territorial governments, commercial publishers
Features: Publications listed here, which are likely to be of interest to schools,
include pamphlets, directories, statistical sources, popular periodicals,
and others. Among entries in the subject index are: agriculture, air pollution, atlases, conservation, courts, ethnic groups, history, Indians, economics
and business, travel guides, urban development, and planning.
Subject terms:
agricultural education
social studies

35-05   Guide to Foreign Information Sources. Chamber of Commerce of
the United States, 1615 "H" Street, NW, Washington, DC 20006,
1974. 51p. $1.00pa.
Purpose: comprehensive
Grade level: all
Arrangement: alphabetical by country; "Selected Bibliographical References"
alphabetical title
Subjects: foreign countries
Entries: names and addresses of government offices, organizations; ordering
information for publications
Indexes: none
Period covered: current
Revision and updating: revised editions at irregular intervals
Media represented: free and inexpensive publications, government publications
Producers represented: governments (U.S. and foreign), organizations
Features: Lists consulates, trade missions, travel offices. [Similar list: *Congressional
Directory* lists foreign embassies only.]

35-05 (cont'd)
Subject terms:
 foreign language
 world cultures

35-06 **Booklist.** American Library Association, 50 East Huron Street, Chicago, IL 60611. $20.00/year.
Purpose: "Government Publications" by Leroy C. Schwarzkopf appears as a monthly feature in the issue dated the 15th of each month; recommendations
Grade level: all
Arrangement: alphabetical title
Subjects: all
Entries: appr. 400/year

 full ordering information, including price; contents annotation
  omitted: grade level suitability
Indexes:
Period covered: current output up to 2 months before publication
Revision and updating: published 11x/year
Media represented: government publications, graphic materials, maps
Producers represented: U.S. government
Features: It is profitable to peruse this selective list to catch titles one may have missed in scanning *Selected U.S. Government Publications* (35-01).
Subject terms: all subjects

35-07 **"State Publications."** Peter Hernon. *Library Journal*, v.97, April 15, 1972, pp. 1393-1398; v.99, November 1, 1974, pp. 2810-2819.
Purpose: "a bibliographic guide for reference collections"; evaluative
Grade level: intermediate, secondary
Arrangement: state-by-state listings in each issue
Subjects: state government publications
Entries: 100

 full ordering information for in-print materials; bibliographic data for others
  omitted: indication of suitability for various ages and audiences
Indexes:
Period covered: current and retrospective
Revision and updating: 1974 article is update of 1972
Media represented: government publications
Producers represented: state governments, commercial publishers
Features: Addressed primarily to the interests of the academic researcher.
Subject terms: social studies

35-08 **School Media Quarterly.** American Association of School Librarians, 50 East Huron Street, Chicago, IL 60611. $15.00/year.
Purpose: "Government Publications," by Christine L. Wynar, a regular feature, recommends "a selective list of publications from federal government sources useful for media center collections"
Grade level: all

35-08 (cont'd)
Arrangement: by topic
Subjects: all
Entries: appr. 100/year

full ordering information; evaluative annotation
Indexes: none
Period covered: currently available
Revision and updating: published 4x/year
Media represented: government publications, graphic materials, maps
Producers represented: U.S. government
Features: In view of the increasing cost of government publications, it is important to have access to recommendations and evaluations before purchase. This is the only listing selected specifically for school use.
Subject terms: all subjects

36—Graphic Materials

Materials included under this heading are all sorts of flat media that do not require equipment for use, with or without accompanying or integral printed matter: charts, pictures, study prints, photographs, posters, illustrations in periodicals. Art reproductions and exhibit catalogs are considered in 20—Visual Arts.

Previews (01-11) occasionally reviews media of this type. These and others are indexed in the "Miscellaneous" portion of *Media Review Digest* (01-03).

The leaflet *Posters, Charts, Picture Sets and Decals* is available free from the Superintendent of Documents, Washington, DC 20402, and *Engraved and Lithographed Printings* from the Bureau of Engraving and Printing, Washington, DC 20228. The services of the National Archives are referred to in 17—Social Studies and 18—Ethnic Groups. Perusal of *Selected U.S. Government Publications* (35-01) is fruitful.

Many guides listed in 34—Free and Inexpensive Publications include graphic materials in their contents. The *Readers Guide to Periodical Literature* indexes illustrations in popular periodicals.

Picture Sources 3: Collections of Prints and Photographs in the U.S. and Canada by Ann Novotny (Special Libraries Association, 235 Park Avenue, New York, NY 10003, 1975. $17.00) describes not only commercial picture services but also those of federal agencies such as the Bureau of Reclamation, Forest Service, Bureau of Land Management, Department of Housing and Urban Development, and others. These generally do not charge print or reproduction rights. Almost 300 commercial and non-profit sources are also listed in the *Writer's Market* (1977. $13.50. pp. 760-789).

36-01   National Geographic Index 1947-1969. National Geographic Society, Washington, DC 20036, 1970. 618p. o.p. LC 71-130451. 1970-1971 Supplement. 1972. 65p. o.p.
Purpose: cumulative index to *National Geographic* (monthly)
Grade level: all

36-01 (cont'd)
Arrangement: alphabetical by subject
Subjects: *National Geographic* magazine
Entries: appr. 10,000

author, title, exact pagination; maps and illustrations indicated
Indexes: none
Period covered: 1947-1971
Revision and updating: v.1 covers 1899-1946
Media represented: graphic materials, maps
Producers represented: 1
Features: covers more and gives fuller data than *Handy Key* (36-02).
Subject terms:
science
social studies

36-02* **Handy Key to Your "National Geographics": Subject and Picture
Locater.** 12th ed. C. S. Underhill, P.O. Box 127, East Aurora, NY
14052, 1976. $3.50pa.
Purpose: index to *National Geographic* (monthly)
Grade level: all
Arrangement: alphabetical by subject
Subjects: *National Geographic* magazine
Entries: appr. 4000

month of publication only; maps and illustrations indicated
Indexes:
Period covered: 1915-1975
Revision and updating: published every other year since 1954
Media represented: graphic materials, maps
Producers represented: 1
Features:
Subject terms:
science
social studies

36-03 **Illustration Index.** Roger C. Greer. 3rd ed. Scarecrow Press, Metuchen,
NJ 08840, 1973. 164p. $6.00. LC 72-10918.
Purpose: indexes illustrations in 12 periodicals (*American Heritage, Ebony,
Grade Teacher, Hobbies, Holiday, Instructor, Life, Look, National Geographic,
School Arts, Sports Illustrated, Travel*) and two National Geographic books
Grade level: all
Arrangement: alphabetical subject order, using Library of Congress subject
headings
Subjects: all
Entries: over 3000

volume, page, date; color or black-and-white
Indexes: none
Period covered: 1963-1971
Revision and updating: 2nd ed. 1966 (by Vance)

36-03 (cont'd)
Media represented: graphic materials
Producers represented: 11 publishers
Features: Schools that have hard-copy backfiles of these heavily illustrated magazines will find this a useful means of retrieving pictorial matter—particularly on events of the 1960s.
Subject terms: all subjects

36-04*   Aerial Photography Summary Record System. National Cartographic Information Center, Reston, VA 22092, 1976. 4v. and covering sheet. free.
Purpose: comprehensive guide to aerial photographs of the continental United States for sale by Geological Survey, Forest Service, Soil Conservation Service, Agricultural Stabilization and Conservation Service, Defense Mapping Agency, National Ocean Survey, National Aeronautics and Space Administration
Grade level: all
Subjects: planned photography   1973 to present
            projects in progress   1972 and earlier
Entries: 7 million photos

        letter symbol for each agency indicates coverage
Indexes:
Period covered: available at time of publications
Revision and updating:
Media represented: graphic materials
Producers represented: U.S. government
Features:
Subject terms:
        earth science
        geography

36-05*   Hart Picture Archives. Volume 1; A Compendium. Hart Publishing Company, Inc., New York, NY 10012, 1976. 396p. $14.95pa. LC 75-31405.
Purpose: pictures, chiefly lithographs and most pre-1907, that are in the public domain and may be reproduced without permission
Grade level: all
Arrangement: 96 topical categories
Subjects: architectural elements   designs and patterns   trades and occu-
            arms and armor   furniture   pations
            bridges .   landscapes   vehicles and
            celebrated persons   music   transportation
            Christmas   ships and boats   others
            coins   tools
Entries: 2228

        identifying caption
Indexes: subject
Period covered: originally published 1800s-1973

36-05 (cont'd)
Revision and updating: first of projected 25 volume set
Media represented: graphic materials
Producers represented: over 130 books
Features: A source for period pictures on almost any topic.
Subject terms: all subjects

36-06* **"Stories Without Words."** Sharon Pheil. *The U*N*A*B*A*S*H*E*D Librarian*, no. 20, 1976. p. 10.
Purpose: Picture books without text; comprehensive
Grade level: primary
Arrangement: alphabetical author
Subjects:
Entries: 68
    title, publisher, publication date
Indexes:
Period covered: 1963-74
Revision and updating:
Media represented: graphic materials
Producers represented: various publishers
Features: [Similar list: "Wordless Booklist" by Children's Book Council (*School Library Journal*, v.21, October 1974, pp. 83-84); see also "Stories without Words" in subject index of *The Elementary School Library Collection* (01-09)]
Subject terms:
    language arts
    visual arts

37-Kits

This term defines a combination of two or more media not necessarily used together (unlike sound filmstrips or slide-tape sets, where words and pictures are coordinated). *Booklist* (01-12) reviews media fitting this classification in the issue dated the fifteenth of each month and *Previews* (01-11) in each issue. These and other reviews are indexed in the "Miscellaneous" section of *Media Review Digest* (01-03). The Media Index locates multi-media lists that include kits. No separate entries are given for kits.

38-Manipulative Materials

A variety of media sometimes labeled and cataloged separately as models, realia, specimens, games, toys, mock-ups, etc., are comprised in this category. Dealers' catalogs must be used almost exclusively to locate them, although *The*

Index to Simulations/Games for Education and Training (41-01) does include
card and board games and mechanical devices. *Booklist* (01-12) occasionally
runs a column reviewing realia. Multi-media lists that include manipulative materials
are found through the Media Index. *Materials for the Open Classroom*, by Skip
Asheim (Dell, 1973. 96p. illus. $3.00pa.) recommended several hundred such
materials for primary and intermediate grades on the basis of their "open-endedness,"
describing and illustrating them in *Whole Earth Catalogue* format.

39—Maps

Display maps generally are sold directly by producers, and vendors' catalogs
must be searched to find suitable choices. Maps in transparency or duplicating
master form may be found through distributors' catalogs.

A vast amount of cartography issues from agencies of federal, state, and
local governments. Much of this is free or quite inexpensive. Almost all of it contains
information and local detail not duplicated on commercial maps. Soil maps, topo-
graphical maps, maps of utility lines, and aeronautical and navigation charts are but
a few of these. To tape the vast resources of the federal government in this respect,
consult *Types of Maps Published by Government Agencies*, issued by the National
Cartographic Information Center, Reston, VA 20092 and request list *SB 102* from
the Superintendent of Documents.

Lists of a few federal agencies are detailed in this chapter. One item dealing
with aerial photography is 36-04, *Aerial Photography Summary Record System*. In
addition, the Geological Survey, Branch of Distribution (Arlington, VA 22202, or
Box 25286, Federal Center, Denver, CO 80225 for states east and west of the
Mississippi, respectively) sells state maps. The Corps of Engineers, Publications
Depot, 890 Pickett Street, Alexandria, VA 22304, has charts of navigable rivers
for sale. Central Intelligence Agency maps are sold by the Superintendent of
Documents, Washington, DC 20402. National Forest Service maps are available
free from the headquarters of each National Forest.

The output of state and local agencies is best located through personal
contact with planning and highway officials. City, county, and regional planning
agencies have working collections of such maps—both their own and those of
other agencies—and can direct the serious inquirer to appropriate sources. Local
soil conservation districts may have soil survey maps for examination or distribution.

Guides for schools listed in 34—Free and Inexpensive Publications access the
promotional publications of states and countries, which generally include free maps.
Several list free oil company cruising charts. Official Canadian maps may be purchased from:

Department of Energy, Mines and Resources, Canada Map Office, 615 Booth Street,
Ottawa, Ontario, Canada K1A OE9 (topographic maps, aeronautical charts,
geological maps and reports, world maps)

Hydrographic Chart Distribution Office, Department of the Environment, 615
Booth Street, Ottawa, Ontario, Canada K1A OE6 (nautical charts)

Canadian Government Travel Bureau, 150 Kent Street, Ottawa, Ontario K1A OH6 (Canada-US highway maps)

UNESCO maps and atlases are published by UNIPUB, Box 433, New York, NY 10016.

Readers Guide to Periodical Literature uses the subheading "maps" under entries for countries, regions, etc. It may be used to locate maps appearing in the periodicals indexed there, particularly for current use.

39-01 **Index to Topographic Maps.** U.S. Geological Survey, Reston, VA 22092, 1977. free.

Purpose: topographic maps for sale by the Geological Survey are indicated on index maps for each state, Puerto Rico, Guam, American Samoa, Virgin Islands; comprehensive

Grade level: all

Arrangement: by state

Subjects: topographic maps

Entries: several thousand

    coverage of each separately published map, scale, size; year of survey, price

Indexes:

Period covered: 1940s-1970s

Revision and updating:

Media represented: maps

Producers represented: U.S. government

Features: Includes order blanks. Index sheet for each state available separately and included in *Teacher's Packet of Geological Materials* (see 16—Science, introduction).

Subject terms: geography

39-02* **Catalog of Aeronautical Charts and Related Publications.** National Ocean Survey, Distribution Division, Riverdale, MD 20840, 1976. 12p. free.

Purpose: National Ocean Survey charts of domestic areas and certain Defense Mapping Agency charts of foreign areas for sale by the National Ocean Survey are indicated on index maps

Grade level: all

Arrangement: geographical

Subjects: low and high altitude charts   world aeronautical charts
          navigation charts   others
          sectional charts

Entries: several hundred

    coverage of each separately published chart, scale, projection, price

Indexes:

Period covered: currently available

Revision and updating: monthly supplements

Media represented: maps

Producers represented: U.S. government

39-02 (cont'd)
Features: Sectional Series provides coverage of continental United States in 37
sheets, Hawaii in one, Alaska in 17, showing relief and contours, and may
be had without aeronautical overprint. Eleven world aeronautical charts,
also available without overprint, cover the continental states, plus seven
for Alaska.
Subject terms:
 earth science
 geography

39-03*   Nautical Chart Catalog. National Ocean Survey, Distribution Division,
          Riverdale, MD 20840. 1976-77. 2 folded maps. free.
Purpose: nautical charts for sale by the National Ocean Survey are indicated on
index maps for the Pacific, Atlantic, and Gulf Coasts
Grade level: all
Arrangement: geographical
Subjects: nautical charts
Entries: several hundred
     coverage of each separately published chart, scale; price
Indexes:
Period covered: available at time of publication
Revision and updating: frequent revisions
Media represented: maps
Producers represented: U.S. government
Features: Includes information on other National Ocean Survey publications,
a state-by-state list of authorized dealers, and order blanks. The National
Ocean Survey incorporates the former U.S. Coast and Geodetic Survey.
The catalog is included in *Oceanographic Packet* (see 16–Science,
introduction).
Subject terms:
 geography
 oceanography

39-04*   List of Frequently Used Federal Government World, United States
          and Historical Maps. 8th ed. National Ocean Survey, Rockville, MD
          20852, 1976. folded sheet. free.
Purpose: descriptive; maps available from seven agencies
Grade level: all
Arrangement: topical
Subjects: historical   United States
           projections   world
Entries: appr. 40
     size, scale, coverage; source, order number, price
          omitted: publication date
Indexes:
Period covered: available at time of publication
Revision and updating:
Media represented: maps

39-04 (cont'd)
Producers represented: U.S. government
Features: Included in *Science Packet* (see 16—Science, introduction).
Subject terms:
American history
geography

40–Microforms

Microfiche is microfilm in sheet form; it generally contains 98 exposures per fiche. It is used for the reproduction of out-of-print titles, primary sources, and otherwise unpublished special reports. Educators are familiar with its application to educational research through ERIC. Backfiles of newspapers and periodicals are preserved on either microfiche or microfilm, and such backfiles are commonplace in libraries.

Examples of special collections on microform geared to school needs are listed in 11—Language Arts (11-02) and 01—Comprehensive Lists (01-25), and are mentioned in the introductions to 16—Earth Science and 17—American history.

Micropublishers' Trade List Annual, Guide to Microforms in Print and *Subject Guide to Microforms in Print* are frequently revised indexes to total microform production. No separate entries are given for microforms.

41–Simulation Games

This chapter considers simulation games only. Table games and the like are included under 38—Manipulative Materials.

Educational games involving simulation and role playing are most frequently used in social studies instruction. Consultation of the guides listed in this chapter is essential for simulation game selection. There are very few reviews in professional journals serving various disciplines, and in *Media Mix* (01-28). They are indexed in *Media Review Digest* (01-03).

41-01*   The Guide to Simulations/Games for Education and Training. Robert E.
Horn. 3rd ed. Didactic Systems, Inc., Box 457, Cranford, NJ 07016,
1977. 2v. $29.00. LC 76-48753.
Purpose: comprehensive; addressed to the potential game user; v. 1—Academic
Grade level: all
Arrangement: alphabetical title within 30 subject groupings

41-01 (cont'd)

Subjects:

communications	geography	mathematics
community issues	health care	practical economics
domestic politics	history	self development
ecology	international relations	social studies
economics	language skills	urban
frame games	legal system	others
futures		

Entries: over 1200 (including college, graduate & professional)

playing time, number of players, grade level, source, copyright date (not in all cases), price; summary descriptions; statement of objectives and decisions (in some cases)

Indexes: title, creators/producers
Period covered: available at time of publication
Revision and updating: previous editions 1970, 1973
Media represented: simulation games, manipulative materials
Producers represented: various commercial, academic, including foreign
Features: Each subject chapter introduced by a summary statement. Simulations requiring computer facilities listed in "computer" chapter and a very few in subject chapters. Some games for grades 3 and up. Games for business use listed in v.2. Fifteen "first games" (p. 507) and some other matter reprinted from earlier editions.
Subject terms: all subjects

41-02   Contemporary Games: A Directory and Bibliography Covering Games and Play Situations or Simulations Used for Instruction and Training by Schools, Colleges and Universities, Government, Business and Management. Jean Belch. Gale Research Co., Detroit, MI 48226, 1973-74. 2v. (v.1, $48.00; v.2, $45.00). LC 72-6353.

Purpose: comprehensive list of instructional games, both manual and computer operated
Grade level: all
Arrangement: v.1 (directory) lists games alphabetically by title; v.2 (bibliography)
Subjects: all
Entries: 900

playing time, number of players, designer, producer, distributor, price, date of publication; availability of instructional manual; grade level, subject terms; bibliographic citations; brief annotation

Indexes: grade level; subject index indicating grade levels
Period covered: current and retrospective, including discontinued games
Revision and updating:
Media represented: simulation games
Producers represented: various commercial, academic
Features: Social sciences, education, languages, and mathematics are subjects most heavily represented.
Subject terms: all subjects

41-03 **Simulation/Gaming.** P.O. Box 3039, University Station, Moscow, ID 83843. $6.00/year.
Purpose: "Games & Fun" reviewing column; evaluations
Grade level: all
Arrangement: random
Subjects: all
Entries: appr. 50/year

producer, price; descriptive annotation; signed review; rating
omitted: number of players, grade level, publication date
Indexes:
Period covered: current releases
Revision and updating: published 6x/year
Media represented: simulation games
Producers represented: various
Features:
Subject terms: all subjects

42–Slides

Here are included photographic slides for use with slide projectors. They may be accompanied by sound recorded on tape or otherwise. Transparencies designed for overhead projection are considered in 44–Transparencies.
Sources of slides on art are suggested in 20–Visual Arts (20-06).
A portion of the current production is reviewed 2-3 times a year in *Booklist* (01-12) and *Previews* (01-11). *Media Review Digest* (01-03) in its "Miscellaneous" section gives title and subject access to reviews in these and other journals. *Films and Other Media for Projection* (01-20) provides comprehensive coverage.

42-01* **Index to Educational Slides.** 3rd ed. National Information Center for Educational Media, University of Southern California, University Park, Los Angeles, CA 90007, 1977. 910pp. $42.50; $22.00 microfiche. LC 76-1599.
Purpose: comprehensive
Grade level: all
Arrangement: alphabetical title
Subjects: all
Entries: appr. 28,000

complete format data, including size, number of frames, etc.; producer, publication date (not in all cases); few annotations; out-of-print titles so indicated
omitted: price
Indexes: classed subject
Period covered: to 1976
Revision and updating: previous editions 1973, 1974; *Update of Nonbook Media*

42-01 (cont'd)
Media represented: slides
Producers represented: appr. 350
Features: Although fine arts listings comprise about two-thirds of the total, the output of major art museums is not included. Slides of the Field Museum of Natural History are also missing.
Subject terms:
 all subjects
 visual arts

42-02*   **Slide Buyer's Guide; 1976 Edition.** Nancy DeLaurier. College Art Association, 16 East 52nd Street, New York, NY 10022, 1976. $5.00pa. LC 76-5632.
Purpose: comprehensive
Grade level: intermediate, secondary
Arrangement: geographic; separate listings for commercial dealers, museums, institutions for each of 26 countries
Subjects: art
Entries: appr. 450 suppliers

 address, description of service, prices; technical quality; subjects
Indexes: subject
Period covered: available at time of writing
Revision and updating: previous editions 1972, 1974
Media represented: slides
Producers represented: appr. one-half are in U.S.; includes government agencies, museums, dealers
Features:
Subject terms:

ethnic studies	visual arts
foreign language	world cultures
history	

43–Television

 Entries in this chapter describe real-time and recorded instructional and educational television programs produced by schools, universities, NET, Public Broadcasting Corporation, and similar institutions. These may consist of entire series or courses or of individual shows. Two entries (43-08 and 43-09) provide information about current showings on commercial and public television.

 Videotape and film make available many programs originally produced for television. In addition to several entries in this chapter and in 32–Films and 45–Video Recordings, almost any list found under these terms in the Media Index will lead to television programs preserved on film or tape. The "TV Programming" heading in *Superfilms* (32-22) indexes about 150 award-winners. Vanderbilt University Television News Archive records news broadcasts in both audio and video formats (17-04). Under the new copyright law taking effect

January 1, 1978, an American Television and Radio Archives is to be established at the Library of Congress.

Public television stations are listed in *Audiovisual Marketplace* (Bowker, 1977). The newsletter of the University of Illinois Visual Aids Service (1325 S. Oak Street, Champaign, IL 61820) in its Spring 1977 issue noted some 65 rental films of programs originally shown on BBC.

43-01   Film Sales Catalog. Audiovisual Center, Indiana University, Bloomington, IN 47401, 1974. 278p. free.

Purpose: catalog of sale, lease, and rental "motion pictures from seven major sources of educational films"

Grade level: all

Arrangement: alphabetical title

Subjects: all

Entries: appr. 1000 (including films based on TV programs and others)

    asterisk identifies new listings; format, running time, purchase and rental price, production date; source; grade level; contents summary; subject terms

Indexes: subject (indicates grade level)

Period covered: 1950-1973

Revision and updating: a 14-page mimeographed supplement

Media represented: films

Producers represented: National Educational Television, Public Broadcast Laboratory, Indiana University Productions, Public Television Library, PTV Stations, National Instructional Television Center, Teaching Film Custodians

Features: Teaching guides available are listed on pp. vi-vii. The subject index, unfortunately, is awkward and uneven ("Alcoholism, see Social Problems"– which turns out to be a very long listing; "Literature, see also Writing"– but there is no entry for Writing; etc.).

Subject terms: all subjects

43-02*   Video Program Catalogue 1976/77. Public Television Library, 475 L'Enfant Plaza, SW, Washington, DC 20024, 1976. 124p. free. ED 119 715. **Supplement March 1977.** 38p. free.

Purpose: sales, rental and reduplication catalog; programs shown on public television available for non-profit and educational use

Grade level: all

Arrangement: alphabetical title

Subjects: American Indian culture   health care   sex education, sex
           art, music   legal system   bias, sexuality
           Black American culture   marriage, parenthood, US culture, history
           China, Japan   motherhood   welfare
           consumerism   psychology   women
           economics   others

Entries: several hundred programs and series

    number of shows, running time; contents annotation; producing station; original production date; subject terms; price

43-02 (cont'd)
Indexes: subject (also in *Supplement*); captioned and signed programs; children's
    programs
Period covered: available at time of publication
Revision and updating: annual, with semi-annual *Supplement*
Media represented: video recordings
Producers represented: public television
Features: [Similar lists: *Television Programs of the Maryland Center for Public
    Broadcasting Available on Video Tape and Film* (The Center, Owings Mills,
    MD 21117. free) lists appr. 35 programs and series on consumer survival,
    economics, biology, English literature and other topics. *WNET 13 Film &
    Videotape Catalog* (356 West 58th Street, New York, NY 10019. free) lists
    several hundred, including series such as MacNeil-Lehrer Report, Black
    Journal, etc. and individual programs.]
Subject terms: all subjects

the arts	health and safety education
consumer education	social studies

43-03*   1977 Recorded Visual Instruction. Great Plains National Instructional
    Television Library, Box 80669, Lincoln, NE 68501, 1977. 158p. free.
Purpose: catalog of school television programs available for sale, rental or duplication
Grade level: all
Arrangement: by grade level; new programs
Subjects: all
Entries: over 200 (excluding college and professional)

    length of series, producer, grade level; course outline, objectives and
    contents; separate price schedules
        omitted: date of original production
Indexes: subject, grade level, title
Period covered: available at time of publication
Revision and updating: published annually
Media represented: films, slides, video recordings
Producers represented: school districts, educational and public television stations,
    BBC, other educational institutions, including Canadian
Features: Includes 8 series produced by the British Broadcasting Corporation
    for The Open University of Great Britain, also slide sets from the collection
    of the National Council for Geographic Education.
Subject terms:
    all subjects
    geography

43-04*   Channel 13 School Television Service Manual for Teachers. School
    Television Service, 356 West 58th Street, New York, NY 10019. 3v.
    membership.
Purpose: program listings
Grade level: all
Arrangement: by grade level and subject
Subjects: all

43-04 (cont'd)
Entries: appr. 70

broadcast time; synopsis of series; detailed contents of each show with teaching suggestions; resource listings for some series
Indexes: title (each volume)
Period covered: current school year
Revision and updating: published annually; monthly bulletins
Media represented: television
Producers represented: instructional and public television
Features: Bulletins alert users to other Channel 13 programs. Includes series from AIT (43-05), Great Plains National Instructional Television Library (43-03) and others.
Subject terms: all subjects

43-05* **1977 Television.** Agency for Instructional Television, Box A, Bloomington, IN 47401, 1977. 112p. free. ED 130 641.
Purpose: catalog of telecourses available from AIT
Grade level: all
Arrangement: alphabetical title

Subjects:	art	science
	communications	social studies
	health & physical education	others
	language arts	

Entries: appr. 100 (excluding adult)

number of programs, running time, producing station, production date; rental and duplication cost; summary of course and of each reel; grade level
Indexes: subject, grade level
Period covered: 1960s-1977
Revision and updating: annual; *1978 Catalog of Television and Audiovisual Materials*
Media represented: films, video recordings
Producers represented: various instructional television agencies
Features: Includes professional and college level courses.
Subject terms: all subjects

43-06* **Movies on TV; 1978-79 Edition.** Steven Scheuer. Bantam, 1977. 816p. $2.95pa.
Purpose: evaluations of feature films cleared for television showing
Grade level: all
Arrangement: alphabetical title
Subjects: entertainment film
Entries: 8,000-9,000

original running time, credits, release date; synopsis; rating (poor, fair, good, excellent)
Indexes: none
Period covered: 1920s-1976
Revision and updating: previous edition 1974, 8th edition since 1958

43-06 (cont'd)
Media represented: films, television
Producers represented: various U.S. and foreign
Features: Includes fewer titles from 1930s and 1940s than previous editions.
Subject terms: film study

43-07   The Family Guide to Children's Television: What to Watch, What to Miss, What to Change and How to Do It. Evelyn Kaye. Pantheon, 1974. 194p. $2.95pa. LC 73-18726.
Purpose: critique of television programs watched by children with suggestions for action; prepared with "the guidance of Action for Children's Television with the cooperation of the American Academy of Pediatrics"; National Association for Better Broadcasting (NABB) "Comprehensive Guide to Family Viewing" for 1974 appears on pp. 169-194
Grade level: primary, intermediate
Arrangement: (pp. 169-194): alphabetical listings in 5 groups: commercial network children's shows, commercial network prime-time shows and selected syndicated programs, excessively violent shows in syndication, old excessively violent crime programs, program series produced for television
Subjects: television programs
Entries: appr. 325

commercial network shows: network, day of week, and brief, critical evaluation; excessively violent shows: title listing only; program series: brief characterization
Indexes: none
Period covered: 1974/1975
Revision and updating: *Action for Children's Television Newsletter*, 46 Austin Street, Newtonville, MA 02160 ($15.00/year quarterly)
Media represented: television
Producers represented: commercial and public television networks
Features: Tool for guiding students' TV viewing at home.
Subject terms: mass media.

43-08*   Prime Time School Television. 120 South LaSalle Street, Chicago, IL 60603.
Purpose: recommendations
Grade level: all
Arrangement: random
Subjects: television programs
Entries: varies

date and time of broadcast, network; contents note; related teaching materials
Indexes:
Period covered: 4-6 weeks following publication
Revision and updating: published monthly as sponsored insert in *Media and Methods* (01-19)
Producers represented: commercial and public networks

43-08 (cont'd)
Features:
Subject terms:
    all subjects
    mass media

43-09*   **Teachers Guide to Television.** P.O. Box 564, New York, NY 10021. $4.00/year. illus.
Purpose: Fall and Spring issues list forthcoming shows on television
Grade level: all
Arrangement: chronological and by network
Subjects: television programs
Entries: vary (12 in Spring 1977 issue)

    date, time, network; synopsis; curriculum area; teaching suggestions; bibliography and related film list in separate section
        omitted: grade level
Indexes: none
Period covered: several months following publication
Revision and updating: published semi-annually
Media represented: television
Producers represented: television networks
Features:
Subject terms:
    all subjects
    mass media

43-10*   **Index to College Television Courseware; A Comprehensive Directory of Credit Courses and Concept Modules Distributed on Video Tape and Film.** W. Werner Prange. 3rd ed. Computerized Courseware Clearinghouse, University of Wisconsin, Green Bay, WI 54302, 1976. 335p. $15.00pa.
Purpose: comprehensive
Grade level: secondary
Arrangement: by subject
Subjects:

all college subjects	literature
art	mathematics
business and economics	music
communications	political science & government
computer science	psychology
history	others

Entries: appr. 300 (including college and graduate)

    instructor, course description, prerequisites; originating institution; number of programs, running time, format data; production date; recommended level
        omitted: price
Indexes: subject, title, cooperating institutions
Period covered: available at time of publication
Revision and updating: previous editions 1974, 1975
Media represented: films, video recordings

43-10 (cont'd)
Producers represented: appr. 80 colleges, universities, educational television agencies and stations
Features: Includes appropriate material from Great Plains National Instructional Television Library (43-03), among others. Range is from semester length courses to 3-program series. Many of the courses intended for underclassmen, community service or independent study may be appropriate for advanced high school students. [Similar list: Associated Western Universities, Inc., 546 Fourteenth Street, Boulder, CO 80302, a consortium of over 30 institutions, published *Televised Higher Education* (*THE*), a periodically updated looseleaf catalog of science, mathematics, engineering, and business courses from over 90 distributors.]
Subject terms: all subjects

44-Transparencies

Prepared transparencies for overhead projection are comprehensively listed in *Films and Other Media for Projection* (01-20). The few reviews in *Previews* (01-11) and other journals are indexed in the "Miscellaneous" section of *Media Review Digest* (01-03).

44-01   **Index to Educational Overhead Transparencies.** 4th ed. National Information Center for Educational Media, University of Southern California, University Park, Los Angeles, Calif. 90007, 1973. 2v. 13 microfiche. $68.50; $49.50 microfiche. LC 75-190634.
Purpose: comprehensive
Grade level: all
Arrangement: alphabetical title
Subjects: all
Entries: 50,000

format data, producer, distributor, release date (in many cases); series note; grade level; out-of-print titles so indicated
   omitted: price
Indexes: classed subject
Period covered: 1960s-current
Revision and updating: 5th ed. 1977; *Update of Nonbook Media*
Media represented: transparencies
Producers represented: appr. 75 commercial, academic, government
Features:
Subject terms: all subjects

45-Video Recordings

Off-the-air videotaping of television programs for future use is a common practice in schools. Commercial networks, the Public Broadcasting System and instructional television agencies each have rules or licensing procedures governing such recordings. They generally require erasure of the tapes after a given period. Educators should be aware of these restrictions and of applicable portions of the new copyright law. However, many commercial and non-profit sources rent or sell television programs recorded on film or video formats (see 43–Television).

The Media Index indicates sources of video recordings, both originals and reproductions. Some rental films may be videotaped on the user's equipment for closed-circuit broadcast. Film catalogs should be consulted regarding permission. Note the policy of the National Aeronautics and Space Administration (16-07).

Booklist (01-12) reviews videocassettes generally in the issue appearing on the first of each month and *Media Review Digest* (01-13) indexes videotape reviews along with those of films.

45-01*   **Index to Educational Videotapes.** 4th ed. National Information Center for Educational Media, University of Southern California, University Park, Los Angeles, CA 90007. 1977. 410p. $29.50; $14.50 microfiche. LC 74-75433.
Purpose: comprehensive listing of "commercially produced educational videotapes"
Grade level: all
Arrangement: alphabetical title
Subjects: (in order of length of listings)

science	literature & drama
social science & sociology	mathematics
psychology	business & economics
fine arts	home economics

Entries: over 15,00 (including adult)

format details, including running time, technical data; producer, distributor; contents summary; grade level; release date (in a few cases); out-of-print titles so indicated
     omitted: price
Indexes: classed subject
Period covered: 1960s-1975
Media represented: video recordings
Producers represented: appr. 400
Features:
Subject terms: all subjects

45-02*   **Video Programs/Index.** Ken Winslow. 923 6th Street, SW, Washington, DC 20024. $3.00/issue.
Purpose: comprehensive directory of sources of video programs
Grade level: all
Arrangement: alphabetical by source
Subjects: all

45-02 (cont'd)
Entries: over 100 sources of programs
available formats, fee arrangements, clearances, subject descriptors
Indexes: subject, equipment format, free loan, free duplication, presentation
rights, off-air recordings
Period covered: available at time of publication
Revision and updating: published 2x/year
Media represented: video
Producers represented: over 100
Features: *Video Blue Book* (Knowledge Industry Publications, White Plains,
NY 10604, 1976. 368p. $29.50) is a comprehensive list of some 4000
programs available in late 1975 from 95 commercial sources, arranged by
subject with title index.
Subject terms: all subjects

45-03* **Videography.** United Business Publications, 750 Third Avenue,
New York, NY 10017. $5.00/year.
Purpose: "Software Reviews" in each issue; descriptive
Grade level: all
Arrangement: random
Subjects: various
Entries: appr. 50/year

format, source, running time, sale or rental fee (not in all cases); contents
summary; code for requesting further information from producer
Indexes:
Period covered: current releases
Revision and updating: published 12x/year
Media represented: video recordings
Producers represented: various
Features: publication began 1976
Subject terms: all subjects

SUBJECT INDEX

Besides indexing items in Sections I (Comprehensive Lists) and III (Lists by Media), the Subject Index also gives more detailed access to the items in Section II (Lists by Subject). Topics described in introductions to certain chapters are cited as, for example, 15-Intro. (15, Introduction). The subject headings used in the index are those named in the entries under "subject terms" with a few additions (e.g. "documentaries"). A cross reference system directs the user to refer to other subject headings for 1) more specific (narrower) terms (NT); 2) broader terms (BT); or 3) related terms (RT). The first column of numbers represents the chapter number; the second column represents item numbers within the chapter, e.g.,

32-   05-06, 16

represents Chapter 32, items 05-06, and 16.

The "All Subjects" category should always be consulted in addition to those for more specific terms.

Subject terms new to this edition are marked with an asterisk (*).

ALL SUBJECTS
01-   01-06, 08-12, 14-18, 20, 22-23,
        25, 27-31
02-   01-02, 04
30-   04-07, 10
31-   01-02
32-   01, 03-04, 06-07, 10, 12-13,
        15, 18, 21-23, 25, 27-28
33-   01-04
34-   01-08
35-   01-03, 06, 08
36-   03, 05
41-   01-03
42-   01
43-   01-05, 08-10
44-   01
45-   01-03

AFRICA
BT   World Cultures
RT   Black studies
13-   22
15-   15
18-   03, 06
19-   10, 13, 17

*AGING
BT   Psychology
RT   Death education Guidance
15-   04, 16, 18, 21

AGRICULTURAL EDUCATION
BT   Vocational education
21-   Intro., 01-02, 10, 14, 16, 21
35-   04

ALCOHOL
Use Drug abuse education

AMERICAN HISTORY
BT   Social Studies
RT   History
01-   26
07-   07
11-   02
17-   Intro., 14, 17, 21
18-   13
39-   04

MEDIA INDEX

The Media Index identifies media encompassed by lists grouped in Sections I and II. Its terms are those of the chapters in Section III. It is designed for simultaneous use with the Subject and Instructional Level indexes.

AUDIO RECORDINGS
01-   01, 04, 08, 14, 16, 19, 21-22,
        25-26, 30-31
02-   03-04
03-   01, 03-04, 07-08, 14-15
04-   03, 07
05-   02
06-   01, 07, 10
08-   01, 06, 11
09-   03
10-   01, 05
11-   Intro., 01, 04-07, 09, 11, 15-19,
        23-26
12-   01, 03, 05-09
13-   Intro., 01-23, 25-26
14-   01, 04
15-   01-02, 09, 11, 14, 17
16-   01, 07
17-   Intro. (American History), 01,
        04, 09, 18-19, 22-23, 25
18-   01, 03, 05, 07, 10, 12, 14,
        16-18, 20-24
19-   02, 04-05, 11-13, 16-17, 19,
        22-23
21-   07, 10, 17, 22-23, 25
22-   01
30-   Intro., 01-13

FILMLOOPS
01-   01-02, 04, 08-10, 14, 22, 25, 31
02-   03
03-   04, 06, 14-15
06-   01, 05, 07
08-   01, 09, 11
10-   01
11-   04
12-   01-02, 06-08
14-   09
15-   01
16-   04
17-   22
18-   01, 03, 07, 10, 12, 16, 21-22
19-   02, 05
20-   07

FILMLOOPS (cont'd)
21-   10-12, 17, 23, 26
22-   01
31-   Intro., 01-02
32-   07

FILMS
01-   01-08, 10-14, 16-25, 27-28,
        30-31
02-   01-04
03-   Intro., 01-04, 06-09, 12, 14-17
04-   Intro., 04-08
05-   Intro., 01-02
06-   Intro., 01-05, 07-12
07-   01-12
08-   01-08, 11-12
09-   02-03
10-   01, 03-05
11-   03, 05, 08-14, 17-18, 20-24,
        26
12-   01-02, 05-09
13-   Intro., 11-12, 16-17, 20, 24
14-   01, 04-09
15-   01-14, 17-21
16-   01-05, 07-13, 15-16
17-   Intro. (American History, Urban
        Studies), 01-03, 05-06, 09-18,
        20-23, 26
18-   Intro. (Blacks), 18-02, 23, 25
19-   01-24
20-   Intro., 02, 04, 07
21-   Intro. (Industrial Arts), 03-04,
        06-13, 17, 21-25, 27
22-   Intro., 02-09
31-   02
32-   Intro., 01-28
34-   07
43-   Intro., 01, 03, 06, 10

FILMSTRIPS
01-   01, 05, 07-17, 19-20, 22-25,
        27, 29-31
02-   02-04
03-   01, 04, 06-09, 12, 14-15, 17

VIDEO RECORDINGS
01-	01-04, 12-13, 19, 21-22, 24-25, 31
04-	07
06-	01, 07
08-	01, 08, 10-11
09-	02
10-	01
12-	01, 07-08
13-	17
14-	01, 09
15-	01-02, 09-10, 18, 21
16-	01, 07

VIDEO RECORDINGS (cont'd)
17-	01, 04, 16, 18
18-	03, 13-14, 16, 20, 22
19-	04-05
20-	07
21-	07, 10, 17, 22
22-	03, 06-07
30-	10
32-	02, 13
43-	02-03, 06, 10
45-	Intro., 01-03

INSTRUCTIONAL LEVEL INDEX

The Instructional Level Index picks up the suitability of a given media list for primary, intermediate or secondary education and is designed for simultaneous use with the Subject and Media indexes.

The "All Levels" category should always be consulted in addition to those for more specific terms.

ALL LEVELS

01-	01-05, 07, 10-12, 14-15, 17, 20, 22-23, 25-27, 29, 31
02-	01-04
03-	01, 03, 14-15, 17
04-	01, 04, 08
06-	01-04, 07-11
07-	10-12
08-	01-02, 05-06, 08
09-	03
10-	01, 05
11-	01-02, 13-14, 18, 22-24, 26
12-	02, 07, 09
13-	02-03, 08-10, 12-18, 20, 22-23
14-	01, 05-08
15-	01, 03-04, 07, 10-11, 17, 19-20
16-	01, 06-07, 11-14, 16
17-	01, 03-05, 07-08, 10, 12, 18-19, 22
18-	01-04, 06, 08-14, 16-17, 19, 21-22, 25
19-	01-02, 05, 07-09, 11-14, 16-18
20-	01-07
21-	10, 14, 22, 25
22-	02-03
30-	01-06, 08, 10, 12
31-	01
32-	01-02, 04-05, 07, 09-10, 12-15, 18-19, 21-22, 25-26, 28
33-	01-04
34-	01-02, 05-06, 08
35-	01-06, 08
36-	01-05
39-	01-04
41-	01-03
42-	01
43-	01-06, 08-09
44-	01
45-	01-03

PRIMARY

01-	09, 16, 18, 30
03-	04, 06, 09
05-	01-03
06-	06
11-	05, 07, 11-12, 19
12-	03, 05
14-	04
15-	05
16-	10
18-	05, 24
21-	08
30-	11
32-	16, 23, 27
34-	03
36-	06
43-	07

INTERMEDIATE

01-	06, 09, 16, 18, 30
03-	04, 06, 09-10, 12
04-	02, 07
06-	06, 12
07-	06-07
08-	03-04, 12
09-	02, 04
11-	05, 11-12, 16, 19
12-	04-05
13-	01, 04-06, 21, 25
14-	04, 09
15-	05, 15
16-	03, 10
17-	02, 17, 20, 23
18-	05, 15, 20, 24
19-	15
21-	08, 11, 23
30-	09, 11
32-	03, 11, 16-17, 20, 23, 27
34-	03, 07
35-	07
42-	02
43-	07

SECONDARY

01-	06, 08, 13, 19, 21, 24, 28
03-	02, 05, 07-08, 10-13, 16
04-	02-03, 05-07
06-	05, 12
07-	01-09
08-	03-04, 07, 09-12
09-	01-02, 04
10-	02-04
11-	03-04, 06, 08-10, 15-17, 20-21, 25
12-	01, 04, 06, 08
13-	01, 04-07, 11, 19, 21, 25-26
14-	09
15-	02, 06, 08-09, 12-16, 18, 21
16-	02-05, 08-09, 15

SECONDARY (cont'd)

17-	02, 06, 09, 11, 13-17, 20-21, 23-28
18-	07, 15, 18, 20, 23
19-	03-04, 06, 10, 15, 19-24
21-	01-07, 09, 11-13, 15-21, 23-24, 26-27
22-	01, 04-09
30-	07, 09
31-	02
32-	03, 06, 08, 11, 17, 24
33-	05
34-	04, 07
35-	07
42-	02
43-	10

TITLE INDEX

The Title Index lists titles in UPPER CASE (all caps) that are entered separately and are fully annotated in Sections I, II, and III. Titles that are briefly mentioned in the text are printed in capitals and lower case. Asterisks identify titles new to or revised for this edition.

AAAS SCIENCE FILM CATALOG, 16-11
"A-V AIDS FOR TEACHING SIXTEENTH CENTURY ENGLISH HISTORY," 11-09
*AV GUIDE, 01-27
*ABOUT AGING: A CATALOG OF FILMS 1977, 15-15
*Action for Children's Television Newsletter, 43-07
*AERIAL PHOTOGRAPHY SUMMARY RECORD SYSTEM, 36-04
*AFRICA FROM REAL TO REEL: AN AFRICAN FILMOGRAPHY, 19-10
*Africa on Film: Myth and Reality, 19-10
*AFRICAN MUSIC: A PEOPLE'S ART, 13-22
AGING: A FILMOGRAPHY, 15-04
*AGING: AN ANNOTATED GUIDE TO GOVERNMENT PUBLICATIONS, 15-16
AGRICULTURAL EDUCATION IN A TECHNICAL SOCIETY, 21-02
AIDS TO ENVIRONMENTAL EDUCATION (GRADES. 7-9, 10-14), 06-05
AIDS TO ENVIRONMENTAL EDUCATION (PRESCHOOL-GRADE 3, GRADES 4-6), 06-06
*ALCOHOL EDUCATION MATERIALS: AN ANNOTATED BIBLIOGRAPHY, 09-04
"ALIVE BUT ALONE," 15-08
*ALL TOGETHER NOW: THE FIRST COMPLETE BEATLES DISCOGRAPHY, 1961-1975, 13-16
ALTERNATIVES, 17-11
*ALTERNATIVES IN PRINT, 01-21
*AMERICAN ANTHROPOLOGIST, 19-21
*AMERICAN BIOLOGY TEACHER, 16-04
*American Dance Band Discography, 13 Intro.
American Film Festival Guide, 32-12
*AMERICAN FILM INSTITUTE CATALOG OF MOTION PICTURES: FEATURE FILMS 1961-1970, 35-21
*The American Film Review Special Bicentennial Issue, 17 Intro. (American History)
*AMERICAN FOLKLORE FILMS AND VIDEOTAPES: AN INDEX, 18-13
*AMERICAN INDIAN REFERENCE BOOK, 18-21

*AMERICAN ISSUES FORUM, 17-21
*American Record Guide, 13-05
*The American West on Film: Myth and Reality, 07-07, 17 Intro. (American History)
*"ANIMATED FILMS: A HISTORY AND FILMOGRAPHY," 07-11
*AN ANNOTATED AND CLASSIFIED LIST OF 16 MM FILMS ON URBAN STUDIES: NEW TOWNS, URBAN PROBLEMS, CITY AND REGIONAL PLANNING, 17-26
*Annotated Bibliography of Commercially Produced Audio, Printed and Visual Career Education Materials, 03-14
*An Annotated Bibliography of Instructional Materials which Emphasize Positive Work Ethics, 03-14
*ANNOTATED BIBLIOGRAPHY OF MULTI-ETHNIC MATERIALS, 18-17
ANNOTATED FILM BIBLIOGRAPHY: CHILD DEVELOPMENT AND EARLY CHILDHOOD EDUCATION, 15-05
*ANNOTATED GUIDE TO VENEREAL DISEASE INSTRUCTIONAL MATERIALS AVAILABLE IN CANADA, 10-05
*ANNUAL INDEX TO POPULAR MUSIC RECORD REVIEWS 1975, 13-01
*APPALACHIAN BOOKS AND MEDIA FOR PUBLIC AND COLLEGE LIBRARIES, 18-20
*"ARCHAEOLOGICAL FILMS: THE PAST AS PRESENT," 19-20
*ARITHMETIC TEACHER, 12-05
*Arizona in Filmstrips, 17 Intro. (American History)
*ASIA THROUGH FILM, 19-18
*"AN ASIAN STUDIES FILMOGRAPHY," 19-07
ASIANS AND ASIAN AMERICANS, 18-02
*AUDIO, 13-21
*"AUDIO-VISUAL AIDS FOR ENGLISH HISTORY SINCE 1750: A CRITICAL REVIEW," 19-22
*Audiovisual Guide to the Catalog of the Food and Nutrition Information and Educational Materials Center, 21-17

NAME INDEX

The Name Index identifies compilers both of separately entered lists and of those mentioned in the text. Authors whose works are cited in the "Introduction to Media Selection" are noted in the references on pages xxviii to xxxi.

Ackermann, Jean Marie, 19-03
Allyn, Mildred V., 15-15
Amberg, George, 32-14
Amelio, Ralph J., 07-03
Aquino, John, 11-13
Armitage, Andrew D., 13-01
Aros, Andrew A., 11-14
Artel, Linda, 18-04, 22-03
Ash, Joan, 08-08
Asheim, Skip, 38 Intro.
Aubrey, Ruth H., 34-07
Axelrod, June M., 20-06

Barsam, Richard M., 32-17
Beale, Thomas Wight, 19-20
Beam, Karen G., 12-07
Bebey, Francis, 13-22
Belch, Jean, 41-02
Bennett, George E., 18-20
Benschoten, Reba Ann, 08-09
Bensman, Marvin R., 30-12
Bernstein, Joanne, 15-17
Betancourt, Jeanne, 22-08
Bird, Gloria, 18-11
Bitter, Gary G., 12-09
Blackmon, Carolyn, 06-04
Blesch, Edwin, Jr., 11-20
Blue, Richard, 19-24
Bologha, Barbara, 11-20
Braun, Susan, 14-07
Brown, Lucy Gregor, 01-08
Brown, Mary R., 21-02
Buchanan, Jim, 18 Intro. (Native
 Americans)
Burke, John G., 06 Intro.
Buteau, June D., 01-24
Butler, Ivan, 19-15
Buttlar, Lois, 18-16

Castleman, Harry, 13-16
Cawley, Rebecca, 06-10
Charles, Cheryl, 17-07

Cooper, B. Lee, 17-25
Coppard, Larry C., 17-28
Covert, Nadine, 16-05, 17-11, 17-13
Cuttill, William J., 32-28
Cyr, Helen W., 19-09

Darino, Eduardo, 32 Intro.
Darrell, R. D., 13-14
David, Nina, 04-06
Davis, Gwendolyn, 15-11
Davison, Susan E., 17-18, 17-24
Dawson, Bonnie, 22-02
deKeijzer, Arne J., 19-04
DeLaurier, Nancy, 42-02
DeLuca, L., 15-16
Dick, Esmé J., 17-06, 17-11
Donelson, Ken, 11-21, 11-22
Drier, Harry N., Jr., 03-01
Dykstra, Ralph R., 08-06

Edwards, Richard, 22-07
Eichman, Barbara, 17-23
Eidelberg, Lawrence, 08-10
Elliott, Peter J., 19-02
Emmens, Carol, 01-30, 11-12, 15-10,
 22-02
Enser, A. G. S., 11-13
Evans, Edward B., 21-27

Falconer, Vera M., 21-06
Feezel, Jerry D., 11-23
Feinman, Jeffrey, 34-07
Fleming, Gladys A., 14-04
Fox, Stuart, 18-25
Fulginiti, Rebecca, 11-10

Gaffney, Maureen, 32-16
Gandy, Clara I., 19-22
Gilman, Robert A., 02-04
Gilmore, Delores D., 18-01